Devolution in the UK

James Mitchell

Manchester University Press

Manchester and New York

distributed in the United States exclusively
by Palgrave Macmillan

Published by Manchester University Press
Oxford Road, Manchester M13 9NR, UK
and Room 400, 175 Fifth Avenue, New York, NY 10010, USA
www.manchesteruniversitypress.co.uk

Distributed in the United States exclusively by
Palgrave Macmillan, 175 Fifth Avenue, New York,
NY 10010, USA

Distributed in Canada exclusively by
UBC Press, University of British Columbia, 2029 West Mall,
Vancouver, BC, Canada V6T 1Z2

British Library Cataloguing-in-Publication Data
A catalogue record for this book is available from the British Library

Library of Congress Cataloging-in-Publication Data applied for

ISBN 978 0 7190 5358 0 *hardback*

First published 2009

18 17 16 15 14 13 12 11 10 09   10 9 8 7 6 5 4 3 2 1

The publisher has no responsibility for the persistence or accuracy of URLs for external or any third-party internet websites referred to in this book, and does not guarantee that any content on such websites is, or will remain, accurate or appropriate.

Typeset
by Action Publishing Technology Ltd, Gloucester
Printed in Great Britain
by CPI Antony Rowe Ltd, Chippenham, Wiltshire

Contents

List of boxes and tables

Preface

This book is the culmination of many years of research and builds on much previous work in which I argued that the UK is best conceived as a union state rather than a unitary state. This drew on Rokkan and Urwin's seminal work on state formation and was developed particularly with reference to the union between Scotland and the rest of Britain. While Rokkan and Urwin focused particularly on the formation of the union, my interests were in how the union evolved, particularly during the twentieth century. In this book, I have taken this forward in two ways: first I have explored the other unions which make up the United Kingdom and secondly considered the implications of devolution for the nature of the state as a whole. I find myself in the unusual position of criticising the notion that the UK is a union state, with which I am closely associated, having witnessed this view become the new orthodoxy after its initial rejection. The significance of how we conceive of the UK is important as it has consequences for how we expect it to evolve.

The approach adopted in this book will be recognised by anyone famil-iar with my earlier work. My focus has been on institutions, both formal and informal, and is historical. In order to appeal to a wider audience, I have avoided emphasising the theoretical literature that has informed this work. I have used primary sources in all empirical chapters, some of which have never before, to my knowledge, been used. This has involved extensive use of public records and I am extremely grateful to the staffs of the National Archives at Kew in west London, the National Archives of Scotland in Edinburgh and the Public Records Office Northern Ireland in Belfast. Hundreds of files were studied and have been referred to, though many others were studied and formed part of my understanding of events and processes which could not be included in the book. I have attempted to balance the need for detail, all too often lacking in the broad overview offered by some political scientists but admirably provided by historian colleagues, with an attempt to ensure that the wood would emerge from the trees. Many other primary sources were consulted. Nigel Smith of *Scotland Forward* allowed me to study papers he had collected over the years which proved extremely interesting.

Occasionally, the products of interviews conducted in recent and not so recent years have been used in the book, though rarely are these explicitly acknowledged but, rather, have helped back up other sources. An array of different newspapers and other primary sources from political parties and other organisations have also been used.

Many people have assisted me over the years with this book and indeed others who have had little direct input into the book have shared thoughts and discussions on material in it. The following deserve particu-lar thanks for reading parts or all of the manuscript and provided criticisms, suggestions and corrections: Sir Kenneth Bloomfield, Jonathan Bradbury, Laura Cram, Russell Deacon, Dylan Griffiths, Charlie Jeffrey, Laura McAllister, Cathal McCall, Bob Purdie, Duncan Tanner, Alys Thomas, John Tomaney, Graham Walker and Barry Winetrobe. Particular thanks also to Eilidh McPhail who read the entire manuscript and Gareth Mulvey who checked the bibliography. The book has evolved from being a short introduction on devolution into a research monograph and during this evolution I was fortunate to receive a grant under the ESRC's Devolution and Constitutional Change Programme. I directed a project on Devolution and the Centre (ESRC L219 25 2026) and was involved in other related programme initiatives with a number of colleagues from whom I gained a great deal. Charlie Jeffrey was an outstanding director of the programme, not least in bringing together various people from different backgrounds. Charlie provided many opportunities to present ideas and work on devolution, not just matters directly related to the project funded by the ESRC. These meetings were invariably useful and interesting.

I would like to thank colleagues at the Constitution Unit, University College London, where I held an Honorary Senior Research fellowship for a period, for the many conversations and discussions. Robert Hazell directed the Leverhulme Project on the Nations and Regions with which I was associated: I headed the Scottish end of the Devolution Monitoring project between 1999 and 2005 (partly funded by the ESRC) and worked with David Bell on a project on territorial finance. Some of the work I did for these projects has found its way into this book. As well as Robert, I should like to thank Alan Trench, Scott Greer, Oonagh Gay and Meg Russell as well as two research assistants, Roger Masterman and Guy Lodge. Richard Wyn Jones in Aberystwyth offered important insights into Welsh politics. Others who deserve especial thanks include Jonathan Bradbury, with whom I have worked intermittently over many years, Dan Wincott and the excellent Scottish Monitoring team: John Curtice, Neil McGarvey, Philip Schlesinger, Mark Shephard and Alex Wright. Despite all my debts of gratitude there will remain errors in this work but these are, of course, my own.

Finally, I must thank my family – Laura, Euan and Kirsty. Laura is always a useful sounding board and critic. Together they have put up with a lot while I have researched and written this book.

Abbreviations

AES	Alternative Economic Strategy
AM	Assembly Member
AMS	Additional Member System
ARS	Alternative Regional Strategy
CEC	Campaign for Equal Citizenship
CPRS	Central Policy Review Staff
CSA	Campaign for a Scottish Assembly
CSG	Consultative Steering Group
CSJ	Campaign for Social Justice
CWM	Council of Wales and Monmouthshire
DEA	Department of Economic Affairs
DEFRA	Department for Environment, Food and Rural Affairs
DETR	Department of the Environment, Transport and the Regions
DTI	Department of Trade and Industry
DTLR	Department for Transport, Local Government and the Regions
DUP	Democratic Unionist Party
EEC	European Economic Community
ERDF	European Regional Development Fund
GLA	Greater London Authority
GLC	Greater London Council
GOR	Government Office for the Region
HIDB	Highlands and Islands Development Board
HMSO	Her/His Majesty's Stationary Office
HMT	Her Majesty's Treasury
ILEA	Inner London Education Authority
IMF	International Monetary Fund
INLA	Irish National Liberation Army
IRA	Irish Republican Army
JEB	Joint Exchequer Board
JMC	Joint Ministerial Committee
LCC	London County Council
MBW	Metropolitan Board of Works
MCC	Metropolitan County Councils
MLA	Members of the Legislative Assembly
MP	Member of Parliament

MSP   Member of the Scottish Parliament
NCC   Nature Conservancy Council
NEC   National Executive Committee
NHS   National Health Service
NICS   Northern Ireland Civil Service
NIO   Northern Ireland Office
ODPM   Office of the Deputy Prime Minister
PESC   Public Expenditure Survey Committee
PIU   Performance and Information Unit
PPP   Private-Public Partnership
PRONI   Public Records Office Northern Ireland
RDA   Regional Development Agency
RSG   Rate Support Grant
SC(DI)   Scottish Council (Development and Industry)
SDLP   Social Democratic and Labour Party
SEC   Scottish Economic Conference
SEPD   Scottish Economic Planning Department
SNP   Scottish National Party
SSP   Scottish Socialist Party
STV   Single Transferable Vote
TECs   Training and Enterprise Councils
TNA   The National Archives
UDA   Ulster Defence Association
UDI   Unilateral Declaration of Independence
UUP   Ulster Unionist Party
UUUC   United Ulster Unionist Coalition
UWC   United Workers' Council
WDA   Welsh Development Agency

1

Constituting the UK

At the hands of its interpreters, the British constitution is an oracle which can only tell you why any and every particular change contemplated will not work. Whereas in some nations the existence of a written constitution means that almost anything can be done (or at least justified), in Britain the unwritten constitution is read to mean that almost nothing can be done. Its principles are ethereal bodies unable to offer any positive guidance but always ready to descend on any change as a violation of their spirit. To summon these Harpies, you need only suggest something different. (Heclo and Wildavsky 1981: 340–341)

What is the UK constitution?

In an article written in 1999, Peter Riddell of the London Times wrote, 'The British dislike thinking constitutionally. It is somehow alien to our much-valued pragmatism' (*The Times*, 18 January 1999). Professor Sir David Edward, former Judge of the European Court of Justice, went further. In a lecture in 2005 he argued, 'We have become constitutionally illiterate, to the extent that we do not understand our own constitution' (Edwards 2005: 9). The reason for this constitutional illiteracy is partly that there is no agreement on what constitutes the UK constitution. De Tocqueville is sometimes quoted as saying that England has no constitution. What this is normally taken to mean is that the UK's constitution is not codified. Conflating two different meanings of constitution – 'how a country is constituted' and 'its constitution' – is common but, according to a leading defender of the pre-devolution constitutional order, should be guarded against (Johnson 2004: 18; see also King 2001: 3–6). One solution to finding the constitution is offered by Neil MacCormick: 'If a state has at some time been set up, "constituted" by some deliberate act or acts, can these constituent acts be other than constitutions?' (MacCormick 1978: 1). Indeed, if a state exists, can it fail to have a constitution, however contested it may be?

In his study of the British constitution, Nevil Johnson distinguished between customary and codified constitutions. Codified constitutions may be open to interpretation but the broad parameters are stated with varying degrees of clarity in some written form. Entrenched constitutions are those which have fixed principles which cannot be changed by normal legislation. The customary constitution 'lays great store by a capacity to leave principles inexplicit, relying instead on what people feel from past experience, to be appropriate in the circumstances' (Johnson 2004: 19). Johnson emphasises the role of elites in both ensuring legitimacy with a wider public and negotiating political accommodations (Ibid.). One critical reviewer of Johnson's work remarked that the 'customary constitution that Johnson celebrates proves elusive' (Russell 2005: 457). This elusiveness was what made it attractive to many of its advocates across the main political parties and amongst the political elite until very recently. Indeed, the customary constitution remains very much alive in the UK today, albeit alongside significant institutional change.

The customary constitution, defended on the right by Johnson, also had its support on the left, though with a very different understanding of what was constitutionally permissible. John Griffith's famous description of the UK constitution as a 'political constitution' highlights this elusiveness: 'The constitution of the United Kingdom lives on, changing from day to day for the constitution is no more and no less than what happens. Everything that happens is constitutional. And if nothing happens that would be constitutional also' (Griffith 1979: 19). Griffith argued for a strengthening of the House of Commons and that the 'fundamental objection [to proposals for a written constitution, Bill of Rights, greater power for the Lords, regional assemblies and Supreme Court] is this: that law is not and cannot be a substitute for politics' (Ibid.: 16). His was an argument for a 'very positivist view of the constitution; of recognising that Ministers and others in high positions of authority are men and women who happen to exercise political power but without any such right to that power which could give them a superior moral position; that laws made by those in authority derive validity from no other fact or principle, and so impose no moral obligation of obedience on others; that so-called individual or human rights are no more and no less than political claims made by individuals on those in authority; that a society is endemically in a state of conflict between warring interest groups, having no consensus or unifying principles sufficiently precise to be the basis of a theory of legislation' (Ibid.: 19). This was a classic leftist statement against comprehensive constitutional reform.

Significant change occurred during the 1980s that resulted in support on the left for a range of constitutional reforms, including devolution. Nonetheless, the UK constitution remains rooted in past ideas, institutions and interpretations. No understanding of today's constitution is complete without an appreciation of these roots. In this sense, the UK constitution is as much a historic constitution as a political constitution.

The unitary state paradigm

At a popular level, people living in the United Kingdom are well aware that it consists of distinct national communities. Yet constitutionally, this diversity often causes confusion. Confusion even surrounds the name of the state itself. Richard Rose noted that it was difficult to name the nation associated with the Government of the UK, stating 'One thing is for certain: No one speaks of the *UKes* as a nation' (Rose 1982: 11). The absence of an adjective associated with the state does not mean the absence of a collective national identity or state nationalism. However, the UK 'stands apart [from other European states] for its lack of an official nationalist ideology' (Keating 1988: 56). When the term 'nationalism' is used in the UK it is more often assumed to refer to one of the sub-state nationalisms – Scottish, Welsh or Irish nationalism. Indeed, British/UK nationalists – state nationalists – quite often rail against 'nationalism' unaware of their own (state) nationalism. UK nationalism operates in a 'banally mundane way' (Billig 1995: 6). It is not only liberal Western academics who 'today find it easier to recognize nationalism in "others" than in themselves', as Billig maintains (Ibid.: 15), but also a wider public in the UK who rarely question the nationalism of the state itself. National identity is not only defined in terms of the state in relation to its external world but internally too. Recent constitutional change has shaken up the sense of identity amongst at least some sections of the UK's population.

The absence of an explicit state nationalist discourse and the rise of sub-state nationalism led to state nationalism in the UK being referred to as 'unionism' in the twentieth century. In earlier times, state nationalism was referred to as 'patriotism' (Weight 2002: 727). Unionism is a term still commonly used in Scotland and Northern Ireland. In both cases, the 'union' originally referred to was the British union with Ireland. The Scottish Tories were known as the Scottish Unionist Party between 1912 and 1965 and for this period the 'union' was explicitly that with Ireland; latterly, the focus of attention in Scotland has been on the Anglo-Scottish union. Opponents of Irish home rule styled themselves as 'unionists', reflecting their support for the union. They did not style themselves as British nationalists. In part, this may be explained by the sense that the state was not entirely integrated. Ironically, then, the term unionist acknowledges the limited nature of the union.

Britain is often inaccurately used as a synonym for the UK. Official and popular understandings are often quite different. This is not surprising given the history of the state and also ambivalence concerning its official designation. In 1961, Duncan Sandys, the Conservative Secretary of State for Commonwealth Relations, sent a memorandum to the Cabinet arguing that public relations with Commonwealth countries were made more difficult by referring to 'the United Kingdom' or 'the UK', as this 'soulless, official designation is totally lacking in popular appeal and inspires no emotions of affection or loyalty' (TNA C (61) 46, 24 March 1961). He proposed the adoption of the terms 'Britain' and 'British' in all official correspondence, public statements and information in relations with the Commonwealth. In Commonwealth countries the Government representative would be called the 'British High Commissioner'. He proposed two exceptions: in treaties and legal documents when the formal designation, 'United Kingdom of Great Britain and Northern Ireland' would be necessary and in the definition of citizenship. He rejected the idea of using 'Great Britain' as that would be abbreviated to 'GB' which he thought would be as 'unattractive as UK'. The Cabinet accepted the proposal though it was thought preferable to make no formal announcement (TNA CC (61), 28 March 1961).

This concern was not confined to Conservative politicians. Labour Premier Harold Wilson recounted how he had fought a battle with the Foreign and Commonwealth Office to prevent the Government being seated at a Commonwealth conference behind a placard marked 'United Kingdom'. Wilson insisted that he represented Britain (Rose 1982: 11). What is striking about these episodes is that nobody appears to have considered how this might be construed in Northern Ireland. As Richard Rose later suggested, any description of the UK as the nation of Britain 'leaves unclear whether Ulstermen are included' (Ibid.). Sandys maintained that before 1939 it was 'rightly felt that other member countries [of the Empire] might resent it, if we arrogated to ourselves the term "British", which was common to them all' but, he felt, changes in the Commonwealth meant this was no longer the case. Northern Ireland was then a largely forgotten part of the UK.

The creation of the UK, like any other state, came about through the amalgamation of previously autonomous or separate entities. The manner in which these amalgamations occurred and the nature of the new political entities influenced future developments. Significantly, the creation of the UK did not mean the eradication of its constituent elements.

In his study of territory and power in the United Kingdom, Jim Bulpitt argued that it was hard not to conclude that the terms confederation, federation and unitary system 'should be pensioned off and left to the second oldest profession, the lawyers, to play with' (Bulpitt 1983: 19). Most text books, even books on Scottish politics, refer to the United Kingdom as a unitary state. The term 'unitary state' has been used rather loosely, and rarely defined. The Royal Commission on the Constitution (Kilbrandon) described the UK as a unitary state:

> The United Kingdom is a unitary state in economic as well as in political
> terms. It has, for example, a single currency and a banking system respon-
> sible to a single central bank. Its people enjoy a right of freedom of movement
> of trade, labour and capital and of settlement and establishment anywhere

within the Kingdom (though there is an exception in Northern Ireland in a restriction on employment imposed in the interests of Northern Ireland workers). Similarly, all citizens are free to participate in trading and other concessions obtained by the United Kingdom abroad. (Kilbrandon 1973: 19, para. 57)

In this respect, Kilbrandon was heavily influenced by conventional academic opinion at that time. What also makes this definition interesting is its application to debates on the future of the European Union today. The notion that a polity with a single currency, various freedoms of movement, even allowing for exceptions, constitutes a unitary state might suggest that the EU has the hallmarks of such a state. The alternative view, however, is that this is an inadequate definition of a unitary state.

The notion that the UK is something other than a unitary state was suggested by Gaspare Ambrosini, an Italian scholar, in the 1930s (Ambrosini 1946). Ambrosini put forward the possibility of an alternative state type, neither unitary nor federal. The third category he proposed was a state characterised by regional autonomy. He maintained that a number of states at certain times conformed with this type. Amongst the constitutions he felt followed a third way were that of Austria before and after 1918, the Spanish Republican constitution of 1931, the Weimar constitution and the Soviet constitutions of 1924 and 1936. He tentatively included the UK, given the status of Northern Ireland and Scotland. Mackenzie and Chapman later suggested that this was accurate and could best be understood with reference to 'Continental jurists' distinction between *autarchic* and *autonomous* bodies within the state' (Mackenzie and Chapman 1951: 186). Each had corporate personality and a measure of discretion. The former drew their powers from the legislatures within the state while the latter drew their powers from the constitution and did not give the central legislature a superior status: the former were polities constituted from laws as distinct from those based on fixed principles. Mackenzie and Chapman noted that regional states are those in which autonomous bodies exist but do not possess any 'national' or 'sovereign' powers as of right. The essence of this third type (Mackenzie and Chapman rather grandly called it a theory) is that there is 'ample constitutional experience to justify the substitution of a scale of unity – for the traditional dichotomy between federal and unitary States; and it is only by applying this criterion that one can obtain what might be called a gradation of Statehood' (Ibid.: 186). Most pertinently, and with prescience, they argued that the UK was a regional state and that

once this is recognised it should be easier to face the issue of Home Rule for Scotland and Wales free from the old bogey of separatism. Regionalism is not a step to separatism, but a safeguard against it. (Ibid.: 198)

For many years, the orthodox view was that the United Kingdom was a unitary state but, as discussed earlier, a new orthodoxy, which viewed the UK as a union state, replaced this. This drew on Rokkan and Urwin's typology of state formation which distinguished between four models: unitary, union, mechanical and organic federal (Rokkan and Urwin 1982: 11). This typology, however, was important for understanding more than state formation and it was argued that it was important in understanding how the state had developed post-union (Mitchell 1997). Even the House of Lords Select Committee on the Constitution identified the UK's union state nature as one of the five basic principles of the constitution (House of Lords 2001). However, while the practice of the UK's territorial constitution may have conformed with the union state conception, which acknowledged its diverse components, it operated alongside a dominant unitary state understanding which was often the 'conceptual lens' through which constitutional politics was viewed and which informed and constrained thinking on which reforms were possible (Mitchell 1997).

The idea of the union state implies, though this is not explicit, that there were two parties to the union when, in fact, the United Kingdom consisted of a number of unions each with a different legacy. Each of these unions has been significant and requires to be taken into account in any understanding of devolution. The new orthodoxy of the UK as a union state already looks rather ragged in its inability to help us conceive of the United Kingdom after devolution. It is now better to conceive of the UK not as a union state but as a state of unions. Indeed, the logic of devolution has differed in each case. As Morgan and Mungham noted, 'The rationale for devolving power to the nations and regions of the UK has involved one or more of the following: a *political* rationale (devolution as a step towards deeper, more pluralistic democracy); an *administrative* rationale (devolution as a means to more efficient, locally-attuned policy-making); an *economic* rationale (devolution as a stimulant to regional development); and a *cultural* rationale (devolution as a means of protecting and promoting civic and ethnic identities' (Morgan and Mungham 2000: 24). Failure to appreciate the different legacies of these diverse unions results in a failure to appreciate these different rationales and the UK's asymmetric nature as well as the likely path of each. The key insight of this conceptual lens is that the UK is far more likely to develop an organic federal constitution, even arrangements in which some part attains some measure of independence, than some more mechanical federal constitution.

England as a unitary polity

England was created as a unitary state and this has had considerable implications for the UK. The assumption that the UK is unitary because England was created as a unitary polity has affected devolution debates.

Ignoring England is perverse not only because it is the largest constituent of the state but it is often seen as the state's core. The medieval historian James Campbell maintains that the history of the United Kingdom cannot be understood without consideration of how 'some thousand years ago, England became a United Kingdom, but failed to incorporate the far West and the long North of our island' (Campbell 1995: 47). That legacy remains relevant. Historians may argue over the beginning of England as a political and social entity (Jones 1998) but there is less argument over the importance of the myth of England as an ancient kingdom. Campbell has argued that England was a nation-state by 1066 and that there is 'no question of there having been anything comparable to the English state in France, Spain or Italy' (Campbell 1995: 31). He distinguishes between three zones in England around the time when England was unified: 'first a zone of palaces and councils; second, a zone lacking palaces and royal meeting-places, but having uniform institutions; third, a frontier zone' (Ibid.: 43). It could be contended that the first is the true heart of the UK, not only England, especially given that the 'ordinary residences of all the rulers of England until Queen Victoria were within the same southern and western zone' (Ibid.: 44). More significant is the claim that a 'system of government which was substantially uniform' existed in the area surveyed by the Domesday commissioners from south of the Tees and the Ribble (Ibid.: 31). England, it would appear, was the prototypical unitary polity from very early times. Provincial particularism and loyalties existed but these marked the success of the state as they had been created by the central authority and 'did not so much contradict as reinforce that authority' (Ibid.: 35).

Of course, this raises questions about the meaning of the state. The state as we know it today is wholly different from that in medieval times. There may well have been a 'substantially uniform' system of government but its reach and remit was so limited as to be almost non-existent by today's standards. Nonetheless, the territorial pattern set by state formation in England lasted. Occasional jocular references to the ancient heptarchy of seven English kingdoms is made by opponents of devolution and federation. This says much about how English history is interpreted in contemporary political discourse. Political regions and regionalism are simply seen as either antediluvian or alien to the English tradition, only relevant in an earlier, more backward period.

The most important legacy of England as the prototypical unitary polity in the context of debates on the territorial constitution in the twentieth century was the myth of parliamentary sovereignty. The idea of parliamentary sovereignty was central to A.V. Dicey's arguments against Irish home rule and would influence debates on Scotland and Wales later. As far as Dicey and later Diceyans were concerned, Parliament at Westminster was sovereign and no other body could be contemplated which might undermine or threaten that sovereignty. For Diceyans, sovereignty was one and indivisible. Though Dicey had a far more sophisticated understanding of the territorial constitution, his legacy has been to limit the scope of autarchic institutions and rule out autonomous bodies.

Union with Wales

Historically, religion and language, rather than the apparatus of the state, made Wales different. The initial union of England and Wales conformed more to the unitary state model of state formation than the union state model discussed above. The Acts of Union of 1536 and 1543 were assimilationist, quite different from the Treaty of Union of 1707 between England (and Wales) and Scotland. From Tudor times, Welsh counties had been run on English lines, subject to English law, with English as the official language and with Wales given representation in Parliament in return (Kiernan 1993: 6). Nonetheless, Welsh continued to be spoken, even if by a declining minority, partly kept alive by the non-conformist denominations, which ensured that this facet of Welsh distinctiveness never entirely disappeared. One problem, however, was that two parts of Wales emerged after 1945 – Welsh Wales, where Welsh was the main language, and English Wales, where English was the main language. Before that, many areas of Wales were mixed. Wales was more fully absorbed into the English core than Scotland ever was but, according to Robbins, neither was 'absorbed in any simple fashion' (Robbins 1988: 11). The intention of the 1536 and 1543 Acts was to introduce 'uniformity in the legal codes of England and Wales, to have uniformity also in their administration' (Williams 1950: 38). The Wales and Berwick Act, 1746 provided that references in Acts of Parliament to England should also be taken to refer to Wales.

But assimilation was never complete and Welsh distinctiveness found expression in different forms. In 1588, the Privy Council ordered that a Welsh translation of the Bible should be placed in every church in Wales (Williams 1950: 76). The nineteenth century was important in terms of tensions between Welsh and British nationalism or, as Thomas expressed it, between particularist and assimilationist attitudes, which followed through into the twentieth century (Thomas 1981). Assimilation in the nineteenth century came to be associated with the Conservative Party and the Anglican Church in Wales. The Conservatives opposed disestablishment and disendowment of the Church. Disestablishment eventually occurred in 1920. But the assimilationist tendency ran deeper than this. In words echoing those of a nineteenth-century Austrian diplomat commenting on Italy, the Bishop of St Davids declared in 1886 that Wales was just a 'geographical expression' (Morgan 1982: 41). Modernisation, or at least developments associated with it, had a mixed effect. It encouraged both assimilation and particularism. As the state's reach stretched beyond that of the night-watchman state, this involved both centralisation and uniformity but also the development of distinct Welsh administration.

The Welsh Courts Act, 1942 allowed for the limited use of Welsh in courts. The Hughes-Parry Report of 1965 on the legal status of the Welsh language, set up in 1963 by Sir Keith Joseph when he was responsible for Welsh affairs, argued for 'equal validity' with English for official, governmental and legal purposes (Ibid.: 389). The Welsh Language Act, 1967 finally carried this through into statute. Wales, it has been contended, has had 'no continuous history of a distinctly Welsh dimension in British political institutions since union with England' (Thomas 1981: 2). This distinguished Wales from Scotland and Ireland (Randall 1972: 353). Wales was reborn (or perhaps only born) as a nation in the twentieth century.

It would be wrong to suggest that Welsh identity grew commensurately with the development of the state's functions. The growth in the state's functions posed threats and opportunities to Welsh identity. Thomas maintains that economic assimilation was dominant in all the major UK parties in Wales. Economic integration with the rest of Britain, which meant England, was something on which Labour, Conservatives and Liberals were largely in agreement even if they differed as to how this should be achieved. Interdependence and redistribution were key elements of integration (Thomas 1981: 14). But state intervention also involved the creation of Welsh public bodies and institutions. The twentieth century witnessed a complex relationship between Welsh and British identities. There was an uneasy, possibly irresolvable, but creative tension between these two identities.

Scotland and the union

The union of Scotland and England involved the creation of a new state without the eradication of pre-existing nations. This was the archetypal union state. The protection afforded to Scottish institutions is frequently commented upon. More significant was the perceived need to enshrine such protection in a treaty, indicating an expectation that assimilation might otherwise occur. Taxation, parliamentary representation, law and legal jurisdictions proved the most contentious issues at the time of union (Ferguson 1990: 47–48). These are also likely to prove the most contentious issues in the era of legislative devolution. As well as providing for a united Parliament, the Treaty of Union prescribed the number of Scottish MPs (45) and members of the House of Lords (16), freedom of trade and a common flag, coinage and system of weights and measures. Taxation would be common and Scotland would receive money for assuming a share in the English national debt. The Scottish Church, Scots law and legal systems were given protection under the Treaty. The provision of education in Scotland would also be treated separately by virtue of the protection afforded to the Church of Scotland, at least so long as a close relationship existed between education and religion. As Dicey and Rait put it, the union was

> the most conservative of revolutionary measures. To put the matter shortly, it repealed every law or custom of England or of Scotland inconsistent with the political unity of the new State, but it did not make or attempt any change or reform which was not necessary for the creation of the new United Kingdom. (Dicey and Rait 1920: 244–245)

Dicey and Rait preferred the term 'Act' of Union, signifying that it was a measure passed by Parliament, upholding notions of parliamentary sovereignty. Others note that the agreement was embodied in a treaty agreed by two parliaments, enshrining rights which could not simply be overruled by the new Parliament and therefore see it as above normal laws, having the status, if in sketchy form, akin to an entrenched written constitution (MacCormick 1978).

Most significant was the attempt to protect institutions which would help maintain a sense of Scottish national identity. The protected institutions were of great significance at the time of union. Over time, changes in politics and society would alter the balance. Scottish private law was protected and public law was to be assimilated but the rise of public law would alter the Scottish–British balance. The decline in the role of the established Church would also diminish the Scottish element in the settlement. As the state gradually took over the role of the Church in the provision of education, especially towards the end of the nineteenth century, another Scottish feature of the union would diminish. It was hardly surprising that the union settlement would become dated and that the desire to protect Scottish distinctiveness would be a recurring feature of British history. The union was not simply a settlement which preserved particular Scottish institutions but an agreement that Scottish institutions should be protected. In other words, the underlying principle was that Scottish national identity should be protected but that might take different institutional forms at different times. The consensus around this view has been widespread throughout most of British political history. Scotland's constitutional status was archetypically that of a component of a union state, not a unitary state.

As in the case of Wales, the nature of the Scottish union with England changed over time. In common with other parts of the UK, economic integration occurred. Gaelic is now spoken by only a tiny proportion of the population (1.4 per cent), concentrated in the west Highlands and Islands, but a strong sense of Scottish cultural identity persists. A Scottish elite exists in business and finance as well as a public administrative elite. The labour movement played its part in Scotland too in the process of integration (Keating and Bleiman 1979) but the development of state intervention, as discussed in a later chapter, has played as much a part in the maintenance of a distinct Scottish politics as it has been assimilationist.

Ireland and the union

The Acts of Union of 1800, passed by the Irish and British Parliaments, created a new state which shall 'for ever after, be united into one Kingdom' (O'Day and Stevenson 1992: 6). It was analogous with the Treaty of Union between Scotland and England, creating a new dimension to the UK union state. The 1800 Union was a less complete union than that of 1707. The Act made provision for Irish representation at Westminster 'consistent with the concept of a United Kingdom. But there was no such positive application of principle in respect of government' (Mansergh 1991: 14). There was little concern for how Ireland would be governed. Consequently, Ireland retained many institutions from pre-1800. As Robert Peel said, Ireland 'is a country separated by nature from that to which she is united by law; a country having once had an independent existence – having within twenty years had an independent legislature – having still her separate courts of justice, and distinct departments of executive government' (Jenkins 2001: 42). Over the course of the nineteenth century, the offices of Lord Lieutenant of Ireland, based in Phoenix Park, and Chief Secretary of Ireland, in Dublin Castle, governed Ireland, overseeing a system of departments and boards which developed incrementally. Normally, either the Lord Lieutenant or Chief Secretary were members of the Cabinet. Mansergh has commented that the 'most lasting impression of Castle administration was of structural confusion' (Mansergh 1991: 15). The 1800 Union had the characteristics of a union state. Its piecemeal evolution reflected changes in state intervention with new and existing Irish bodies given new and extended roles. But unlike the development of the institutions of union with Scotland, the politics of the Irish union were inseparably linked with Catholic emancipation, land reform and, indeed, famine.

In 1968, Harry Calvert argued that though the Acts of Union are no longer in force in the Republic of Ireland, 'they retain their full vigour so far as Northern Ireland is concerned' (Calvert 1968: 10). The issues of Ireland's relations with Britain and the civil rights of Catholics dominated Irish politics, were interconnected and had 'already assumed a recognized shape in the 1780s and 1790s' (Jackson 1999: 23). This relationship has run through the history of the politics of Irish home rule and devolution. The plantation of Ulster in the seventeenth century by Protestants, mainly from Scotland, was to create a population of immigrants who would continue to look to Britain as its own in a way that the rest of the population did not. In the case of Ireland, it was not simply that the process of creating a single state was incomplete. There never was a serious effort to integrate Ireland with the rest of the state; it was treated more as a colony than an integral part. The legacy of this approach remains. Czeslaw Milosz could have been referring to Northern Ireland's relations with Britain in his Nobel lecture when he said that it is possible that there is no other memory than the memory of wounds (Milosz 1980: 20). Collective memories and interpretations of the past have been more important in recent history than the institutional arrangements themselves.

Whereas Scotland was allowed to retain its own church, Irish Catholicism after the Reformation was seen as disloyal and even a threat to London. Land ownership became enmeshed in the troubled relations. The minority who identified with London did so on the basis of religion or rights granted by London rather than geography. In the twentieth century, however, a territorial dimension emerged with the creation of Northern Ireland but, as Lee has noted, 'Ulster' was 'less a place than a state of mind, however insistently this mentality expressed itself in the idiom of the territorial imperative' (Lee 1990: 5).

From its creation, Northern Ireland had a relationship with the rest of the UK that had the characteristics of a union state. It had been created by treaty. Integration was imperfect and indigenous elite recruitment existed, including a political elite elected to Stormont. However, the nationalist community looked to Dublin and maintained a sense of community with the rest of Ireland. The unionist community did not so much look to London but to the Protestant elite in Northern Ireland. Northern Ireland's autonomy and lack of integration were not, of course, a sign of regional nationalist agitation. The unionist majority were adamant in their support for the union but one with union state characteristics. The irony has frequently been noted that home rule came to that part of the UK where greatest opposition to it had existed.

Structure of the book

Each component nation of the UK developed its own distinctive institutions separate from the others. Occasionally one would influence another but there was remarkably little formal attempt to coordinate these developments. This is not to say that developments were centrifugal. This distinctiveness was evident in autarchic, rather than autonomous institutions in Scotland and Wales and operated with a core executive under Cabinet government. This all operated within the myth of parliamentary sovereignty. However mythical parliamentary sovereignty may have been, it fuelled a strong centralist mentality that severely constrained the parameters of the autarchic institutions of the UK's state of unions. The extent to which autarchic institutions spawned expectations that sat uneasily with notions of parliamentary sovereignty became clear in the years leading up to devolution. This book follows these developments by considering each component nation in turn. There were occasions in the 1970s when debates on devolution were relevant to more than one component of the United Kingdom. To avoid repetition, these debates are discussed in whichever chapter seemed most appropriate, with the use of cross referencing and comparisons with other components of the UK where relevant. This structure is not only a useful means of organising a complex pattern of institutional development but also largely reflects the way in which institutions developed.

Territorial management was *ad hoc*, operating within a customary constitution, and each chapter on Scotland, Wales, England and Northern Ireland draws out the issues and pressures for change that recurred over time. The first section attempts to describe the nature of the pre-devolution institutions of the component nations of the UK. Too much that has been written about devolution adopts what might be called Year Zero assumptions: that devolution has no predecessor institutions and that the politics of devolution can be understood without any historical background. This error leads to all sorts of mistaken claims – exaggerations concerning devolution's novelty and failure to appreciate the continuities from pre-devolution institutional arrangements. Much that is thought to be new has merely come to wider notice or has become formalised, codified or more pronounced. It also becomes clear that while the customary constitution has a 'capacity to leave principles inexplicit' (Johnson 2004: 19), there were remarkable similarities in the broad outlines of territorial management, especially in the three non-English components of the UK. Though Northern Ireland had autonomy, its Unionist rulers imposed self-constraints in many areas which resulted in its Assembly resembling the autarchic institutions which existed in Scotland. Where it operated autonomously, it often did so in an unrestrained manner which undermined its legitimacy. The inexplicit principles that emerge might best be captured in the notion of parliamentary sovereignty, which may have been a legal fiction but operated as a powerful idea that informed behaviour, limiting autonomy.

This is not to understate the extent to which devolution has been new, as becomes clear in the second section in which the devolved polities are examined. However, formal institutions do not exist in isolation. The questions to be addressed are whether the inexplicit principles of the customary constitution remain, whether they have been altered or whether new competing principles now operate. Formally, it appears that new competing principles do exist but these operate alongside the old principles of the customary constitution. The context of the early years of devolution needs to be taken into account: Northern Ireland's institutions operated sporadically, public money was plentiful relative to what went immediately before and after, and Labour was in power in London as well as in Edinburgh and Cardiff. While context is vitally important, intimations of the operation of distinct autonomous institutions growing out of autarchic bodies are evident. The diverse institutions which operated fairly successfully under the terms of the customary pre-devolution constitution were untested in these early years as compared to what might be expected in a very different context, which is only now beginning to emerge. It is not difficult to identify the areas in which tensions might emerge.

Conclusion

United Kingdom constitutional development has never been uniform. As MacCormick has noted (1999: 49), an 'evolved state' is bound to differ from a deliberately constituted one based on a historic constitution. The unions which contributed towards the establishment of the United Kingdom differed markedly. The most significant was that which created England. It was most significant for three reasons: first, it was the founding union; secondly, a unitary state was created and thirdly, England would become the largest component of the United Kingdom. This resulted in a widespread assumption that the United Kingdom was and is a unitary state, one and indivisible despite other quite different unions which contributed towards its creation. At its heart lay the notion that Parliament at Westminster was sovereign. It would be wrong to conclude that England is perverse within the United Kingdom. It is the asymmetrical nature of the United Kingdom, its competing centripetal and centrifugal pressures, and the differing experiences and understandings of union that are relevant.

However, England's size and perceptions of its experience have had profound effects on territorial government in the UK as a whole. F.W. Maitland commented that the 'State that Englishmen knew was a singularly unicellular State, and at a critical time they were not too well equipped with tried and traditional thoughts which would meet the case of Ireland or of some communities, commonwealths, or corporations in America which seemed to have wills – and scarcely fictitious wills – of their own' (Maitland 1900: Introduction). This myth of centralisation and uniformity in its largest component would be a significant hurdle in reforming the territorial constitution.

Two different types of pressure have affected the territorial distribution of government functions in the UK as elsewhere. The first has its origins in how the state was formed. The UK was formed through the amalgamation of territories. In England, this meant the near eradication of regional and local autonomy and the creation of a unitary state. However, in the case of the other constituent nations of the UK, there was always some attempt to allow for or even encourage distinctiveness. This created tensions. There were different models of state formation and evolution operating within the same state. The English model of the unitary state was important if only because England was by far the largest component of the state but this ran contrary to other models, particularly in Ireland and Scotland. This became more significant as the state's intervention in society and the economy increased. The second pressure came about as a result of social and economic forces which resulted in changes in state intervention. These altered the balance between diversity and integration, often undermining the former but, ironically, also requiring local and regional administration and thereby potentially creating greater diversity.

The new devolved institutions cannot be understood by simply looking at their founding legislation, policy output or the resources available to them. They did not involve a revolution in constitutional design though they represent significant change. They owe far more to past practice and the informal customary constitution than is often appreciated; continuities have tended to be played down in the early discussion of the new arrangements. Devolution retains the features of a state of diverse unions rather than characteristics of a federal (organic or mechanical) state, but it makes any drift towards a unitary state unlikely. The term 'union state' is no longer adequate to capture the variety of forms that devolved government takes and the different institutional forms and practices that have been adopted at the centre in response. A more accurate conceptualisation of the UK today is as a state of unions.

2

Approaching to Arch-angelic: administrative devolution in Scotland

Even the Stewarts rarely attempted to place the management of Scottish government in the hands of Englishmen; a Scottish tyrant or a Scottish bigot would, they felt, be likely to give less offence to Scotsmen than would an energetic and fair-minded Englishman who failed to understand the feeling of a country with which he was not connected by descent or education. The care with which this conviction has been followed since the Union is the more remarkable when contrasted with the free admission of Scotsmen to every form of governmental or official life throughout Great Britain, or the British Dominions. (Dicey and Rait 1920: 329)

... the men who drafted the Treaty of Union carefully left every institution in England and every institution in Scotland untouched by the Act, provided that the existence of such an institution was consistent with the main objects of the Act. Hence the extraordinary success of the Act. It destroyed nothing which did not threaten the essential unity of the whole people; and hence, lastly, the supreme glory of the Act, that while creating the political unity it kept alive the nationalism both of England and of Scotland. (Dicey and Rait 1920: 362)

What are your feelings about the Secretaryship for Scotland? The work is not very heavy – the dignity (measured by salary) is the same as your present office – but measured by the expectations of the people of Scotland it is approaching to Arch-angelic. We want a big man to float it – especially as there is so much sentiment about it. (Letter from Lord Salisbury inviting the Duke of Richmond and Gordon to become the first modern Scottish Secretary, 7 August 1885: Hanham 1965: 229)

Introduction

Administrative devolution is the term used to describe the Scottish and Welsh Offices. Significantly, a different term – direct rule – is used to describe the Northern Ireland Office. Though similar in many respects, there are differences between the two British territorial departments and the Northern Ireland Office. The Scottish Office has always been headed by politicians with a political base in Scotland and since 1945 always with a Scottish seat in the Commons. The Scottish Office was a concession catering for Scottish distinctiveness. It had both a symbolic and a substantive function. Symbolically, it represented recognition by government at the centre that Scotland was different. Substantively, it developed a considerable range of responsibilities.

Towards the end of the First World War, the Haldane Committee on the Machinery of Government considered the organisation of central government. Haldane saw two main alternatives: organising according to the persons or classes to be dealt with, or by function, according to the services to be performed. The Committee preferred the functional basis of organisation (Cd. 9230 1918: 8) but acknowledged later in the report that Scotland and Ireland should be treated separately (Ibid.: 58). Acknowledging this territorial dimension for Scotland and Wales cut across the functional basis. Education, for example, was a function which, according to Haldane's preference, would have been the responsibility of a single Whitehall department, but recognising the territorial dimension meant that it would be split between a functional department (covering England and Wales) and Scottish and Welsh central administrations. The territorial dimension was an aberration from the functional norm and was endorsed over fifty years later in another significant official document, a White Paper on the reorganisation of central government issued by Edward Heath's Government in 1970. Once more, though more explicitly this time, the territorial basis was accepted as a departure from the dominant method and only because there were 'strong reasons for moderating its [functional] application' (Cmnd. 4506 1970: para. 10).

The evolution of separate Scottish and Welsh administration was not simply a consequence of responding to sentiment, though that played its part. Questions of good government were also important. It was the interaction of the two – national sentiment and governmental efficacy – which led to the evolution of a very unusual structure of British central government and what later came to be called 'administrative devolution'. But not all matters affecting Scotland came under the Scottish Office. A Treasury memorandum prepared for the Royal Commission on Scottish Affairs in the 1950s outlined the factors which have 'favoured the retention of a Great Britain basis of administration for many services':

(a) First, there are what may be described as the consequences of the Treaty of Union. Scottish affairs are determined by the Parliament of the United Kingdom and in the executive field by a United Kingdom Cabinet, that is to say, by bodies which have regard to the well-being of the United Kingdom as a whole. This inevitably colours the administrative pattern.

(b) As the Haldane Committee (Cmd. 9230 of 1918) pointed out, it has usually been thought better that the functions of Departments should be allocated according to the services to be performed rather than according to the persons or classes to be dealt with. This arrangement of business has ensured that the acquisition of knowledge and the development of specialised capacity by those engaged in the several Departments could be encouraged to the full. It follows that, in allocating business between Departments, there have been strong arguments for dividing the work, by services, on a Great Britain basis rather than by the nationalities of the persons with whom a Department deals. In any event, the small size of Scotland, in comparison with England, has meant that the separation of the Scottish work would not afford much relief to an over-burdened Great Britain Department.

(c)   The expansion of regional devolution during and after the late war has greatly improved the adaptability of Departments covering Great Britain as a whole. The regional organisation has made it possible for administrators to be more closely in touch with local conditions and more accessible to those affected by their work. Moreover, since the principle of devolution of authority from the centre has been accepted, the extent to which this is done can to some extent be regulated according to the circumstances of different parts of the country; and in some cases it has been thought right to give a greater measure of devolution to Scottish branches of Great Britain Departments than has been accorded to the corresponding English regional offices. (TNA T 222/632)

Establishing the Scottish Office

In a lecture in 1885, a prominent Scottish judge remarked on the state of the union just before the establishment of the Scottish Office. The union had succeeded, he maintained, for two reasons: access to Empire and because London had decided that there should be 'no attempt to interfere unduly with our domestic institutions, or to frame them on the English pattern'. The establishment of the Scottish Office would restore a separate administration and it 'secures to us for the future the Scotland of the past' (Smith 1885: 233). The Scottish Office did not quite 'restore a separate administration' as Smith claimed. A number of boards appointed by patronage existed dealing with a range of matters. The use of boards was favoured by London because of the difficulties of communication, with the consequence that Dublin and Edinburgh had a degree of administrative independence (Willson 1955: 44). The Scottish boards were based in Edinburgh and, at least in theory, accountable to Government Ministers in London. Poor law and public health, education, prisons, fisheries, lunacy and mental deficiency (to use the language of the times) and agriculture were all administered by these boards, largely made up of Edinburgh lawyers (Milne 1957: 212–215). This conformed with the pattern of central administration that had existed in England until the Northcote-Trevelyan reforms towards the end of the nineteenth century which marked a move towards a professional civil service appointed by competitive examination.

The pressure for a Scottish Secretary emerged in the mid–late nineteenth century because a growing body of Scots felt that Scottish distinctiveness was being ignored. Changes in the range of central government intervention were believed to have undermined this distinctiveness. There had been special procedures catering for Scottish distinctiveness but these were thought to have become ineffective. Both the Conservatives under Lord Salisbury and the Liberals under Gladstone accepted that the office should be established (Hanham 1965; Mitchell 2003: 11–28). However, there was less agreement on the administrative functions of the office. Under one set of proposals, education would come under its remit and under another law and order was proposed. While Scotland appeared fairly united on the need for a Scottish Secretary, sectional interests could not agree on its administrative tasks. The teachers' professional body, the Educational Institute for Scotland (EIS) argued against education coming under its remit while lawyers did not want it to include law and order. Both sets of interests feared that their interests might be relegated to a parochial backwater but both supported a Scottish Office in principle.

Prime Minister Salisbury invited the elderly Duke of Richmond and Gordon to be the first holder of the office. In fact, Richmond and Gordon was Salisbury's fourth choice. His first choice, the Marquess of Lothian, had been a supporter of the office and was later to accept the post (Roberts 2000: 351). Richmond and Gordon was privately opposed to the office's establishment (Hanham 1965: 228). Salisbury summed up the nature of the office better than he probably realised: '... the dignity (measured by salary) is the same as your present office – but measured by the expectations of the people of Scotland it is approaching to Arch-angelic ... It is really a matter where the effulgence of two Dukedoms and the best salmon river in Scotland will go a long way' (Ibid.: 229). In a further letter to Richmond and Gordon, Salisbury remarked that the 'whole object of the move is to redress the wounded dignities of the Scotch people – or a section of them – who think that enough is not made of Scotland' (Ibid.: 230). The office's symbolic function would always be important.

Salisbury had accepted that Scottish opinion had to be taken into account; Scotland may have been an irritant but it was not irrelevant. His description of the expectations of the 'Scotch' with reference to the Scottish Secretaryship as 'approaching to Arch-angelic' was adopted as the title for an article by a future Scottish Secretary over a century later (Ross 1978). Scottish Secretaries would be expected to articulate Scottish interests regardless of whether the department had legal jurisdiction in the area in question. The Scottish Secretary was Scotland's representative in the Cabinet.

The development of administrative devolution in Scotland

Over time, the office's functions grew. The turnover of politicians to hold the office was high in the first few years after its establishment. A.J. Balfour became Scottish Secretary in 1886 for seven months. He was to be the only Scottish Secretary to go on to become Prime Minister (1902–06). During his brief tenure at the Scottish Office, he took advantage of disturbances on Skye to widen the scope of competencies to include law and order. This began a long process of accumulating responsibilities. In 1912 agriculture was added and health, including housing, was added after the First World War. A Parliamentary Under-Secretary, a junior minister, was also attached to the Scottish Office at this time. Over the course of time, other responsibilities were added and the scope of central government expanded in these and many other areas already devolved. The Scottish Office's extensive scope was noted by Robert Munro, Scottish Secretary between 1916 and 1922:

> A Secretary for Scotland must put a severe curb upon his personal predilections, and endeavour to deal with those branches of his activities, whatever they may be, that call for immediate attention. He cannot, being merely human, expand habitually to the width such a catalogue would demand. He has to live from day to day, to attend Cabinets, to think of Upper Silesia as well as, let us say, Auchtermuchty. (Munro 1930: 282)

Membership of the Cabinet had its advantages, most obviously bringing access to the centre of power, but it also added to his burdens, requiring the Secretary to consider wider matters. The multi-functional character of the office limited the nature of the Scottish Secretary's role. He could leave initiatives to his officials or follow English precedents. However, much depended on the predilections and personal influence of the individual holding the office.

By the 1930s, the office's responsibilities had grown but some boards continued to exist semi-independently, although the Scottish Secretary had formal responsibility for their activities. Scottish central administration had grown incrementally with no clear pattern. An official enquiry was set up under Sir John Gilmour, a former Scottish Secretary, which reported in 1937 (HMSO 1937b). It noted a number of significant developments since the office's establishment. The Scottish Secretary was 'popularly regarded as "Scotland's Minister"' (Ibid.: 19). Some years before, the London *Times* had commented on that 'great Pooh-Bah, the Secretary for Scotland, who combines in his person, in respect of half the kingdom, all those offices for which a more complex England requires half a dozen separate Ministries' (*The Times*, 7 April 1925). More than this, the Gilmour Report noted the 'increasing tendency to appeal to him on all matters which have a Scottish aspect, even if on a strict view they are outside the province of his duties as statutorily defined' (HMSO 1937b: 19). Twenty years later, Sir David Milne, Permanent Secretary at the Scottish Office, 1946–59, commented on this 'no-man's land' into which the Scottish Secretary had to venture because he is popularly regarded as Scotland's Minister. Matters on which the Scottish Secretary is 'most violently assailed in Parliament or in the Scottish press' were often ones which he has 'no direct duty to defend':

> If [the Scottish Office] seek to intervene unduly in matters for which other Ministers are directly responsible, they will be an intolerable nuisance to their colleagues; if they fail to intervene when their close acquaintance with Scottish conditions makes intervention seem desirable, they will be blamed, and probably justly. (Milne 1957: 7)

Gilmour's recommendations in 1937 rested on three arguments: that Scots wanted to see Scottish administration in Scotland; that the 'haphazard growth' had developed without any clear principle; and that the construction of a new headquarters in Edinburgh would facilitate the consolidation of responsibilities. The vast bulk of work had long been done in Edinburgh but it was scattered throughout the city with little co-ordination. The system of boards was criticised and it was proposed that the boards should come directly within the Scottish Office under the Scottish Secretary. The Reorganisation of Offices (Scotland) Act, 1939 was duly passed coinciding with the opening of St Andrew's House on Edinburgh's Calton Hill. What emerged was a mini-Whitehall almost all under one roof. In the event, St Andrew's House was not big enough to house all Scottish Office civil servants. The Scottish Office was organised along functional lines with divisions and departments corresponding loosely with English departments of state. Twenty years later, there was still a tendency to regard the Scottish departments as separate from the Secretary of State which, as the Scottish Office's most senior civil servant then suggested, was probably a survival of the days when the boards or departments had a legally independent existence prior to 1939 (Milne 1957: 6).

The reforms of 1939 have frequently, but inaccurately, been seen as transferring people and power to Scotland. This was the way in which the Government wanted to present the changes. Administrative devolution was presented as a form of Scottish self-government, serving to appease Scottish demands for greater control over Scottish affairs. This coupling of administrative needs with the expression of national identity in the development of the Scottish Office was most evident in the use of the term 'administrative devolution'. The term started to be used in internal Scottish Office discussions of the office's reforms in the early 1930s though the idea that the administrative arrangements represented a form of self-government pre-dated this. In the 1920s, defenders of the board system argued that the Edinburgh boards, appointed by patronage, were a form of 'Scottish control of Scottish affairs' in so far as they consisted of Scots governing Scotland in Scotland. That they were unelected and unrepresentative was overlooked.

The development of the Scottish Office's responsibilities had not always been smooth. On some occasions there was strong resistance in Whitehall to giving the Scottish Office more responsibilities. An example occurred at the time when the Scottish Board of Agriculture was set up under the Scottish Office in 1912. There was a fear in London that the Scots might be less stringent in administering the Diseases of Animals Acts, resulting in sick animals straying over the border and infecting healthy English animals, thus starting an epidemic which would sweep throughout England. This led to animal health being withheld from Scottish Office jurisdiction. Animal health was only transferred to the Scottish Office from the Ministry of Agriculture in 1955.

The post-war Scottish Office

The scope of government intervention expanded with the development of the welfare state after 1945 with repercussions for Scotland's position within the union. Agitation for Scottish home rule at this time was an important backdrop to these changes, forcing Attlee's Labour Government to pay attention to the Scottish dimension of state intervention and welfare. Separate legislation was required for the National Health Service in Scotland: the new NHS came under the Scottish Office but other aspects of the developing welfare state, most notably changes in National Insurance, resulted in uniformity across the state. National Insurance was a rare example of reverse devolution, an expanding policy which was removed from a distinct Scottish body and placed under a UK-wide ministry and therefore deserves special attention. Separate National Insurance Commissions had been established for England, Scotland, Wales and Northern Ireland in 1911 under the National Insurance Act. This Act introduced a system of compulsory, though restricted, insurance. In 1919, the Scottish Insurance Commission came under the Scottish Board of Health within the Scottish Office. That same year, the English and Welsh Commissions came under the newly established Ministry of Health. In 1945, National Insurance in Scotland was moved to the UK Ministry of National Insurance.

In December 1943, the Cabinet's Machinery of Government Committee argued, 'We consider that unified responsibility in this sphere [social insurance] is essential; we agree that careful arrangement will be necessary for local administration in Scotland ... Scotland should be regarded as a special case ... it is desirable that sufficient authority should be devolved to enable Scotland's position to be strong on the spot with the minimum of reference to London and that in the settlement necessary in London on large matters of principle Scottish aspects should be fully considered ... the official in charge in Scotland should be carefully selected and should have sufficient standing to make his advice valuable and his voice effective in the higher councils of his department in Whitehall: he should visit London frequently in order to share in the formulation of general policy' (TNA PIN 8/83). The Committee recognised the sensitivities involved. An inevitable Scottish backlash against centralisation had to be met by some concessions. In Parliament, Walter Elliot, former Scottish Secretary, challenged this reversal of devolution (Hansard, Commons, col. 1875, 14 November 1944). He was supported in sections of the Scottish press (*The Bulletin*, 15 November 1944).

Correspondence between the Scottish Office, including Scottish Secretary Tom Johnston, and the Ministry of Reconstruction focused on what might be conceded. Johnston warned that the view expressed in *The Bulletin* 'indicates an attitude which may so develop that it will completely bedevil and sabotage the new Ministry' (TNA PIN 8/83). Scottish officials asked for a number of special procedures but the general attitude was to avoid making any specific concessions. One official, in a note to Sir William Jowett, Reconstruction Minister, argued that it was 'not really necessary (except for reasons of national prestige) that this position should be recognised by way of a special official rank or salary, and the concession of such rank or salary would impair the efficient organisation of the Regions generally. Similar demands have been made, and resisted, in connection with the Regional Office of the Ministry of Labour for Scotland, though there is not in that case the argument from past practice which can be argued in connection with Health and Pensions Insurance' (Ibid.: Note to Minister, 22 November 1944). Refusing Scottish institutions in new areas of government activity was easier than removing existing arrangements, even when these existing arrangements would necessarily have to be overhauled due to major changes in workload.

In October 1947, Arthur Woodburn, Scottish Secretary, wrote a Cabinet memorandum noting cross-party support for greater Scottish control of Scottish affairs. He proposed changes in parliamentary procedures to take greater account of Scottish affairs and that 'in association with the Minister for Economic Affairs I should seek to bring about a greater co-ordination of economic affairs in Scotland' (TNA CAB 21/3329). He noted that those pressing for a review of Scottish administration were primarily concerned with economic affairs and the organisation of the nationalised industries. He proposed the creation of a Scottish Economic Conference under his chairmanship to provide a forum for discussion of economic questions, to enable the Scottish Secretary to keep in touch with Scottish economic issues and to advise ministers, particularly the Chancellor of the Exchequer.

A Cabinet Office civil servant noted that the Scottish Secretary had no responsibility for economic affairs and that an 'official Council which is dealing with a Minister without responsibility is likely to become a focal point for irritation and annoyance rather than an assistance to the Government' (TNA CAB 21/3329). As President of the Board of Trade, Stafford Cripps had attempted to 'rid himself of some of the tiresome Scottish economic problems by pushing responsibility (but not power) on to the Secretary of State for Scotland' (Ibid.). This had been resisted by the Scottish Office under Joseph Westwood but Arthur Woodburn, appointed Scottish Secretary in 1947, took a different line. The Cabinet Office memorandum warned that Woodburn would be 'very foolish if he takes on these tasks and then finds, as he will find, that he is absolutely power-less to give effect to any economic recommendations which may be made to him' (Ibid.). The warning sounded remarkably similar to that given by Lord Salisbury back in 1885 when he suggested that as far as the Scottish Office was concerned, 'power limped lamely behind responsibility' (Ross 1978: 9). The problem was, as a future Chief Economic Adviser to the Secretary of State noted, that successive Scottish Secretaries over the post-war period became concerned with economic matters 'although largely lacking statutory economic functions' (McCrone 1985: 207).

Nonetheless, a White Paper on Scottish Affairs was issued in 1948 (HMSO 1948). It proposed changes in parliamentary procedure to take greater account of Scottish affairs. As Woodburn had recommended, the Government also proposed to set up a Scottish Economic Conference (SEC) to meet regularly under the chairmanship of the Secretary of State (Ibid.: 3). An annual review of the main developments and trends in Scot-tish economic affairs was also proposed. This was a significant landmark. Not only was it accepted that there was a distinct Scottish central admin-istration but also a distinct Scottish economy with attendant expectations. The machinery of government would be kept under continuous review. Special procedures within the nationalised industries for Scotland were also proposed (Chester 1975: 1031). The Scottish Economic Conference's terms of reference were that it 'would meet from time to time for the inter-change of information on developments and trends in economic affairs and to confer with the Secretary of State on questions of economic impor-tance in Scotland'. However it had little impact and was quietly forgotten about until its revival in the 1990s by Michael Forsyth, Conservative Secretary of State for Scotland, who was seeking a means of demonstrat-ing to the Scottish public that his party took the Scottish dimension seriously.

Taking account of Scottish demands without conceding too much was difficult. Compared with Wales, where expectations were lower and insti-tutional development less advanced, Scotland was seen by Whitehall officials as presenting more challenges. Demands were articulated around substantive public policy concerns. A Cabinet Office official remarked to a colleague in March 1950, that though the Scots felt strongly about 'their national rights', this did not mean 'they would relish the kind of flattering, flamboyant but untruthful document which might appeal to the Welsh' (TNA CAB 21/3329).

The Scottish Office at mid-century

In 1950, the four main Scottish central departments were: the Department of Agriculture for Scotland; the Scottish Education Department; The Department of Health for Scotland; and the Scottish Home Department. The scale of Scottish Office activities was considerable. In June 1946, a Treasury memorandum was issued to departments on the status, organisation and staffing of regional offices in Scotland which stated that 'Departments with a strong regional organisation throughout Great Britain should devolve upon their Scottish Representatives sufficient authority for business to be settled on the spot' (quoted in Mackenzie and Grove 1957: 275). Departments should strengthen their Scottish offices 'even if the result is an official or an organisation of greater weight and standing than on ordinary staffing canons would be thought more appropriate' (Ibid.: 275–276).

The Conservatives came back to power in 1951. In opposition, they had played the Scottish card. They were critical of the unwillingness of the Attlee Government to cater for Scottish distinctiveness and had produced a document, 'Scottish Control of Scottish Affairs' in 1949, making four recommendations:

i.   the establishment of a Minister of State, a 'Deputy to the Secretary of State for Scotland';
ii. the appointment of an additional Parliamentary Under-Secretary of State;
iii. the appointment of a Royal Commission 'to review the whole situation as between Scotland and England in the light of modern developments, and to make recommendation'; and
iv. the creation of separate executive authorities for Scotland 'for those industries which it will be impossible to denationalise' (Scottish Unionist Party 1949).

In office, the Conservatives established a Minister of State with Lord Home, future Prime Minister, the first Minister of State. Prime Minister Churchill told Home to 'Go and quell those turbulent Scots, and don't come back until you've done it' (Home 1976: 103). Labour now played the Scottish card – a common electoral strategy of parties in opposition – and noted that the office of Minister of State was not quite as powerful as Conservative rhetoric in opposition had suggested. The new Minister's access to the Cabinet proved no different from that of the Parliamentary Under-Secretaries at the Scottish Office. An additional Parliamentary Under-Secretary was also appointed.

In addition, the Conservatives in opposition had announced that they would set up a Royal Commission on Scottish Affairs, which they did in 1952 under Lord Balfour. It reported two years later. The Balfour Commission argued that Scotland's 'needs and points of view should be known and brought into account at all stages in the formation and execution of policy' (Balfour 1954: 12). It considered why discontent had become evident:

> It has, we think, been aggravated by needless English thoughtlessness and undue Scottish susceptibilities, but deeper than this lie some more tangible causes. First, there has been a profound change during the last forty years in the functions of government and consequently in the machinery necessary to exercise them. But since then its encroachment on private activities has mounted with what has seemed to be ever-increasing intensity. Restrictions arising from two world wars, steps to meet the depression and unemployment in the inter-war period, the allocation of scarce materials, the rationing of capital investment, the need to channel production – all these have called for regulations and controls, most of which have been organised on a Great Britain basis with ultimate authority resting in London. (Ibid.)

A book on central administration in Britain published four years later made a similar point: 'it is natural that the Scotsman should resent what he, perhaps wrongly, regards as insensitive "English" government' (Mackenzie and Grove 1957: 275). As Balfour argued, 'When the State's interference with the individual was insignificant, it mattered little to the Scotsman whether this came from Edinburgh or London. But when so many domestic affairs are no longer under control of the individual and so many enterprises require some form of official authorisation, he begins to wonder why orders and instructions should come to him from London, to question whether Whitehall has taken sufficient account of local conditions and to criticise not government but what he regards, however, erroneously, as the English government' (Balfour 1954: 13, paras 17–18).

Some proposals were made to tidy up the arrangements for administrative devolution. In October 1954, the Cabinet agreed proposals from the Chancellor of the Exchequer and Scottish Secretary accepting Balfour's recommendation that responsibility for roads, piers and ferries should be transferred from the Minister of Transport to the Scottish Office, the appointment of justices of the peace from the Lord Chancellor's office and animal health, except in the case of control of epidemic diseases among animals throughout Britain, from the Ministry of Agriculture (TNA CC (54) 71 (3)). Home rule pressure had subsided by the time Balfour had reported and this was evident in his conclusions. It was an unexceptional enquiry with unexceptional conclusions. Nonetheless, there were some unintended consequences of the few transfers of responsibilities it proposed. Added together with existing Scottish Office responsibilities, they would give the office a more comprehensive remit for economic planning when it became fashionable in the 1960s.

In 1957, Sir David Milne's official study of the Scottish Office was published as part of the New Whitehall series of books on Whitehall departments. Milne had been Permanent Secretary at the Scottish Office from 1946. He commented on the evolution of the office:

> Some of the alterations may have been made for political reasons, others out of a desire for administrative tidiness; the river may have flowed erratically, but its main course has been clear. There has been a definite and increasing tendency to assign to a Scottish minister matters in which there is a distinctive Scottish tradition of body of law or where Scottish conditions are notably different from those in England and Wales. The present administrative structure is not the result of design, but of constant change and adjustment over a period of 250 years. It is unlikely that it is complete but no one can say what the future changes will be. Time finds its own solutions. (Milne 1957: 20–21)

The era of planning

Further changes did indeed occur. The Scottish Council (Development and Industry), a body set up in the 1930s bringing together local authorities, trade unions, business and the Scottish Office, set up an enquiry under John Toothill, which produced an influential report (Toothill 1961) that led to the establishment of the Development Department within the Scottish Office in 1962. That year also saw the introduction of economists into the Scottish Office, though an annual White Paper on industry and employment had long existed and the Secretary of State had long had an economic adviser. In 1964, the Scottish Economic Planning Board was set up within the Scottish Office, consisting of officials from relevant Scottish and UK departments. This was seen as the Scottish equivalent of the ill-fated Department of Economic Affairs. In addition, the Scottish Economic Planning Council, chaired by the Secretary of State, was set up in 1965 (MacDonald and Redpath 1979: 103). By the late 1960s, the Scottish Office consisted of four departments: the Development Department; Home and Health Department; Agriculture and Fisheries Department; and Education Department.

With an economic and statistics unit added in 1970, the Scottish Office seemed well kitted out to plan the Scottish economy, create economic growth and provide jobs. The discovery of North Sea oil gave impetus for this role. In May 1973, a minister with special responsibility for oil development was appointed to the Scottish Office and the Scottish Economic Planning Department (SEPD) was set up alongside the existing four departments. The SEPD took over regional development and economic responsibilities from other departments within the Scottish Office. The scene seemed set for a major period of economic growth with the Scottish Office playing a central role. This was not to be. Just as the Scottish Office acquired the institutional machinery to act, the economic situation changed dramatically. Governments across the world were hit by economic crises following the first oil crisis in late 1973. Crisis management became the objective.

One significant institutional innovation was the establishment of the Highlands and Islands Development Board (HIDB) in 1965. The area the Board had responsibility for was vast – one-sixth of the land mass of the UK and just under half of Scotland's – but with a small population of about 320,000 people. Like the Scottish Office, the HIDB had its institutional antecedents. In 1918, a book on public administration in the Highlands and Islands noted that this area had 'become something of a laboratory for administrative and legislative experiments' (Day 1918: 6). The Scottish Office argued from the 1920s for more money from the Treasury on the grounds that the Highlands and Islands were a special case (Cameron 1996: 158). An Advisory Panel on the Highlands and Islands had been set up in 1946 and produced a report that fed into the idea that emerged in the 1950s of some over-arching Highland development authority, but the Balfour Royal Commission on Scottish Affairs rejected the idea (Balfour 1954: 83–85, paras 284–289). This long series of efforts to tackle the problems of the crofting communities, congested districts and Highlands and Islands culminated in the establishment of the HIDB (Cameron 1996; Mitchell 2003: 81–83) with a remit to assist the local population to improve their economic and social conditions and enable the area to play a more effective part in the economic and social development of the country.

Responding to the Scottish National Party

Following the victory of the Scottish National Party (SNP) in the Hamilton by-election in 1967, Harold Wilson set up a committee to explore further devolution to Scotland and Wales (TNA CAB 164/658). Dickson Mabon, the Scottish Office's Minister of State, produced a paper proposing that the Scottish Office should take over the Ministry of Public Building and Works' responsibilities in Scotland and have a general responsibility for tourism. In April 1968, a Cabinet Office official noted that the Scots were 'in some difficulty' as 'their proposals amount to much less than possible devolution for Wales, since they already control most of the domestic functions of Government' (TNA CAB 165/298). In a book published that year, John Mackintosh, political scientist and future Labour MP, echoed this point in his warning that extending administrative devolution would be inadequate as, 'it is precisely where this process has gone furthest, in Scotland, that the rejection of the present system of local and central government has gone furthest' (Mackintosh 1968: 130–131).

North Sea oil played a significant part in the SNP's electoral success in the early 1970s and the Labour Government felt it had to respond. There was reluctance in Whitehall to allocate oil funds specifically to Scotland but it was felt necessary to make some concession. Towards the end of 1974, it was decided that the Industry Department's responsibility for some aspects of regional assistance should be transferred to the Scottish Office. More symbolically significant was the decision to create a new economic regeneration body for Scotland. In July 1974, a Treasury official pointed out that the Treasury could not 'concede [that] a great deal of extra expenditure can be provided for the Scots from North Sea oil' but, the creation of a development agency 'would be attractive just because it might make it possible to buy off some of the pressures from Scotland without a substantial addition to expenditure there' (TNA T 328/1031). The idea of a Scottish Development Agency (SDA) emerged. As Sir Douglas Henley of the Treasury remarked in a note in late summer 1974, the SDA was 'intended to contain the pressure for benefits to Scotland "associated with" North Sea oil without, as we sincerely hope, an undue proportion of resources and environmental development in Scotland' (TNA T 227/4253). In a letter to Tony Benn, Scottish Office Minister Bruce Millan reminded the Industry Minister that, 'the SDA concept had its genesis in the necessity we all saw of demonstrating to Scottish public opinion that Scotland would receive tangible benefits from North Sea oil. We must not lose the initiative and momentum on this as our opponents will be ready to seize on any opportunity of denigrating what we are trying to achieve' (TNA PREM 16/266). Concern that Scotland should not receive too much from North Sea oil was also voiced by politicians. In November 1974, Tony Crosland, Environment Secretary, warned Wilson that, 'Opinion in the North of England is on the watch to see that Scotland and Wales do not steal a march, and we shall be very hard pressed indeed unless we have something on offer' (TNA PREM 16/266).

The SDA came into existence as a political response to Scottish nationalism but cut out an important role for itself. While party political motives explain the political logic of its establishment, this built on a long-standing planning tradition (Halkier 2006: 187–191). It went through a number of changes, reflecting the changing economic environment and economic policy thinking. Most significantly, from the perspective of administrative devolution, it became an institutional expression of central government's recognition of the existence of a Scottish economic dimension requiring Scottish institutions.

The Scottish Office under the Conservatives

The election of Margaret Thatcher and the Conservatives in 1979 marked an unusual period in the history of the Scottish Office. Throughout its history, governments of all complexions had presented themselves as supporters of administrative devolution and each further responsibility gained for the office was presented as a major victory for the Scots. Willie Ross, Scottish Secretary under Harold Wilson, had, for example, made sure that he was given credit in 1968 for the establishment of the Scottish Transport Group. Under Mrs Thatcher, the Conservatives continued the long process of administrative devolution but singularly failed to capitalise on it. This may have been because it was felt that there was less pressure given that the SNP were in the electoral doldrums. Nonetheless, George Younger gained a reputation in sections of the London-based media for warning of a nationalist threat when he felt it necessary (*Daily Telegraph*, 21 March 1984). The perception developed that the Conservatives were 'anti-Scottish' and Mrs Thatcher particularly so (Mitchell and Bennie 1996). Yet after 1979, Scotland was increasingly used not simply as a regional unit of a British-wide department or body but as a separate unit from England (Hogwood 1995: 288). This was evident in housing, nature conservancy, training and enterprise, higher education and the arts. Some of these had involved the transfer of programmes with large amounts of public expenditure.

One reason for the perception that the Conservatives were anti-Scottish was the length of time they were in power; parties in Opposition, as we have seen, tend to 'play the Scottish card'. The rhetoric and attitudes of the Conservatives did not help. Mrs Thatcher's views became explicit after she left office but nevertheless these views were far from hidden while she was Prime Minister. Though the Conservatives had been in power when the Scottish Office was established and played a greater part than any other party in its development, she had less sympathy for a distinct Scottish dimension than any of her predecessors. Her perception of the Scottish Office was outlined in her memoirs: 'The pride of the Scottish Office – whose very structure added a layer of bureaucracy, standing in the way of reforms which were paying such dividends in England – was that public expenditure per head in Scotland was far higher than in England' (Thatcher 1993: 627). To a politician who set out to cut public spending and roll back the state, the Scottish Office was bound to appear more than just an impediment: it was a cause of problems. But at no stage was there any serious prospect of it being abolished by Mrs Thatcher. This reflected the enormous difficulties and costs which would have been involved in integrating Scottish public administration into the rest of Whitehall.

Scottish Office ministers

The number and status of Scottish Office ministers changed over time too. The initial demand in the 1880s had been for a Secretary *of State* for Scotland. The 'of State' signified a senior minister who would, it was assumed, be a member of the Cabinet by right. The legislation establishing the office created a Secretary for Scotland, a minister with a more lowly status. In practice, Scottish Secretaries more often than not were in the Cabinet and, war cabinets apart, were continuously members of the Cabinet from 1892. In 1926, the Secretaryship for Scotland was finally upgraded to a Secretaryship of State and much was made of this symbolic gesture by the Conservative Government at the time (Mitchell 1990: 21–22) though, in fact, little really changed. Even the Secretary's salary remained less than that of other Cabinet Ministers, and it was only upgraded in 1937. Additional junior ministers were added as the office's portfolio grew. A Parliamentary Under-Secretary was added to the office in 1919 and a further in 1940, then a third in 1952 at the same time as the Minister of State was appointed. The tendency to have a Minister of State in the Lords was established though this has not always been the case. From the 1920s, the Scottish Secretary was a member of the Commons. The one exception was the brief period between May and July 1945, between the end of the wartime coalition and the 1945 election, when the Conservatives were in power and the Earl of Rosebery held the office. The office of Scottish Secretary did not rank highly in the Cabinet hierarchy. One study written over forty years ago on ministerial hierarchy noted the lowly position of the Scottish Secretary in the inter-war period and concluded that the Scottish Secretary always 'brought up the rear' throughout the 1950s (Heasman 1962: 325).

The junior minister attached to the Scottish Office in 1919 had specific responsibility for health. This was written into the legislation but very soon the remit widened beyond that defined by statute. The definition of responsibilities was changed when the Secretaryship was upgraded in 1926 and the junior minister was given a more general responsibility. The Gilmour Committee considered a proposal to add another junior minister to the Scottish Office but made no specific recommendation (HMSO 1937b: 52). After the war, when the Scottish Office had two junior ministers, the Secretary of State, Joe Westwood, proposed that one should be given special status and recognised as directly responsible for housing and town planning in Scotland and be answerable to the Cabinet and the House of Commons. It would have represented a return to the period between 1919 and 1926. The idea proved unacceptable. Amongst those opposed was David Milne, later Permanent Secretary at the Scottish Office, who had a private meeting with Edward Bridges, Cabinet Secretary, and made it clear that he disagreed with his Secretary of State.

During this meeting the idea emerged of allowing the junior minister to attend Cabinet committee meetings in place of the Secretary of State. This would include special meetings on housing presided over by the Prime Minister, but the junior minister would not be able to attend the full Cabinet (TNA CAB 21/3328). In his paper to the Prime Minister, Bridges noted the problems which would arise from Westwood's proposal:

> If legislation for this purpose were introduced, it would give rise to a number of awkward questions. Thus, what would be the status of the Under Secretary charged with these duties? Would he be on a level with the Secretary of State for Scotland, or intermediate between a Minister of Cabinet rank and an Under Secretary? Either solution would be troublesome, since, if he were of intermediate rank, it would be complained that housing had been depressed by being assigned to a Minister of lower rank. If he was on the same level, the Secretary of State for Scotland would lose his general oversight over all Scottish affairs.
>
> Further, if a special Bill were introduced to assign responsibility for housing in Scotland to a single Minister charged with these duties and no other, would this not stir up the old controversy – happily now dormant – that a separate Minister of Housing should be appointed in England? (Ibid.)

Stuart Murie, Milne's successor as Permanent Secretary at the Scottish Office, then at the Cabinet Office, wrote a memorandum responding to the Secretary of State's desire for a Minister of State in which he conceded that the Scottish Secretary's job was a 'very hard one, since it means switching one's mind among a wide variety of subjects and suffering the wear and tear of frequent journeys to Scotland'. However, he argued that conditions had recently been unusual with a series of significant bills going through Parliament and that this would change. He also questioned the assertion that the Scottish Secretary and the two Parliamentary Under-Secretaries could not count on being in Scotland on more that one day each week. Murie argued that the Scottish Secretary would normally be able to spend Friday, Saturday and Monday in Scotland. The Scottish Secretary could also be there for considerable periods in the recess as Cabinet and committees usually met on Tuesdays and Thursdays. Murie's objections to an additional Cabinet-ranking Scottish Office Minister were that the Scottish Secretary would continue to be the main source of grievance and would not get 'much more protection than from a good Under Secretary of State'; there would be friction between the Secretary of State and the Minister of State as indeed there had been between Secretaries of State and ambitious Under-Secretaries of State; and any new legislation would 'open up the whole question of more devolution to Scotland at an awkward time' (Ibid.). The awkwardness of the timing referred to the growing demand in Scotland for home rule. These arguments were simply ignored when the Conservatives came to power in 1951. Having played

Table 2.1   Scottish Secretaries, 1885–1999

Name	Party	Period
Duke of Richmond and Gordon	Conservative	Aug. 1885 – Jan. 1886
George Otto Trevelyan	Liberal	Feb. 1886 – March 1886
Earl of Dalhousie	Liberal	April 1886 – July 1886
Arthur Balfour	Conservative	Aug. 1886 – March 1887
Marquess of Lothian	Conservative	March 1887 – Aug. 1892
George Otto Trevelyan	Liberal	Aug. 1892 – June 1895
Lord Balfour of Burleigh	Conservative	June 1895 – Oct. 1903
Andrew Murray	Conservative	Oct. 1903 – Feb. 1905
Marquess of Linlithgow	Conservative	Feb. 1905 – Dec. 1905
John Sinclair (Baron Pentland)	Liberal	Dec. 1905 – Feb. 1912
Thomas McKinnon Wood	Liberal	Feb. 1912 – July 1916
Harold Tennant	Liberal	July 1916 – Dec. 1916
Robert Munro	Liberal	Dec. 1916 – Oct. 1922
Viscount Novar	Conservative	Oct. 1922 – Jan. 1924
William Adamson	Labour	Jan. 1924 – Nov. 1924
Sir John Gilmour	Conservative	Nov. 1924 – June 1929
William Adamson	Labour	June 1929 – Aug. 1931
Sir Archibald Sinclair	Conservative	Aug. 1931 – Sept. 1932
Sir Godfrey Collins	Conservative	Sept. 1932 – Oct. 1936
Walter Elliot	Conservative	Oct. 1936 – May 1938
John Colville	Conservative	May 1938 – May 1940
Ernest Brown	National Liberal	May 1940 – Feb. 1941
Thomas Johnston	Labour	Feb. 1941 – May 1945
Harry Primrose, Earl of Rosebery	Conservative	May 1945 – July 1945
Joseph Westwood	Labour	Aug. 1945 – Oct. 1947
Arthur Woodburn	Labour	Oct. 1947 – Feb. 1950
Hector McNeil	Labour	Feb. 1950 – Oct. 1951
James Stuart	Conservative	Oct. 1951– Jan. 1957
John Maclay	Conservative	Jan. 1957 – July 1962
Michael Noble	Conservative	July 1962 – Oct. 1964
William Ross	Labour	Oct. 1964 – June 1970
Gordon Campbell	Conservative	June 1970 – March 1974
William Ross	Labour	March 1974 – April 1976
Bruce Millan	Labour	April 1976 – May 1979
George Younger	Conservative	May 1979 – Jan. 1986
Malcolm Rifkind	Conservative	Jan. 1986 – Nov. 1990
Ian Lang	Conservative	Nov. 1990 – July 1995
Michael Forsyth	Conservative	July 1995 – May 1997
Donald Dewar	Labour	May 1997 – May 1999

the Scottish card in opposition and promised a Minister of State, they were obliged to deliver. This office owed more to electoral politics than to anything else and never assumed the significance which the Conservatives had attached to it when in opposition.

From Goschen to Barnett

In common with other Whitehall departments, Scottish central administration's relations with the Treasury could be tense, with private disputes occasionally spilling into the public domain. The Scottish central administration's allocation of public expenditure was based primarily on what had been spent in the past year, altered each successive year by a mixture of the outcomes of battles elsewhere in Whitehall, a formula, and an element of political manoeuvring. Heclo and Wildavsky's comment on balancing decisions on spending – 'highways versus hospitals versus schools versus houses' – can be applied to determining Scottish Office spending: 'Avowed empiricists by profession, British political administrators are at times secret idealists ... They love politics, but they are secretly disappointed at their inability to substitute a rational formula for political conflict' (Heclo and Wildavsky 1981: 360).

Most attention, both within Whitehall and in wider public debates, has tended to focus on the formulae used, whether the old Goschen formula or the more recent Barnett formula. In neither case was the formula designed for the purpose it subsequently acquired. Goschen was introduced in 1888 as a convenient tool with which to decide the allocation of public funds to the component parts of the UK (for its origins and development see Mitchell 2003: 149–181). Goschen's intention had been to transfer tax receipts to local government. Local government found itself burdened with responsibilities as a result of law and policy decided by the centre but without the necessary financial capacity. However, the prior existence of markedly different structures of local government in the components of the state required that some intermediary device between the Treasury at the centre and the local authorities themselves was necessary. There was no such need in the case of Wales which was well integrated into the English system, but both Ireland and Scotland required to have their own Local Taxation Accounts. Determining the method of payments into each Local Taxation Account (for England and Wales, Ireland, and Scotland) was the first stage of the process and it was this which came to be known as the Goschen equivalent or formula. Relative share of population was not used but instead, as Goschen explained in Parliament, each would receive a share 'in proportion to the general contributions of that country to the Exchequer. On this principle, England will be entitled to 80 per cent, Scotland to 11 per cent, and Ireland to 9 per cent' (Hansard, Commons, vol. 324, 26 March 1888, col. 301). As the poorest component of the state, Ireland was treated generously. The formula survived Ireland's departure from the UK and Goschen became a relationship between English and Welsh expenditure and that for Scotland, the 11/80ths formula. It was convenient to use it well after it was first introduced to determine changes in educational spending in the Education (Scotland) Act, 1918. Though it was never applied across all lines of Scottish Office expenditure, it attained totemic status. Relative need was lost in arguments as Goschen assumed an importance beyond its original purpose. The Scottish Office, Scottish politicians and the media would all invoke Goschen to make the case for more money for Scotland as did the Treasury when it suited its opposite purpose. Even after its formal demise in the late 1950s, there were signs that it continued to be used simply for convenience and it remained for many years the yardstick of fairness.

But as noted, Goschen was only a small part of the story of Scottish Office funding. The absence of transparency in these matters probably contributed to an emphasis in public (or at least elite) preoccupations with Goschen. Simple politics, the art of negotiation and lobbying were vital in ensuring that during the Scottish Office's long history, it managed to gain significant, often cumulative, expenditure increases. Scotland's unique status within the union, relatively small compared with the state as a whole and with little prospect of its victories leading to comparable demands elsewhere, was exploited by successive Scottish Secretaries and, more often, officials. Scottish Secretaries took pride in winning funds from the Treasury. This applied across time and the political spectrum. In 1955, for example, Tory Scottish Secretary James Stuart was credited with increasing Scotland's share of expenditure (Hutchison 2001: 76).

However, the opportunities to gain additional resources had to be set against the constraints imposed by the same institutional arrangements. An example from a response from John Simon, Chancellor of the Exchequer, to the Scottish Secretary following a request for special support for a housing initiative in 1938, typified the prevailing view: 'I feel quite certain that it would be impossible to apply a special stimulus to Government assistance to Scotland without arousing demands from the rest of the United Kingdom for corresponding treatment. In fact we should see the reverse of the familiar process under which England initiates a series of social schemes and Scotland demands that a proportion of the expenditure contemplated should be applied to her needs' (NAS, HH/36/120). It was not only the lack of political leadership nor problems of legitimacy that account for the absence of policy initiatives. Institutional impediments stood in the way of allowing Scotland scope, especially where spending money was concerned, for innovation.

Scottish Office expenditure had traditionally been determined functionally, that is by each Scottish Office function, with the Scottish Office reaching agreement with the corresponding functional department for England and the Treasury. This arrangement encouraged the adoption of the same priorities and policies across Britain. In the late 1960s, John Mackintosh remarked that the 'great pride of the civil service is not that it has developed special methods or a different emphasis in Scotland, but rather that no gap can be found between Edinburgh and London methods so that no politically awkward questions can be raised' (Mackintosh 1968: 132).

There were, nonetheless, opportunities for the Scottish Office to prioritise spending across the services for which it was responsible in a different manner from priorities in England. In the late 1960s, with the backdrop of Scottish nationalist pressure, it was suggested that this flexibility might be increased. Douglas Haddow, Permanent Secretary at the Scottish Office, responded to this idea in a letter to the Treasury in late 1968 in which he pointed out that it was 'rarely possible for us to depart markedly from the pattern of expenditure in England save in special circumstances' though there were occasions when 'at the margins of our programmes, Scotland and Wales may wish to shade the allocations a little differently from England' (TNA CAB 151/45). Willie Ross, Scottish Secretary, was opposed to any formal change:

> I see no reason for thinking that, either presentationally or in terms of practical benefit, there is anything to be said for a system under which Scotland and Wales are given total allocations for public service spending, and left to distribute these as they wish. Apart from anything else, I cannot imagine on what basis the size of such allocations could be fixed, except by aggregating the existing allocations for particular services or projections of these allocations. I do not believe that we should commission a major official exercise on this, for which the current official work on control of public expenditure has not produced even a relevant starting point. What matters is that Scottish (and Welsh) needs should be, and should be seen to be, the basis for Scottish (and Welsh) allocations. (Ibid.)

The existing arrangements suited Ross. These discussions heard what would become a familiar call in meetings discussing territorial levels of spending in debates on legislative devolution with Social Services Ministers and officials insisting that 'common GB standards' had to be maintained across a range of services (Ibid.).

The Barnett formula was credited to Joel Barnett, Chief Secretary to the Treasury from 1974 to 1979, by David Heald: 'All formulae need a name. In the apparent absence of an official one, I now name this the "Barnett formula", after Joel Barnett MP, the then Chief Secretary of the Treasury with responsibility for public expenditure. Perhaps, some day, this will make Joel Barnett as famous as Lord Goschen!' (Heald 1980: 12). Barnett has willingly taken credit for the formula, although since it became politically salient after the establishment of the Scottish Parliament, he has argued that it should be abolished. However, in 1985 in response to questions about the formula, his answer corresponded better with the public records:

> I was aware of what you describe as the 'Barnett Formula' but I had not been aware that the particular formula has been thought of as my special creation. My understanding is that the allocations in the proportions of England 85%, Scotland 10%, and Wales 5%, is a fairly long standing formula that has been used over many years before I became Chief Secretary to the Treasury. All I can tell you is that the formula was indeed used during the whole of my period in office and to the best of my knowledge and belief is still being used. (Barnett 1985)

Barnett made no reference to the formula in his book on his years as Chief Secretary (Barnett 1982) but explained this in evidence to the Treasury Select Committee in 1997, 'When I wrote the book I was not too concerned with that particular issue. I was concerned with many more' (Barnett 1997: 1).

The formula had been used before Barnett became Chief Secretary. A paper prepared by a Treasury civil servant in response to the Kilbrandon Commission on the Constitution in January 1974 noted, 'For some services, notably health and the personal social services, there are very few objectively defined standards for the provision of services, and significant differences in the levels of provision. Present policy is designed to ensure that the growth rates in England, Scotland and Wales are broadly comparable, and that additional expenditures on reduced allocations are calculated on a population basis (85 England, 10 Scotland, 5 Wales)' (TNA T 227/4253). This was the formula. Changes in expenditure would be determined functionally across Britain, that is for each service, and then these changes would be applied to amounts spent in previous years on this 85:10:5 ratio between England, Scotland and Wales or, depending on the service, 90:10 between England and Wales, and Scotland.

Barnett took on particular relevance in the devolution debates in the late 1970s. Jim Ross, Scottish Office civil servant in charge of devolution policy in the late 1970s, explained that the background to Barnett 'reflected the devolution debate in that it reflected the conviction of all Departments other than the Scottish Office and all MPs other than Scottish ones that the Scots had been getting away with financial murder' (Ross 1985). Scotland had done well because it was allowed to negotiate each of the functional blocks individually and there had been little interest in how Scotland had done overall:

> The purpose of Barnett was both to simplify the Treasury's bargaining processes and to ensure that, when increases in Votes were negotiated, the total Scottish increase over all Votes should be no more than a reasonable one. The 10/85 formula was intended gradually to reduce the then existing Scottish advantage

in terms of public expenditure without creating a degree of disturbance that would have created a row ... In other words, the Barnett formula established a new pattern of negotiation between the Treasury and Departments, a pattern which had already been partly in operation but which was legitimated by Barnett. The Treasury settled with the main English Departments what alterations were to be made in the various functional Votes. The total Scottish Votes were then altered by the formula, and it was left to the Secretary of State to sort out the balance within the Scottish Votes. (Ibid.)

Ross's account of the introduction and operation of Barnett lays emphasis on the convergence intentions of the formula, the pressures from outside for change and the backdrop of devolution. In its origins, Barnett involved far more continuity with past practice than has generally been appreciated. Its long-term convergence consequences would have been well understood by Treasury officials but as an interim measure these would not have been seen as important. As happened with the Goschen formula, a temporary expedient took root. During the Conservative years, as the formula attracted attention, it became less significant. Ian Lang, as Secretary of State, maintained that the formula was often by-passed in special deals with the Treasury (Lang 2002: 194). Indeed, the evidence suggests that the Barnett formula only existed as an expedient and was not applied rigorously with the effect that converging levels of expenditure did not occur at any time prior to the establishment of the Scottish Parliament. Nevertheless its symbolic importance grew throughout the period and, like Goschen, it has generated more heat than light in discussions of levels of territorial public spending.

Conclusion

John Mackintosh set out a number of tests to measure the success of administrative devolution:

The first is whether being closer in geographical terms to the field of operation, and having a smaller population to deal with, enables the Department to know more about its tasks and its subject and so to have a better intelligence service. Secondly, there is the question of how far being under a single minister permits swifter co-ordination and action. Then there is the test of whether national policies when applied through St. Andrew's House [Scottish Office headquarters] can be and are adapted to any particular circumstances in Scotland which do not arise elsewhere, and finally, does this remove the grievance about remote government? Is the electorate conscious of a difference, a greater sense of local flavour about the administration and does this satisfy, in any way, the desire for more local control? (Mackintosh 1968: 112)

The ability of Scottish Office officials to know local conditions, local councillors and local officials is inevitably greater than that of functional departments in Whitehall simply by virtue of the smaller size of Scotland. The Scottish Office adapted policies to suit Scotland. However, as Mackintosh further noted, 'financial, administrative and heavy political pressures brought to bear' on the Scottish Office 'make it operate in a manner and according to priorities which are as close as possible to those of Whitehall' (Ibid.: 132). Public policy in Scotland may not have paralleled that south of the border but operated within a broad notion of parity while acknowledging diversity. However, it was never clear how aware Scots were of the impact of the Scottish Office. The Kilbrandon Commission conducted a poll asking whether people were aware of the Scottish Office, which showed that is appeared not to have a high profile. Another poll in 1985 had similar findings (Mitchell 1996: 44). But even if the Scottish public were unaware of the Scottish Office, it played a central part in Scottish politics, contributing to a sense of a Scottish 'political system' (Kellas 1973).

The Scottish Office was established because it fitted with the nature of the union, that 'most conservative of revolutionary measures' as Dicey and Rait had called it (1920: 244). It allowed for the preservation of Scottish distinctiveness while maintaining the essential supremacy of Parliament. It had been created in the nineteenth century in large measure in response to Scottish demands and developed as a consequence of tate intervention in the twentieth century. It remained an essentially nineteenth-century institution. Although it allowed for Scottish distinctiveness, it failed to cater for Scottish democracy in the sense that it remained accountable to Parliament at Westminster, a UK rather than a Scottish forum. In large measure it proved significant as a symbol of central government's willingness to accept that union did not mean uniformity, but there was always the danger that the Scottish Secretary would be seen as the Cabinet's man in Scotland rather than Scotland's man in the Cabinet though, in fact, every holder of the office has attempted to perform both roles. But it was more than merely symbolic. Once established, a precedent had been set. Indeed, the boards and administrative arrangements which preceded it had already created the precedent, so that new public responsibilities and government duties would be provided for on a Scottish basis. The Scottish Office, more than any other institution, represented the union state nature of the Anglo-Scottish relationship. That was its strength but ultimately became its prime weakness. Formal acceptance of a distinct Scottish politics had been given. This would strengthen the case for legislative devolution, especially when its political head was out of sympathy with the Scottish public.

3

Staggering forward little by little: administrative devolution in Wales

Wales was a separate nation and not just a region, province or appendage of England. Time and again we were made to realise that the problems of administration in certain fields were different from those in England and that there was therefore a clear and unmistakable need to secure for Wales a different system of administrative arrangements to deal with these special problems. (Council of Wales and Monmouthshire, *Fourth Memorandum*, para. 13, January 1959)

The story of the development of the Welsh Office is particularly illuminating of the process by which devolution of governmental responsibility within Britain has staggered forward little by little. (Rowlands 1972: 334)

Introduction

The history of Welsh central administration and the Welsh Office resembles that of Scotland. Campaigns for a Welsh Office used Scotland as a precedent. The Welsh Office was created in 1964 when Labour came to power under Harold Wilson but its roots lay deep in institutional developments earlier in the twentieth century. In the 1890s, Alfred Thomas, Glamorgan MP, with the support of Lloyd George, argued unsuccessfully for a Welsh Secretary of State (Hansard, Commons, 24 February 1890, cols 1069ff). His various proposals were, as Coupland remarked, 'somewhat clumsy measures, of administrative devolution ... no more than a gesture, a demonstration that a body of Welsh opinion wanted a measure of national self-government and had begun to think out its practical implications' (Coupland 1954: 230). It is no coincidence that this happened only a few years after the establishment of the Scottish Office. The campaign for a Welsh Office was more drawn out, more controversial and less certain than that which led to the establishment of the Scottish Office, reflecting the relative historical positions of Wales and Scotland within the union. As the state increased its role in delivering services over the course of the twentieth century, distinctly Welsh institutions might have been created for their delivery, but the Welsh base was never as great as its Scottish equivalent. At the start of the twentieth century, the assimilationist nature of the original Anglo-Welsh union was still evident, though there was politically, as well as culturally, much that set Wales apart from England. By the end of the twentieth century, at the point when the Welsh Assembly was being set up, Welsh political institutions had cut out a remarkable place in Welsh society signalling a significant transformation in the nature of Wales's place in the union.

Educational administration

As in Scotland, educational provision was the first significant matter to be dealt with by the emerging modern machinery of central government. National sentiment, non-conformist religion and education were inter-twined in the emergence of Welsh central education administration. The establishment of the University Colleges in Cardiff and Bangor followed an enquiry into the condition of intermediate and higher education in Wales and Monmouthshire in 1880. This, in turn, contributed to the Welsh Intermediate Education Act of 1899. In 1890, an all-Wales confer-ence of education committees met for the first time (Watkins 1944: 53). This body argued for a united body responsible for the inspection and examination of all Welsh intermediate schools. The Central Board had its first meeting in Shrewsbury in November 1896. As Sir Percy Watkins, who became Permanent Secretary of the Welsh Department of Education, later recollected:

> the 16 years from 1880 (Aberdare report) to 1896 (formation of Central Welsh Board) represent the finest flowering period of statesmanship and effective performance in the whole history of Welsh Education. It was a period when we took our own line as Welsh people, without clamouring for separation; it was a period when by judicious planning and intelligent persua-sion we won support from all quarters and all political parties; it was a period when, in the main, we moved together as a nation, pursuing the national good, without forgetting to enlist the active goodwill and co-operation of the small localities in every nook and corner of Wales. (Ibid.: 58)

Watkins' comments hint at some of the problems confronting attempts to create all-Wales bodies. Local particularism and divisions within Wales were to prove enduring impediments in debates on Welsh administrative and legislative devolution. However, his comments also highlight the importance of administrative efficacy as a factor in the case for an all-Wales body.

The period from 1906 until after the First World War was marked by an increase in central government activities. This involved a degree of deconcentration of central government activities to Welsh bodies. Admin-istrative efficacy required new machinery as the state took on roles and responsibilities it had not hitherto performed. The public provision of education, health and insurance, as well as agriculture, had implications for territorial government. In 1907, under the Liberals, a Welsh Department within the Board of Education in London was set up. Randall has argued that this 'formally began a process of departmental decentralisation which eventually led, over half a century later, to the establishment of a Secretary of State for Wales with direct responsibility for a range of Welsh affairs' (Randall 1969: 2). This is too deterministic but there was a long line of Welsh institutional innovation prior to the creation of the Welsh Office which helped facilitate its establishment, although there was never any certainty that it would do so. The Conservatives had considered something along the lines of a Welsh Department for Education in 1902. Lord Londonderry, President of the Board of Education, had submitted a proposal to the Cabinet to establish a Welsh branch of the Education Department (Ibid.: 21). Despite this, the establishment of the Welsh Department under the Liberals five years later was strenuously opposed by the Conservatives. This contrasted with the situation in Scotland where Conservatives had joined with Liberals in supporting the establishment of the Scottish Office in 1885.

Alfred Davies, a Liverpool solicitor and Welsh educationalist, became Secretary of the new Welsh Department. In addition, a Welsh Inspectorate was established. The Inspectors' role as 'street level bureaucrats' (Lipsky 1980) would prove as important in developing educational policy as it did in Scotland (MacPherson and Raab 1988: 134–153). In a memorandum to the President of the Board of Education in 1909, Davies outlined the achievements of the Welsh Department. The outstanding feature, he maintained, had been the 'definite recognition of the Welsh language and Welsh literature in the curriculum of the schools and training colleges of Wales' (Randall 1969: 51). Administrative efficacy may have played a part in its foundation but clearly those involved saw it as having a role in maintaining a distinct sense of Welsh national identity.

Insurance, health and agriculture

The administration of health insurance under the National Insurance Act, 1911, introduced by Lloyd George, required new machinery of government. This might have been provided on a UK basis but instead was provided for each of the constituent parts of the UK. This excited little interest in Wales. Lloyd George regretted having to create these national bodies instead of one Commission as it would introduce an 'additional complexity into the working of the measure' (Hansard, Commons, 13 November 1911, col. 61) but he agreed to 'defer to sentiment' (Ibid.) when he agreed to set up Irish and Scottish Insurance Commissions and decided that it made sense to have a separate Commission for Wales as well. A Joint Committee of the four Commissions co-ordinated work and ensured some uniformity under the Financial Secretary to the Treasury.

William Braithwaite, a key figure involved, wrote in his diary that Scotland, Ireland and Wales had 'wrecked the [Insurance] bill, splitting it up into four separate parts, but this was not because they were not given full consideration; it arose simply out of the nationalist position' (Bunbury 1957: 148). However, Sir Henry Bunbury, who later edited Braithwaite's diary, felt that experience contradicted these fears. Bunbury accepted that Irish nationalist pressure explained the origins of the plan but that the separate Commissions were 'in the first critical year a powerful influence against defeatism in London. They were uncooperative but they were also resolute; they meant to make the Act work and they believed that they could' even though it 'added somewhat to the cost of central administration'. It had been, according to Bunbury, 'not only a necessary but a very successful experiment in applied home rule' (Ibid.: 31).

At the end of the First World War, the Welsh Insurance Committee favoured a Welsh Ministry of Health. However, in 1918, the Government proposed that the powers of the Welsh Insurance Commission should be transferred to the Minister of Health with provision only for an office of the Ministry in Wales. Supporters of a Welsh Ministry drew comparisons with Scotland, where a Scottish Board of Health was being established. In February 1919, the *South Wales News* maintained that, 'Whilst Wales is wiped out, so to speak, Scotland is endowed with new powers of autonomy' (Randall 1969: 118). The following month the Government conceded an amendment establishing a Welsh Board of Health but critics noted the absence of a Welsh Minister (though Scotland was given a Parliamentary Under-Secretary), the lack of clear powers and duties, especially compared with the Insurance Commission, and that membership was nominated by the Minister (Ibid.: 78–80). Addison, the minister responsible, admitted that Wales was not being treated as generously as Scotland but this was because it did not have administrative machinery of its own.

The Welsh Board of Health consisted of three members. A fourth, with responsibility for housing, was added shortly afterwards and further matters were devolved to the Board a year later. In 1922, the Geddes Committee, charged with proposing savings in national expenditure, recommended the abolition of the Board on the grounds that it duplicated work done elsewhere. This was resisted by the Cabinet 'for reasons of national sentiment and policy' (Ibid.: 86). However, centralist impulses in London came to the fore during Neville Chamberlain's time as Minister of Health in the late 1920s. Chamberlain often dismissed the Scottish Office as irritating and incompetent and his attitude towards Welsh central administration was little different. In 1928, he abolished the chairmanship of the Welsh Board of Health because the Board had not operated as an executive body since its foundation and had met on average only three times a year (Ibid.).

The example of Ireland proved more important than Scotland in early debates on agricultural administration in Wales. The Irish Department of Agriculture had been set up in 1899. In 1910, the Glamorgan Chamber of Agriculture passed a resolution favouring a Welsh Board of Agriculture along the lines of the Irish Department (Ibid.: 92) but thereafter the Scottish example came to the fore. The following year an Act was passed which brought the Scottish Board of Agriculture into existence, provoking demands for something similar for Wales. Opinion amongst Welsh MPs was then divided between those who favoured the Scottish model, with a separate minister, and those who wanted a Welsh Department within the Board of Agriculture in London along the lines of educational administration.

In 1912, the President of the Board of Agriculture proposed the appointment of an Agricultural Commissioner for Wales to advise the Board and an Agricultural Council for Wales to meet biannually. Opinion was hardening in Wales. A Welsh Parliamentary Party, representing all Welsh MPs, was established in December 1911 and supported a separate Board of Agriculture. The outbreak of war temporarily removed the issue from the political agenda. Towards the end of the war a committee appointed by the President of the Board of Agriculture recommended the creation of a Welsh Office. Administrative efficacy rather than national sentiment came to the fore. In 1919, the Council of Agriculture for Wales was set up but many Welsh MPs felt that this was insufficient.

That the central administration of education, health, insurance and agriculture developed distinct Welsh machinery of government was more coincidental than co-ordinated. These were pragmatic, incremental developments and not some plan to create a Welsh Office. Randall (1972) identified three factors giving rise to the creation of separate institutions. These were similar to those which explain the development of a separate Scottish central administration. First was the acceptance that Wales was distinctive; this was in marked contrast to earlier periods in history. Secondly, national sentiment played its part, and thirdly these developments were part of a larger process of administrative change in British central government. There was reluctance in Whitehall to concede reforms based on territory, but nonetheless it sometimes made practical sense. Once a precedent had been set, it was much easier to make the case for further reforms based on territory. Much of this early work done by the Welsh administration was regulatory and supervisory, involving routine work rather than policy-making (Randall 1969: 112) but this paved the way for later developments.

In the inter-war period, further demands to acknowledge Welsh distinctiveness were heard. Support for a Welsh Secretary often existed uneasily alongside support for a Welsh Parliament. Administrative devolution was a first and necessary step towards legislative devolution for home rulers while it was an end in itself for others. In 1920, a bill was introduced for the appointment of a Secretary of State for Wales, but it made no progress. In 1928, Prime Minister Baldwin was called on to establish a Welsh Office, as was Ramsay MacDonald on a number of occasions in the early 1930s. In 1937, the North Wales Liberal Federation criticised the existing arrangements as inadequate and incapable of 'independence of administration' (Randall 1972: 361). Two Liberal MPs introduced a short bill that year to establish a Welsh Office along the lines of the Scottish Office. Earlier bills had been introduced but the 1937 Bill was a 'less ambitious but far more practical measure than its predecessors' (Chappell 1943: 41). The Bill had cross-party support and the case for it was made in terms of tackling Welsh social and economic problems. The following year, a cross-party group of Welsh MPs met Prime Minister Neville Chamberlain. Chamberlain appeared sympathetic but opposed a Secretary of State for Wales (Randall 1969: 145). Jim Griffiths, the first Welsh Secretary in 1964 and Welsh MP from 1936 to 1970, later described the meeting. Chamberlain's letter replying to the deputation set out reasons which, Griffiths noted, were to be heard time and again. The Prime Minister had sympathy for the argument 'from national sentiment' but Welsh affairs were already dealt with through offices in Wales and there would be considerable cost involved. Parity with Scotland was also discussed by Chamberlain:

> ... the two cases are not parallel. For Scotland has always had different systems of law and administration from those in force in England; indeed, even before the institution of the Scottish Office, most of the Scottish administrative work was performed in Scotland and the Lord Advocate was, for all practical purposes, the head of a distinct Scottish Department in London. Wales, on the other hand, since Henry VIII's Act of 1535, has been closely incorporated with England and there has not been, and is not now, any distinct law or administrative system calling for the attention of a separate minister. (Griffiths 1969: 159)

It was clear that the emerging Welsh central administration was not seen by everyone as leading to the establishment of an office of Secretary of State for Wales.

The Attlee Government and Wales

As in Scotland in the 1880s, the local authorities were important in the establishment of a Secretary of State. The Conference of Welsh Local Authorities adopted a motion urging the appointment of a Welsh Secretary of State in June 1943. In October, a memorandum sent by Welsh MPs to Prime Minister Churchill argued that a Welsh Secretary would give institutional recognition to Welsh nationality; allow for policy co-ordination in the fields of health, education and agriculture; provide a 'cohesive' outlook on Welsh affairs; and safeguard Welsh interests in post-war reconstruction (Randall 1969: 209). In November, an all-party group of Welsh MPs tabled an amendment to the King's Speech regretting that it contained no mention of proposals for a Secretary of State for Wales. However, not everyone was convinced. Percy Watkins, a leading figure in Welsh educational administration, pointed out that political feeling in Wales 'very seldom' coincided with the feeling of the rest of Britain, that Wales consistently sent a 'large majority of progressive members, whilst the rest of Britain is much less stable' (Watkins 1944: 221–228). A Conservative Secretary of State for Wales would be the 'chief opponent of the wishes of Wales' as well as the 'official advocate of Wales in the Cabinet'. In addition, by virtue of the size of Wales, the Welsh Office would not be very influential. Instead, his model of devolution involved existing Whitehall departments decentralising operations, Welsh officials having direct access to ministers and senior officials in Whitehall, and the creation of an Advisory Council (Ibid.). The Association of Welsh Local Authorities sent a questionnaire to all members asking for opinions on the idea of a Council of Wales and Monmouthshire. Of the replies, 13 approved of the proposal, 72 approved of it as an experiment and 68 disapproved (Gibson 1968: 32). There were other reasons for believing that the matter remained unresolved.

There were important developments under Attlee's Labour Government. Changes in the structure of British central government at this time emphasised the Welsh dimension. Most major Whitehall departments were in the process of decentralising, with regional offices being established or expanded. In March 1946, the Welsh Parliamentary Party repeated a request that the Government should create a Welsh Office and a Secretary of State for Wales. In May 1946, the Cabinet Committee on Machinery of Government under Herbert Morrison, the Lord President, rejected the Welsh Parliamentary Party's request. This was accepted by the full Cabinet. Ness Edwards, Parliamentary Secretary at the Ministry of Labour and MP for Caerphilly, argued that the 'chief need' was for 'machinery for treating questions of administration in Wales as a single problem'. Senior officials of Whitehall departments met in the 'course of normal inter-departmental consultation' but there was 'no higher authority to co-ordinate their actions'. Edwards saw a need for a 'superior co-ordinating official' reporting annually to a non-departmental minister with an opportunity for an annual debate on Welsh problems in Parliament (TNA CAB 134/504) but doubts were expressed as to the viability of the degree of co-ordination Edwards proposed. A more informal arrangement was thought preferable (Ibid.). At full Cabinet, Joseph Westwood, Scottish Secretary, gave strong backing to a proposal that officials should be appointed to regional offices in Wales and said that Scottish experience showed that it was 'most desirable that the official in charge of such an office should be sufficiently senior to be able to represent direct to his Minister the special problems and difficulties of his Region'. Attlee invited the committee to consider whether any means could be found of improving Welsh central administration consistent with this and which would satisfy a desire for a more effective demand for national self-expression (TNA CAB 9 (46) 5). But alongside these developments, recognition of Wales as a unit for administrative purposes was not common; the Regional Hospital Board and Wales Gas Board were unusual examples of such recognition (Davies 2007: 603). Major developments in the government and administration of coal, electricity, road transport, and railways failed to recognise the unity of Wales but were instead organised by splitting Wales and combining parts of Wales with parts of England.

Attlee promised an annual debate on Welsh affairs in the Commons, the publication of a White Paper prior to such debates, and that 'material and important changes in administrative machinery' would be carried out to ensure 'skilled and sympathetic attention to the application of Government policy to Welsh conditions and the avoidance of unnecessary reference to Whitehall' (Gibson 1968: 11–12). Attlee opposed a Welsh Office, repeating Chamberlain's arguments of a decade earlier and refuting comparisons with Scotland: 'Scotland, unlike Wales, had codes of civil and criminal law and a system of administration which are different in important respects from those of England. Moreover all who have the welfare of Wales at heart are particularly concerned with differences in the economic sphere, and it is in just this sphere that there is no separate Scottish administration. Economic matters for Britain as a whole have been handled, as they must be, by departments covering the whole country' (Ibid.: 13).

The first Welsh debate in the Commons took place in October 1946. Stafford Cripps, President of the Board of Trade, stressed the economic disadvantages of the appointment of a Welsh Secretary of State (Hansard, Commons, vol. 428, 28 October 1946, cols 310–317). Aneurin Bevan, Minister of Health, argued that the Welsh Secretary would be 'nothing but a Welsh messenger boy' (Ibid.: 315). However, the issue did not disappear. The Labour Party in Wales presented the Government with a paper on 'Democratic Devolution in Wales' in 1947, written by its secretary Cliff Prothero. Prothero was hostile to Welsh nationalism. Heavily steeped in the language of socialism, the paper noted that while Labour in Wales was a predominantly working-class party, it should also appeal to 'that important strata of middle-class intellectual opinion which has at present strong nationalist tendencies' (TNA CAB 124/325). It recommended a Wales Regional Advisory Council. Its functions would be:

(a) To meet with the regional controllers of the Government Departments regularly in an advisory and consultative capacity.
(b) To make a collective approach on behalf of the whole or any of its

constituent interests to the Welsh Parliamentary Party where necessary
in order to lay the case before Parliament and bring influence to bear on
the legislature.

(c)   To encourage the formation of group associations on a regional basis.
(Ibid.)

It sought the appointment of Welsh Parliamentary Secretaries to government departments 'other than those dealing with "national" reserved
subjects, such as Foreign Affairs, Defence and Finance' to liaise between
Welsh interests and Government Ministers. In December 1947, Government Ministers and representatives of the Welsh Labour Party met under
the chairmanship of Herbert Morrison. Morrison argued that the case
against Welsh Parliamentary Secretaries was the same as against a Secretary of State for Wales. Wales, he maintained, 'although the home of a
nationally conscious people was indissolubly bound up with England'.
North Wales had more connections with Lancashire and Cheshire than
South Wales with its 'natural connections to the Midlands and Glouces-
tershire'. Unlike Scotland, there was no 'natural "border" dividing
England and Wales'. He told those present that Ellen Wilkinson, as Minister of Education, had once told him that she had appointed a
Parliamentary Secretary with special responsibility for Welsh education
only to be told by Welsh members that they did not want to be 'fobbed
off' in this way. He told the meeting of the Government's plans for Wales,
which involved the creation of an Advisory Council, quite different from
the Welsh Reconstruction Committee set up during the war which had
'died for lack of something further to do' (TNA CAB 124/325). Aneurin
Bevan, Health Minister and Welsh MP, warned that these 'unwise concessions' would give Welsh nationalism impetus. There were 'enormous
advantages accruing to Wales' from government policy, halting emigration
caused by chronic unemployment. He dismissed the Scottish example for
different reasons to those given by Morrison. Separate ministerial office
'seemed to have led to a progressive deterioration in Scottish public life.
There were plenty of able Scots but they were no longer to be found in
Scotland. The Scottish Grand Committee was now a parochial minded
body not much superior in standard to an average County Council', all a
'direct consequence of Scottish separation and of the existence of a Secretary of State' and he did not want the same thing to happen in Wales. He
had 'trouble enough with the Welsh Board of Health' (TNA CAB
124/325).

In late 1948, the Cabinet endorsed the Machinery of Government
Committee's recommendations: an annual White Paper on government
activities in Wales would be published; there would be an annual Welsh
Day debate in the Commons; and a quarterly conference of the heads of
government departments in Wales. However, calls for an elected Council
of Wales or a Secretaryship of State were rejected, provoking the main

Welsh newspaper to complain when the Government issued its White Paper on Scotland, '... at the very moment when the Government are unresponsive to, and even silent on, Welsh demands for administrative devolution and a Minister responsible for Welsh affairs, Scotland is given a vast new measure of self-control. It exceeds the most sanguine demands of the Scottish members and startled Parliament by its character' (*Western Mail*, 30 January 1948). This was not how it was seen in Scotland where modest proposals to reform parliamentary procedure, a few administrative changes and an enquiry into Anglo-Scottish financial relations was proposed. But what mattered was that Scotland was thought to be getting more than Wales.

In opposition, the Conservatives played the Welsh card just as they were doing in Scotland, and with as little substance. They criticised Labour for not going far enough and promised that they would create a minister responsible for Welsh administration. In January 1948, Rab Butler stated that while the Conservatives were opposed to a Secretary of State, he believed that some arrangement was needed in the form of a 'watchdog' or 'Ambassador for Wales' in the Cabinet (Hansard, Commons, vol. 446, 26 January 1948, cols 693–696). In February, the Conservatives published the 'Conservative Charter for Wales', advocating a minister in the Cabinet who would exercise a 'general responsibility for ensuring that as far as possible Welsh interests and needs are taken into account in the administration of all and not merely some departments of government' (quoted in Randall 1969: 218). This marked a change in Conservative attitudes towards Wales. By the late 1940s, a critical stage had been reached in Welsh politics: it was no longer possible for whichever party was in government to ignore the Welsh dimension in British politics. It may not have taken centre stage, not even in Wales, but an important turn on the ratchet had occurred.

The Council of Wales and Monmouthshire

Two factors were crucial in the establishment of the Welsh Office in 1964: a report by the Council of Wales and Monmouthshire in 1957 and Labour's return to power (Thomas 1981: 45). In November 1948, Herbert Morrison announced the establishment and terms of reference of a Council for Wales and Monmouthshire in Parliament:

i. to meet from time to time, and at least quarterly, for the interchange of views and information on developments and trends in the economic and cultural fields in Wales and Monmouthshire, and

ii. to secure that the Government are adequately informed of the impact of Government activities on the general life of the people of Wales and Monmouthshire. (Hansard, Commons, 24 November 1948, col. 1269)

Box 3.1 Membership of Council of Wales and Monmouthshire

Twenty-seven Members selected by the Prime Minister:
Twelve selected from a panel of persons nominated by Welsh local
authorities
Four representatives of management/employing side of industry
and
agriculture
Four representing the work people in industry and agriculture
One nominated by the University of Wales
One nominee from the Joint Education Committee of Wales and
Monmouthshire
One from the Welsh Tourist Board
One from National Eisteddfod Council
Three others could be proposed by Prime Minister in order to

The Council reported on a wide range of matters. In 1951, it came up with proposals for administrative devolution and its first chairman, Huw Edwards, suggested that a committee on the economic and financial relations between Wales and the rest of the UK, modelled on the Catto Committee on Scotland, should be set up (TNA CAB 124/63). Prime Minister Attlee had ruled out an enquiry to assess revenue and government expenditure in Wales in June 1950 (Hansard, Commons, 13 June 1950, cols 22–23). A deputation from the Council was due to meet Ernest Bevin, Lord Privy Seal, that year just before Bevin died. Bevin had been sympathetic to Edwards' idea of an economic and financial committee but the idea was then dropped. The Council drew up short-term and long-term policies on administrative devolution. In the short term it aimed to increase the Welsh dimension in Whitehall and long term it aimed for 'parity with Scotland', subject to differences reflecting the different legal and administrative systems but including a Secretary of State for Wales and a Welsh Office (TNA CAB 124/63). In April, Edwards told Bevin's successor that the Council were 'strongly of the view that Wales should have a Capital and that the choice should fall to Cardiff' (Ibid.). An official noted that none of the departments mentioned by the Council suggested any changes. This was only the first attempt by the Council to raise the issue of administrative devolution.

The Council's greatest impact came with the publication of its Third Memorandum, published in January 1957 (Council of Wales and Monmouthshire 1957). The Council had considered investigating central government administration in Wales for some time and had indicated that parity with Scotland was a long-term aim. The report recommended the appointment of a Secretary of State for Wales responsible for agriculture, education, health, housing and local government and it argued that there was a need for greater co-ordination of government activities in Wales (Council of Wales and Monmouthshire 1957: 183). This was, according to Gowan, the 'most remarkable contribution the Council made' (Gowan 1965). Randall maintained, 'From this date onwards an irresistible demand for a Secretary of State was set in motion which, in the end, was impossible to deny' (Randall 1969: 238).

The thinking behind the report was motivated by a mixture of administrative concerns and national sentiment. It was not clear from the report whether it proposed a Welsh Office mainly to influence policy or for symbolic recognition of Welsh nationhood (Thomas 1981: 51). But the depressed state of the Welsh economy was an important part of the backdrop to the Council's deliberations and though it may have been unclear as to how a Welsh Secretary of State might go about reviving the Welsh economy, this was an objective and one which gave impetus to the cause. It also meant that when the office was established there would be high expectations, similar to those noted in Scotland, that it would tackle economic problems.

In November 1956, Sir Frank Newsam, Home Office Permanent Secretary, described the report, which Whitehall had seen, as a 'matter of some urgency' and a committee of senior Whitehall civil servants was set up to consider the proposal (TNA T 222/839). A year earlier, in order to forestall demands for a Welsh Office, the Home Office had asked departments to devolve as much to their Welsh offices as possible (TNA T 330/2). The committee of civil servants warned that it would be difficult to fill the new ministerial offices especially if, on the Scottish analogy, only Welsh MPs were appointed. They doubted whether a convincing administrative case could be made that there was enough work to make it viable and felt that co-ordination would not be improved. They noted, 'It is difficult to suggest to Welshmen that their claim is weaker than Scotland's because their country is smaller, or because they were united with England by conquest in 1285 and not by Treaty in 1707.' There were already two ministers for each area for which the Welsh Office would take responsibility – an English Minister and the Scottish Secretary: 'To add a third would make the achievement of a common policy in the very many cases where this is desirable, an extremely difficult and cumbrous process.' Of more concern to the civil servants, 'parity with Scotland' would, they felt, strengthen the claim for a separate Scottish Parliament. Finally, they expressed concern that the Welsh Secretary would 'naturally want to take different decisions from his English colleagues' (Ibid.). In December 1957, Prime Minister Harold Macmillan rejected the Council's proposals. The Conservatives claimed that Scotland's different system of law and local government made a separate system of administration headed by a Secretary of State necessary. The Prime Minister acknowledged that Wales was a distinct community within the United Kingdom. Wales, he accepted, had

'... not only her language but her distinctive needs and culture, and there-fore the system of Government administration must be based on full recognition of these acts' (Thomas 1981: 46). In 1959, the Council responded:

> Wales was a separate nation and not just a region, province or appendage of England. Time and again we were made to realise that the problems of administration in certain fields were different from those in England and that there was therefore a clear and unmistakable need to secure for Wales a different system of administrative arrangements to deal with these special problems. (Council of Wales and Monmouthshire 1959: para. 13)

In October 1958, Huw Edwards, the chairman of the Council, resigned when the Government refused to accept the change and subsequently joined Plaid Cymru for a number of years. Henry Brooke, Minister of Housing and Local Government and Minister for Welsh Affairs, was appointed in his place as temporary chairman, leading to further resignations.

The impact of thirteen years of Conservative rule

In the 1950 and 1951 elections, the political parties offered distinct alter-natives for Wales. The Liberals proposed a Secretary of State for Wales as an interim measure on the road to a Welsh Assembly. The Conservatives were committed to a minister in the Cabinet with general responsibility for Welsh affairs. Labour defended its record of establishing the Advisory Council. The return of the Conservatives in 1951 proved disappointing to those hoping for major changes. David Maxwell-Fyfe was appointed Home Secretary and designated Minister for Welsh Affairs. David Llewellyn, Conservative MP for Cardiff North, was appointed Parliamen-tary Under-Secretary to assist on Welsh affairs. In 1954, Maxwell-Fyfe was replaced by Gwilym Lloyd George as Home Secretary and Minister for Welsh Affairs. Following the publication of the report of the Royal Commission on Scottish Affairs in 1954, he insisted that Wales should be treated according to the same principles: 'i. the machinery of government should be defined to dispose of Welsh business in Wales; ii. Welsh needs and points of view should be known and brought into account at all stages in the formulation and execution of policy' (Randall 1969: 233). These principles had proved sufficiently vague in Scotland to allow the Govern-ment to appear to be doing much when they did little. Lloyd George hoped to do the same, though with even less substance in Wales.

Labour policy evolved in opposition, although tensions existed inside the party. A 'Parliament for Wales' campaign had the support of initially five, then six, mostly Welsh-speaking Labour MPs. But it was officially opposed by the party, especially the Welsh organiser Cliff Prothero (Jones and Jones 2000: 252–253). In a significant *volte face* in 1954, the 'Labour

Policy for Wales' was published, supporting the appointment of a full-time Minister for Welsh Affairs with a seat in the Cabinet. Over the next five years the policy firmed up. In 1959, James Griffiths, deputy leader of the Labour Party and Welsh-speaking MP, was asked by Labour's National Executive Committee (NEC) to draw up a programme for Wales before that year's election. The NEC unanimously accepted the policy document, 'Forward with Labour', which promised to create the office of Secretary of State for Wales. This was carried through to the 1964 election. In line with developments in British central administration generally, Labour was renewing its interest in regional matters ahead of coming to power in the 1960s. The Conservative response was largely symbolic. In April 1963, it was announced that the Welsh office of the Ministry of Housing and Local Government would be known as the Welsh Office and would include an economic intelligence section. That same month, Labour published 'Signposts to the New Wales' in which it reaffirmed its commitment to a Secretary of State for Wales, now including responsibility for agriculture.

For the Labour Party, class remained the key cleavage in society. National identity was of far less significance. Indeed, many Welsh Labour figures remained hostile to the national question which they saw as a distraction. The UK was a centralised state for good reason. Macro-economic policy-making necessitated a strong centre and devolution, in almost any form, was thought to endanger Welsh interests. This had been evident in Attlee's response to demands for a Welsh Secretary in the 1940s but two things changed in the 1950s. The long years in opposition encouraged Welsh Labour to back the Welsh cause. Nation and class coalesced against the Tories. The other change was more subtle. Labour did not abandon its belief in a strong centre or in central demand management but Welsh administrative devolution came to be seen to complement traditional Labour views of government.

The fact that Scotland had its own Secretary of State helped. The Scottish Secretary had not undermined the Treasury's control of the economy but was thought to have gained preferential treatment for Scotland. James Callaghan, future Prime Minister and MP for Cardiff South-East, had seen the way in which the Scottish Office had campaigned successfully for the Forth Road Bridge in the 1950s while there had been no Welsh Office arguing for a bridge over the Severn (Morgan 1997: 197). Welsh administrative devolution came to be seen as wholly compatible with parliamentary supremacy, Treasury control of the economy and Welsh interests. The establishment of a Welsh Office would involve a fairly conservative revolution made easier by changes in administration over the course of the twentieth century.

The establishment of the Welsh Office

Labour was elected to power under Harold Wilson in October 1964 and James Griffiths became the first Secretary of State for Wales. The Labour Party in Wales had published its 'Signposts to the New Wales' in 1962, which became part of its 1964 manifesto, pledging to 'appoint a Secretary of State for Wales, who will be a senior member of the Government with a seat in the Cabinet . . . in addition to his overall supervision of Welsh affairs, the Secretary of State will have executive responsibility over a wide field, including education, health, housing and local government, and agriculture' (Labour Party 1962: 22). The Conservatives accepted the office and made it clear that they had no intention of abolishing it on returning to power, but they sounded some warnings. Sir Keith Joseph argued that a Welsh Office would offer more limited career prospects for civil servants and a more limited voice for the minister appointed (Hansard, Commons, vol. 697, 25 June 1964, col. 755). Dick Crossman, otherwise a staunch supporter of regionalism, expressed the irritated voice of metropolitan Labour in his diaries. The Welsh Office was an 'idiotic creation . . . a completely artificial new office for Jim Griffiths and his two Parliamentary Secretaries, all the result of a silly election pledge' (Crossman 1975: 117). Years later, a Conservative MP who had served as a junior Welsh Office Minister, reflecting on the office's establishment, described it as a 'strong and heady apperitif for Plaid Cymru' (Roberts 2006: 113). According to Griffiths, aged 74 when he became the first Secretary of State for Wales, the office had been created primarily out of a 'recognition of our nationhood' which aimed at a 'new status for Wales within the constitution of the United Kingdom' (quoted in Randall 1972: 358). As we have seen, the Welsh Office was preceded by a long debate and pressure over many years as well as a slow process of creating Welsh administrative machinery. Much of the office's early administrative responsibilities were inheritances from these developments but it was not given responsibility for all areas which Labour had proposed in 'Signposts for the Sixties'.

There was some debate on the functions of the new Welsh Office, as had been the case with the Scottish Office in 1885. There was a view that it should not have any specific transfer of powers but have a general watchdog role overseeing the work of all departments. Griffiths did not share this view and was convinced that 'a minister without a department is seriously handicapped in his work; moreover that a roving commission is almost bound to create friction between him and his colleagues' (Griffiths 1969: 166). Sir Thomas W. Phillips, the Permanent Secretary at the Ministry of National Insurance when Griffiths had been Minister under Attlee, wrote suggesting that he ought to have a watchdog function but 'in order to do this effectively you ought to have a department of your own, with a competent civil service staff' (Ibid.: 166).

Initially, the office was given responsibility for matters which had previously been administered by the Welsh Office at the Ministry of Housing and Local Government and the Ministry of Transport, including town and country planning, housing, water, sewerage and other local government services, economic planning and roads, but notably not education. However, as with the Scottish Office, a general 'oversight' function was attached to the office. Matters affecting Wales which came under the Ministries of Agriculture, Fisheries and Food, Health, Labour, Transport, the Department of Education and Science and the Board of Trade would come under this general heading.

On succeeding Griffiths in April 1966, Cledwyn Hughes raised the powers of the Welsh Office with the Prime Minister. Griffiths wanted health transferred immediately, followed by education in a year and agriculture at some later date. Wilson remitted the matter to Sir Laurence Helsby, Joint Permanent Secretary to the Treasury, who produced a paper three months later (TNA BA 25/47). Helsby's lengthy memo considered the case for and against enlarging the Welsh Office. While it gave both sides of the argument, there was no doubting where his sympathy lay. He noted the Treasury's doubts about the administrative success of the Welsh Office and its opposition to transfers as they would 'entail both increased expenditure and reduced administrative efficiency'. In an accompanying note to the Prime Minister, Helsby argued that if administrative efficiency was the criterion, 'my own view is that the arguments point towards leaving responsibility for these services where it is'. Arguments for more powers 'relate mainly to the political standing of Welsh Ministers in Wales' (TNA T 330/101).

Three and a half months later, ever aware of the political dimension, Wilson responded by proposing to set up a small *ad hoc* committee of ministers. He asked Jim Callaghan, Cardiff MP and Chancellor of the Exchequer, to chair the committee but progress was slow due to Callaghan's other commitments. After five months Wilson asked Patrick Gordon Walker, Minister without Portfolio, to take charge and 'press ahead with this work fairly quickly'. As Helsby had done eight months before, Gordon Walker sought the views of Whitehall, but he also went to Wales to speak to various public figures. The Treasury view was summed up by an official: 'this is very nearly a straight conflict between efficiency and nationalism', and he claimed that Jim Callaghan shared this view (TNA T 330/2). Gordon Walker presented his paper to the Prime Minister in December 1967. In it he identified four arguments for transferring education, health and agriculture: i. 'we were pledged to do so'; ii. transfer of housing and roads had 'worked successfully'; iii. the Government should give the Secretary of State for Wales 'effective powers'; iv. at that time the Welsh Office was 'too small to be adaptable to sudden pressure of work or to attract good staff' (TNA BA 25/47).

He argued that the case for transferring health was strongest, followed by agriculture and lastly education. He estimated that the number of additional staff involved would be 20 for health, 100 for education and 220 for agriculture. He maintained that the case should be considered 'solely on its merits, not as a gesture to extreme nationalism which cannot in any case be placated' and concluded that any transfer 'need not lead to any significant divergence of national policies, save perhaps in the field of education'; it would 'bring no practical benefits to the people of Wales and no improvement in administration'; it 'might prove to be against the interests of staff other than the professional classes'; and it would 'cause an overall increase of work and an increase of some 340 in the staff' (Ibid.). His recommendation was to do nothing. Predictably, Cledwyn Hughes challenged many of the 'unjustified arguments' and 'wrong conclusions' but limited his argument to making the case for the transfer of health 'as soon as possible', deferring any decision on agriculture and education (Ibid.). Hughes had written to Gordon Walker after seeing a draft of the report in August. He was 'shocked' and could not agree to the Government's 'reversal of its existing Labour Party policy for Wales' (Ibid.).

In the interim, the political context had changed dramatically. Not only had Plaid Cymru won Carmarthen in July 1966 but Winnie Ewing had taken Hamilton in November 1967 for the Scottish National Party. Dick Crossman, Lord President of the Council, wrote to Wilson within a fortnight of Hamilton, agreeing with the Prime Minister's view that it would be 'unwise to disregard the growing feeling that Wales and Scotland are not getting a fair deal from Whitehall and the growing demand for further devolution including some kind of Scottish and Welsh Parliament' (TNA CAB 164/658). Home rule was now on the agenda. Extending administrative devolution no longer looked like a significant change but a reluctant concession. Another important part of the backdrop was the reorganisation of local government. Wilson had set up Royal Commissions on Local Government in England and Scotland. Proposals for the reform of Welsh local government were caught up in debates on functional regionalism and responses to nationalism. The idea of a Council for Wales was discussed in Cabinet committee. Peter Shore, Secretary of State for Economic Affairs and Anthony Greenwood, Minister of Housing and Local Government, opposed the idea while Dick Crossman was the main supporter. In January 1968, Sir Burke Trend, Cabinet Secretary, reported to the Prime Minister that Crossman was proposing to chair a Cabinet committee on devolution consisting of junior ministers. Trend supported the idea: 'I am not quite sure what might come out of a body like this! On the other hand, I believe that this is a subject which might benefit from a fresh and perhaps unconventional approach' (Ibid.). The terms of reference excluded England though Crossman hoped that English regionalism would eventually be brought into the discussions (TNA CAB 165/297). In February 1968, Wilson set up the committee, chaired by Dick Crossman, to 'examine the implications of further devolution for Scotland and Wales, and to report their conclusions to the Home affairs Committee [of the Cabinet]' (TNA T 224/1764).

In February 1968, two months before leaving office as Welsh Secretary, Cledwyn Hughes sent Wilson another memorandum arguing for an elected Council of Wales. This included a passage setting out his understanding of administrative devolution: 'General policy – for example, that underlying new legislation – is mainly the work of the Minister with the subject responsibility but the Secretary of State [for Wales] is able to participate in its formulation. After general policy has been determined, its administration in Wales is done by him while his officials keep in close touch with their opposite numbers in the main Whitehall Departments so as to ensure that the method of handling casework does not deviate in an unnecessary or embarrassing way from the method of handling it in the rest of Britain. There is also full Treasury control of all that is done' (TNA CAB 164/658).

The existence of a Welsh Office complicated territorial management, a view privately conceded in interviews with retired Scottish Office staff. It was fine so long as the Secretaries of State for Scotland and Wales agreed, but problematic when they differed. The Scottish Office feared the precedent set by establishing a Council For Wales, even if it was an 'organ of local government and as such complement[ed] rather than contradict[ed] a strengthened Welsh Office' (Ibid.). Added to this were concerns about the implications for the English regions of any proposals for reform in Scotland and Wales. Northern Ireland was the only part of the United Kingdom that barely featured in discussions.

In July 1968, Crossman produced a paper on 'Devolution to Scotland and Wales' setting out two plans: Plan A could be implemented in the lifetime of the existing Parliament; Plan B would have to wait until the next but might be proposed in a White Paper (Ibid.). There were three elements to Plan A: educating public opinion on the merits of the 'present unitary system of government'; further administrative devolution; and 'Parliamentary devolution' involving Welsh and Scottish Grand Committees meeting in Cardiff and Edinburgh respectively. The 'educative' element would involve the Treasury, Scottish and Welsh Offices providing material to be used by the Labour Party. The Welsh Office would gain responsibility for health, ancient monuments and historic buildings, and tourism, and share responsibility with the Ministry for Agriculture. The Government had already committed itself to a Welsh Council with advisory and promotional functions, as a development of the Welsh Economic Council, in its White Paper on local government (Cmnd. 3340 1967). The scope of the Council might be extended depending on the reports of the

Redcliffe-Maud and Wheatley Commissions on local government for England and Scotland. Plan B, Crossman argued, might involve a National Assembly for Scotland or a Royal Commission on Scottish Government with a wide remit but this would be for later discussion. In Wales, Elystan Morgan, Labour MP for Cardiganshire and former Plaid Cymru candidate, had argued strenuously for a Royal Commission.

Harold Wilson was unenthusiastic. The Prime Minister proposed that Dick Crossman, Willie Ross and George Thomas should get together and produce a 'more warm-hearted' paper. In June 1968, Crossman told Wilson that he feared that such 'tripartite collaboration' would be the 'lowest common denominator and not the highest factor of consensus' (TNA CAB 164/658). The lowest common denominator was that the Treasury should assist in 'bashing the nationalists', to use Willie Ross's phrase. In a letter to Wilson in June, Crossman argued that 'all the embellishments' listed in the earlier Cabinet committee paper could accompany such a campaign and balance the 'purely negative character of this propaganda campaign' to show the 'attractions of unitary UK government'. Crossman repeated his preferred model of a quasi-federal constitution which, he felt, might not satisfy Scottish nationalism but might appeal to the Welsh. Thomas repeated his case for a Welsh Council which, he maintained, might become a model for the English regions but Willie Ross opposed a Welsh Council, especially if elected, as a 'dangerous concession to separatism, quite apart from the major difficulties I see in maintaining the status of the Scottish (or for that matter the Welsh) Office alongside such a Council' (Ibid.). He was concerned that such a council would have greater legitimacy than a Whitehall department: 'One or other would have to be in the lead, and in democratic terms it is very hard to see how a department of central government – i.e. the Welsh Office or Scottish Office – could retain effective control over a body deriving authority from the electorate in the area' (Ibid.).

Civil servants were also involved in the debate. In July 1968, Sir William Armstrong, head of the Home Civil Service, admitted that further devolution might be 'politically desirable' but most proposals would be 'at the cost of some administrative efficiency' reflected in increased staff numbers (TNA CAB 164/658). The same month, Burke Trend drew up a paper setting out the key issues. He too agreed with 'bashing the nationalists'. The 'thorniest issue for the short term' was whether to set up a Council for Wales, and he acknowledged Ross's strong opposition to this (Ibid.). Trend raised a question which reverberated through all subsequent debates on devolution: 'The history and the institutions of the two areas are so different that it will be difficult to fit them into the same pattern. Is it really impossible to distinguish them and to give each a pattern of devolution appropriate to its own circumstances but demonstrably, and defensibly, not appropriate to the other?' (Ibid.).

By August, Wilson was reportedly 'dead set' on some form of 'Parliamentary devolution' (TNA CAB 164/658). However, Fred Peart, Lord Privy Seal and John Silkin, Chief Whip, opposed the idea of the Grand Committees meeting in the respective capital cities. Various options to allow the Grand Committees to meet in Edinburgh and Cardiff were considered but each was found wanting. George Thomas too expressed reservations. Plans to extend administrative devolution in Scotland and Wales proceeded over the summer. Sir William Armstrong addressed the issue in a paper in early September in which he noted that the Minister of Health opposed health being transferred to the Welsh Office. It highlighted problems and identified areas which should not be devolved, including specialist health advisers and negotiations on pay and conditions. The Departments of Health and Social Security were in the process of being merged at this time and it was assumed that social security matters would be unaffected. As far as shared responsibilities were concerned, it was 'assumed that in exercising his functions the Secretary of State would not require separate policy advisers' and that the Permanent Secretary of the Ministry of Agriculture, Fisheries and Food would 'retain full responsibility as Accounting Officer for expenditure in Wales as well as in England' (TNA CAB 164/658). It was clear that the Welsh Office would remain a junior partner.

What remained after the long series of meetings and memorandums were proposals for extending administrative devolution. In October 1968, Harold Wilson announced that the Welsh Secretary would take on responsibility for health and tourism and would share responsibility for agriculture with the Minister of Agriculture, Fisheries and Food. The Minister of State at the Welsh Office was appointed chairman of the Welsh Economic Council and the Welsh Office, rather than the Department of Economic Affairs, provided the chairman of the Welsh Planning Board. The addition of health became part of the reform of the central administration of health and related services in Whitehall. As in the English regions, an economic council was set up in Wales but economic policy remained largely under the control of the Treasury.

By autumn 1968, the Whitehall machine had ground down Crossman's more radical proposals but, despite this, some significant changes, especially affecting administrative devolution to Wales, had emerged. Wilson had come round to thinking that most of Crossman's Plan A should be abandoned and efforts concentrated on Plan B. In late September, Crossman told Wilson that George Thomas now had doubts about Plan A and there was 'no great enthusiasm for them in Scotland'. There was, he felt, no alternative to waiting for the reports of the Royal Commissions on local government. The focus now shifted to the idea of a Royal Commission.

The process of transferring responsibilities to the Welsh Office had been slow. Ted Rowlands, Welsh Office Minister of State 1969–70 and 1974–75, commented that in the case of health the reason lay 'chiefly in the jealous guardianship exercised by Whitehall departments over the principle of a centralised administration' (Rowlands 1972: 334). But over time a number of other matters were devolved. Primary and secondary education were transferred to the Welsh Office in 1970 and child care the following year. Some industry functions were transferred from the Department of Trade and Industry in 1975 and higher and further education, apart from the universities, were transferred in 1978 along with agriculture and manpower functions. By 1979, the Welsh Office had gained those responsibilities which the Council of Wales and Monmouthshire had proposed in 1957 (Griffiths 1996: 52).

The Welsh Office after 1979

In the 1980s, the Welsh Office's functions grew further. Russsell Deacon argues that in its first fifteen years, the Welsh Office 'had to cope with predatory Whitehall departments, anxious not to lose any of their powers. Over its final 20 years it developed into a multi-functional ministry carrying out the majority of non benefit-related, revenue raising and social security government functions in Wales' (Deacon 2002: 39). Though 'slightly less dramatic' than in Scotland (Hogwood 1995: 288) the trend after 1979 continued to be to use Wales as a separate unit.

Table 3.1 Division of functions between Whitehall and the Welsh Office (1996)

Whitehall	Whitehall and the Welsh Office	Welsh Office
Defence	Europe	Natural resources
National security	Agriculture	Economic development
Foreign affairs	Industry and training	Roads and transport
Economic policy	Employment	Local government
Monetary policy	Environmental protection	Housing
Taxation		Education
Transport		Social services
Air and rail		Planning
Criminal law		Health
Police		Welsh language
Prisons		Arts and culture
Probation		
Fire		
Civil law		
Courts		
Social security		
Broadcasting		

Source: Constitution Unit 1996: 37

Responsibility for the urban programme, non-university institutions of advanced and further education, the Manpower Services Commission and public libraries were given over to the Welsh Office. In 1989, the responsibilities of the Housing Corporation in Wales were transferred. In 1991, Training and Enterprise Councils (TECs) were transferred from the Department of Employment and the Nature Conservancy Council was split into three bodies including one for Wales. In 1992, the Welsh Arts Council was transferred and a Welsh Higher Education Funding Council was set up. After 1979, the Welsh Office had indeed 'come of age' (Griffiths 1996: 54). A steady accumulation of functions had taken place. Its watchdog role remained as important as the Scottish Secretary's role as 'Scotland's Minister' which the Gilmour Committee on Scottish public administration had noted in 1937 (Cmd. 5563: 19).

Welsh Office ministers

James Griffiths, the first Welsh Secretary, had been a key figure in the Parliamentary Labour Party and Welsh Labour politics. His successor was Cledwyn Hughes. Hughes had expressed doubts about administrative devolution in a debate in Parliament in 1955. He was 'extremely suspicious of administrative devolution' and disliked the idea of 'bureaucracy being projected into the Principality without simultaneous answerability to an elected body there' (Hansard, Commons, vol. 537, 4 March 1955, cols 2449–2450). In time this would become more relevant but so long as Labour, the dominant party in Wales, was in power, the issue of Welsh ministers' accountability to a Welsh elected forum seemed irrelevant. Even when the Conservatives, a minority in Wales, were in power it seemed less important at least so long as the Welsh Office was run by MPs from Wales. When that changed, the nature of administrative devolution appeared to change. George Thomas, Griffiths' successor at the Welsh Office and future Speaker of the Commons, was adamantly opposed to legislative devolution. A comparison is often made between Aneurin Bevan and Jim Griffiths (Morgan 1989) but the more relevant one as far as Welsh government is concerned may be that between Thomas and his two predecessors as Welsh Secretary. The reshuffle which brought Thomas to the Welsh Office was not universally welcomed. Richard Crossman reported a meeting in his diary in which he noted this: 'I found an atmosphere of complete chaos as a result of Harold's reshuffle. First of all George Thomas, who comes from South Wales and regards Cledwyn Hughes's views as sheer treason, had taken Cledwyn's place' (Crossman 1976: 771).

In 1970, Edward Heath appointed Peter Thomas, a Welshman representing Hendon South, as Secretary of State for Wales. Thomas had strong Welsh connections and had represented a Welsh seat in Parliament.

Nationalism appeared to have waned at the general election, making his appointment less controversial than the appointments made by Heath's Conservative successors. Under John Morris, Labour's Welsh Secretary 1974–79, the Welsh Office gained further responsibilities. This was intended to preserve a substantial role for the office in the event of a Welsh Assembly being established (Griffiths 1996: 51). There was clearly no consensus on the nature of the office.

The Conservatives staged a recovery in the 1979 election in Wales partly because they had unambiguously opposed Labour's proposals for a Welsh Assembly. Nicholas Edwards (later Lord Crickhowell), Secretary of State for Wales from 1979 to 1987 represented Pembroke in Parliament. Edwards and Sir Hywel Evans, Permanent Secretary from 1971 to 1980, were later described by the *Economist* as the two men who had 'shaped the Welsh Office' (*Economist*, 13 August 1988). In retrospect, what they achieved was the continued legitimacy of the Welsh Office. It was a minor office whose senior politicians and officials succeeded in avoiding controversy. Edwards paved the way for Peter Walker's headline-grabbing approach on his appointment in 1987 after Walker was demoted to become Welsh Secretary in Margaret Thatcher's Cabinet. Walker managed to convince many journalists that he was protecting Wales from Thatcherism (*Observer*, 21 February 1988; *Scotsman*, 17 June 1988; *Observer* 12 February 1989; *Sunday Times*, 16 April 1989) but was less successful in convincing Welsh voters. From Mrs Thatcher's point of view it was the equivalent of sending a troublesome but effective commissar to Siberia. Even she conceded that Walker was 'ever ingenious' (Thatcher 1993: 602). His ingenuity and presentational abilities at the Welsh Office ensured that the appointment of an Englishman representing an English constituency did not provoke the kind of reaction that might have happened had a less astute or sensitive politician been appointed. Walker made the office more visible and raised expectations which it could only fail to deliver, leaving a mixed legacy to his successor. He was aided by Thatcher's lack of interest in Wales, especially compared with Scotland. According to Walker, Thatcher had agreed to let him govern Wales in his own, un-Thatcherite way: 'old-style unionism, in which government sought to adapt central policies to the distinctive needs of the territory concerned, both in terms of policy content and political style' (Bradbury 1997: 88). Walker's successor, David Hunt, attempted to maintain the consensual approach to governing Wales (Ibid.: 89).

The appointment of John Redwood as Welsh Secretary in 1993 marked a dramatic change in style. Redwood had been head of Thatcher's Downing Street Policy Unit in 1984–85 and was a staunch Thatcherite with little knowledge of Wales. Welsh local government was by-passed by unelected public bodies appointed by the Welsh Secretary. While it may have been under John Redwood that the 'abuses of the Welsh quangoc-

Table 3.2 Secretaries of State for Wales

Name	Party	Location of Constituency	Years
James Griffiths	Labour	Wales	October 1964 – April 1966
Cledwyn Hughes	Labour	Wales	April 1966 – April 1968
George Thomas	Labour	Wales	April 1968 – June 1970
Peter Thomas	Conservative	England	June 1970 – March 1974
John Morris	Labour	Wales	March 1974–May 1979
Nicholas Edwards	Conservative	Wales	May 1979 – June 1987
Peter Walker	Conservative	England	June 1987 – May 1990
David Hunt	Conservative	England	May 1990 – May 1993
John Redwood	Conservative	England	May 1993 – June 1995
David Hunt	Conservative	England	June 1995 – July 1995
William Hague	Conservative	England	July 1995 – May 1997
Ron Davies	Labour	Wales	May 1997 – October 1998
Alun Michael	Labour	Wales	October 1998 – July 1999
Paul Murphy	Labour	Wales	July 1999 – October 2002
Peter Hain	Labour	Wales	October 2002 –

racy came to light' (Ibid.: 92), this had been practice for some time. Redwood was less inclined to develop close relations with the Welsh media than either of his predecessors (Williams 1998: 48), serving to emphasise his appearance of being an outsider. His own adviser described Redwood's attitude to his party in Wales: 'a decadent Party weaned on, and therefore weakened by, governmental largesse. Conservatives were quango-crazy. Unelected to public office, either at Westminster or on local councils, they sated their political ambition in the hunt for a quango' (Ibid.: 51). Redwood had identified the key weakness of administrative devolution, power over Wales without elected accountability, but so too had the Welsh electorate. William Hague, Redwood's successor, had a less confrontational style but by 1995 there was little that the Conservatives could do to shore up their support. The Welsh Secretary now appeared more like a colonial governor than the watchdog for Wales, an impression not helped by Redwood's embarrassing attempt to mime the Welsh national anthem in 1993 (http://uk.youtube.com/watch?v=RiwBvjoLyZc). However differently each Welsh Secretary approached the post, as Deacon has remarked, 'All Welsh Secretaries between 1964–1997 were expansionists, bringing fresh powers and functions to the Welsh Office' (Deacon 2002: 40). Periods of growth were followed by periods of consolidation. Jim Griffiths would, argues Deacon, have been 'proud of the development and expansion of the Welsh Office at its end. It achieved and surpassed his dreams for a Welsh Office ... he would have been more delighted still to see the Welsh Office consumed by the Welsh Assembly' (Ibid.: 40).

Financing the Welsh Office

The public expenditure process affecting Wales was more integrated than that in Scotland. As with so much of Welsh public administration, England generally meant 'England and Wales'. The establishment of the Welsh Office meant that spending lines had to become disentangled as each function was added to the department's responsibilities. Within a short period of time, the Welsh Office was seeking to increase the degree of flexibility in how it could allocate its total expenditure. This was resisted in Whitehall but also by the Scottish Office which already enjoyed a degree of flexibility in practice. The Scottish Office feared that making different spending priorities and existing flexibility more transparent would create problems. The Welsh Office, on the other hand, required formal agreement on flexibility to achieve anything approaching what the Scottish Office already enjoyed. In January 1969, George Thomas maintained that an argument in favour of flexibility was that it was of 'great presentational importance' in 'dealing with the Nationalists' (TNA T 331/438). However, Willie Ross, the Scottish Secretary, could see little advantage presentationally or 'in terms of practical benefit' (Ibid.). The arguments for and against more flexibility were well rehearsed in Whitehall. The 'price-tag' of flexibility, according to a note prepared by a Treasury official in February 1969, included a 'weakening of Great Britain [*sic*] public expenditure control and management'; 'widening of the gap between available information and techniques, and the assessments and decisions for which they are needed'; 'accentuation of the conflict between pressures for greater choices in different areas and pressures for uniform or at least high standards in all areas – with a consequent upward pressure on expenditure overall'; and 'greater scope than at present for complaint from some areas that their standards are lower than elsewhere' (Ibid.). The 'compensating benefits' included 'presentationally to nationalist opinion'; 'operationally in relation to annual settlement of estimates';

and 'experimentally as a guide to some of the possibilities and snags' of devolution (Ibid.).

A paper prepared by Welsh Office officials in March 1969 set out how the system operated. The Welsh Office controlled a little over half of identifiable public spending in Wales (identifiable expenditure excluded matters such as defence, overseas commitments and social security for which Welsh figures either did not apply or did not exist separately). However, as the paper made clear, 'The word control used in this context needs qualification. A large part of the total expenditure is the direct responsibility of the local authorities, hospitals and other agencies such as the Forestry Commission, and only a part is the direct responsibility of the Welsh Office. The extent to which the Welsh Office effectively controls the total expenditure of £206 million for which it has responsibility varies from service to service and is greater for capital than for revenue expenditure' (TNA T 331/660). There was no integration or analysis of needs and objectives across the field of areas of expenditure for which the Welsh Office had responsibility, leading to a number of weaknesses. First, the relative priorities of Wales could not be taken into account. Secondly, Welsh spending needs were small compared with both English and Scottish needs for the same services, resulting in difficulties in accommodating variations in spending necessary for large projects such as motorway building and hospitals, especially as the Welsh spending was not expected to vary significantly in percentage terms each year from the amount spent in England. Thirdly, there was no general power of flexibility to overcome these problems by allowing the Welsh Office to re-prioritise its spending commitments, though some allowance had been made, such as in 1968 when it was agreed to allow the Secretary of State to produce his own mix of spending cuts required as part of the general spending cuts at that time. Fourthly, the system discouraged anything other than increasing spending as each service was viewed as independent of other services and considered in relation to English and Scottish programmes for each comparable service (Ibid.).

The problem had been that when the Welsh Office was established it had simply inherited the practices and institutions for determining spending limits from the functionally-based service ministries whose responsibilities it had inherited. The Welsh Office was simply added on to existing institutional arrangements. The Welsh Office was a formal institution operating within well-established informal institutions, rules and norms which prevented much scope for flexibility other than that which developed incrementally. Additionally, there remained a strong belief in the need for uniform standards at least across England and Wales and any flexibility might undermine this principle. A Treasury official responsible for these matters conceded in a note to colleagues in March 1969 that 'there is no very obvious or rational explanation of the reasons why some programmes are allocated to the responsibility of the Secretary of State for Wales, and some remain the responsibility of UK Ministers. Why, for example, is health a Welsh national programme, but neither education (after all there is a Welsh language), nor Law and Order?' (Ibid.).

Conclusion

The process of institution-building in Wales was dynamic, as had been the case in Scotland. At the start of the twentieth century, Wales appeared much less distinctive than Scotland but Welsh administrative distinctiveness developed over the course of the century. The changing functions of the state provided the dynamic that ensured a highly distinctive Welsh central administration came into being by the end of the twentieth century, which contributed to a distinct Welsh politics that in turn facilitated the establishment of the Welsh Assembly. There was never any inevitability about the establishment of the Welsh Office but there was a clear trend towards the acceptance of Wales as a distinct administrative and political entity which made the establishment of the Welsh Office more likely. At times, Scotland stood in the way of progress towards the creation of a Welsh Office, but at other times it acted as a useful precedent. It was frequently pointed out that Scotland had always been distinct whereas Wales was historically more integrated or even assimilated into England. Welsh offices of London ministries and the establishment of new Welsh institutions undermined the assimilationist myth and provided an institutional base for a Welsh Office. There was, of course, also the matter of electoral and party political competition. Playing the Welsh card in opposition became increasingly attractive.

The Welsh Office lacked autonomy in important respects, most notably financial, which placed limits on the degree to which policy differences were possible (Griffiths 1996). In 1988, the *Economist* remarked, 'Wales has virtually no legislation of its own, no distinctively Welsh policy. In all essentials, laws and policy spring from London (as do responsibility for the police and social security)' (*Economist*, 13 August 1988). This understanding of the Welsh central administration was to be the basis on which an elected assembly was built in 1999. Distinct formal Welsh institutions existed with limited autonomy but high expectations of people in Wales.

4

Encouraging conformity, not emphasising differences: Northern Ireland

The true watchwords which should guide English democrats in their dealings with Ireland, as in truth with every other part of the United Kingdom, are not 'equality', 'similarity', and 'simultaneity', but 'unity of government', 'equality of political rights', 'diversity of institutions'. Unless English democrats see this they will commit a double fault: they will not in reality deal with Ireland as with England, for to deal with societies in essentially different conditions in the same manner is in truth to treat them differently. (Dicey 1886: 30–31)

Oddly enough, I would say that the main task of the separate government in Northern Ireland has not been to emphasise differences but to encourage conformity of standards. (O'Neill 1969: 77–78)

Introduction

The irony has frequently been noted that the most vehement opponents of devolution came to support it for Northern Ireland. Amongst these was A.V. Dicey, the constitutional lawyer and leading opponent of Irish home rule. Towards the end of his life, his efforts, as those of other Unionists, focused on Ulster. Though often caricatured, Dicey's thinking on home rule was both subtle and sophisticated. He did not argue that the state was one and indivisible, though some of his writing on sovereignty may have implied this. He rejected the proposition that relations with Ireland should be governed by equality, similarity and simultaneity but instead proposed three 'watchwords': unity of government, equality of political rights, and diversity of institutions (Dicey 1973 [1886]: 30–31). Given Dicey's status, both as a formidable intellectual opponent of home rule and the leading exponent of parliamentary sovereignty, it is worth considering the evolving constitutional status of Northern Ireland against his three 'watchwords' as well as the relationship between devolution and sovereignty. To what extent did devolution to Stormont operate within Dicey's terms?

Dicey supported the establishment of a Northern Ireland Parliament so long as it did not attack the minority Catholic community (Cosgrove 1980: 242). This view was echoed by Edward Carson, another Unionist hero. On resigning from the Ulster Unionist Council in 1921, Carson advised its members, 'From the outset let us see that the Catholic minority have nothing to fear from Protestant majority. Let us take care to win all that is best among those who have been opposed to us all in the past. While maintaining intact our own religion let us give the same rights to the religion of our neighbours' (Stewart 1981: 120). The success or failure of devolution would depend on whether this advice was heeded. Legitimacy lay at the heart of the politics of Northern Ireland. Would Northern Ireland attain legitimacy across its intra-communal divide?

Establishing Northern Ireland

The three statutory foundations of Northern Ireland were the Government of Ireland Act, 1920, the Anglo-Irish Treaty, 1921 and the Agreement of 1925. The first had provided for parliaments in Dublin and Belfast. The second allowed for the creation of the Irish Free State as a British Dominion while Northern Ireland could opt out of this new state, and the third dealt with outstanding issues regarding the boundaries and operation of Northern Ireland. The Irish Free State left the Commonwealth in 1949 and declared itself a republic under the Republic of Ireland Act, 1948, passed by the Irish Parliament. Westminster responded in the Ireland Act, 1949 by acknowledging this but stating that 'the Republic of Ireland is not a foreign country for the purposes of any law in force in any part of the United Kingdom' (Ireland Act, 1949: 2(1)). Sir Basil Brooke, Stormont Premier, insisted that Northern Ireland's status within the union should be guaranteed (Mansergh 1991: 340). The Act affirmed Northern Ireland as part of the UK and that 'in no event will Northern Ireland or any part thereof cease to be part of His Majesty's Dominions and of the United Kingdom without the consent of the Parliament of the United Kingdom' (Ibid.: 1(2)).

The classic Imperial device was used to define powers of the subordinate Parliament. The Northern Ireland Parliament would have authority to make laws for 'peace, order and good government'. Certain restrictions were listed in the legislation. Section 5 prohibited laws which 'establish or endow any religion, or prohibit or restrict the free exercise thereof, or give a preference, privilege, or advantage, or impose any disability or disadvantage, on account of religious belief or religious or ecclesiastical status ...' Section 75 of the Government of Ireland Act preserves the 'supreme authority of the Parliament of the United Kingdom ... over all persons, matters, and things in [Northern] Ireland'.

Throughout Northern Ireland's turbulent history, supporters of continued union with Britain differed on the best course for the territory. The continuum of views ranged from what amounted to an assimilationist path through to independence for Northern Ireland, all competing within the broad 'Unionist' coalition for support. That supporters of independence for Northern Ireland could in any meaningful sense have been described as 'Unionist' tells much about the main motivation of those who have operated under this banner. The one, over-riding objective which unites Unionists has been opposition to Dublin rule. Jennifer Todd distinguished between the Ulster loyalist and Ulster British traditions (Todd 1987). Each tradition had its own 'Other', against whom it defined itself, and its own values. Ulster loyalism's 'imagined community' is primarily Northern Protestants with a secondary sense of belonging to Britain with the Roman Catholic Church being its 'Other'. Ulster British identify primarily with Britain though have a secondary identification with Northern Ireland. Their 'Other' 'reject Britishness, that is in Ulster British eyes they do not value individual freedom, social progress or democracy or share the moral virtues of patriotism and political principledness which the Ulster British see as essential to civilised society' (Ibid.: 18). Another distinction within Unionism is that between integrationists who believe the union is 'best maintained by the legal, political, electoral, and administrative integration of "the province" with the rest of the United Kingdom' and devolutionists who argue for 'extensive self-government – if only to provide a bulwark against potential British treachery' (McGarry and O'Leary 1995: 93). Recently, a distinction has been drawn between primordial and instrumental unionism (McLean and McMillan 2005: 135). A primordial unionist 'regards the Union as a value in and of itself' while an instrumental unionist regards the union 'as good because it has good consequences' (Ibid.). This distinction applies equally amongst nationalists.

Republicans and Irish nationalists have made much of the invention of Northern Ireland. However, nations and states are invariably artificial constructs. None is 'natural'. Arbitrary lines are drawn on maps to create states and provinces and levels of sub-state government. The Government of Ireland Act, 1920 had legislated for the creation of parliaments in Dublin and Belfast, the latter a concession to Unionists in the north who opposed Irish home rule, but the Act proved unworkable in Dublin. As Ken Bloomfield has written, if the 1920 Act was 'pragmatically partitionist, it was aspirationally unitary' (Bloomfield 2007: 6). The Parliament in Northern Ireland continued to operate even though its original purpose disappeared with Dublin's secession from the UK. As one commentator remarked in the 1960s, 'There seems no good reason why the provision for a Northern Parliament, which the Unionists had not sought, should not also have been repealed. It would have been, then as now, the truest demonstration that Northern Ireland wanted to be what its political leaders said it was – namely, British' (Wallace 1967: 159). However, the new Northern Ireland Parliament and the new polity of Northern Ireland created their own *raison d'être*.

What is striking about Northern Ireland is that little effort was made by the majority's leaders to build a sense of loyalty amongst the minority population. In its essentials, province-building, the development of loyalty to a newly created territory (Black and Cairns 1966: 27), is no different from nation-building. What was significant about province-building in Northern Ireland was that conscious efforts focused almost exclusively on the Unionist community. It is not Northern Ireland's artificiality that led to a crisis of legitimacy but that its legitimacy was continually questioned because its leaders failed to engage in province-building amongst the minority community.

The history of creating Northern Ireland is little different from other histories of boundary drawing. Compromises, efforts to take account of physical geography, demography and practical government, fed into its creation. Around the same time that Northern Ireland was created, the map of Europe underwent dramatic change. The issue, as elsewhere in Europe, was whether the new territorial order would attain the levels of legitimacy required for long-term stability and survival. Though the Anglo-Irish Treaty of 1921 had stated that the boundary should be 'in accordance with the wishes of the inhabitants, so far as may be compatible with economic and geographical conditions' (Stewart 1989: 171), its prime rationale was to create a polity in which Protestant Unionists were a majority. The constitutional losers, the minority community in the new Northern Ireland, were excluded from debate, their consent never sought.

Constitutional and administrative matters needed to be resolved at its establishment. Sir Ernest Clark's 'swift and highly efficient formation of Northern Ireland' (Follis 1995: 6) may have been a bureaucratic success but more significant in its creation was the constitutional thinking that informed its establishment and development. In his study of the government of Northern Ireland, Mansergh discussed the 'influence of political theory' on the demand for devolution (1936: 27–40) and argued that of the 'two quite distinct motives' behind devolution – constitutional and political – the latter was 'obviously predominant' (Ibid.: 307). Decentralist or federalist thinking was absent. The need to placate the Unionist community while initially delivering a measure of home rule to Ireland was paramount and was to a cast a shadow over Northern Ireland from the start.

In discussing the first twenty years of Northern Ireland's existence, Buckland noted that 'devolved government in Northern Ireland proved incapable of reconciling regional development with the essential unity of the United Kingdom' (Buckland 1979: 279). A similar point was made by Home Office officials in a paper prepared for the British cabinet in 1968:

> The conclusion seems inescapable that a financially autonomous regional government can only be truly independent if services in the region reflect the

resources of the region, even if this means that they differ from those in other regions; complete domestic autonomy may not be compatible with parity of public services and social benefits throughout the Kingdom. (TNA T 333/184)

However, devolution in Northern Ireland was not created with public policy considerations in mind; it was not set up to ensure that local circumstances and priorities would be accommodated in the system of government. Once established it would create its own public policy logic, but one rooted in its original purpose. At no stage did it break free of these roots.

In his study of the government of Northern Ireland, Lawrence stated that devolution's origins produced a 'singularly inept scheme of self-government and also the conditions that could secure its frictionless operation' (Lawrence 1965: 34). The 'frictionless operation' was a reference to the desire of Unionist leaders to avoid conflict with London. However, this 'inept scheme of self-government' inevitably meant that significant issues would require immediate attention, most obviously its financial provisions. The financing of services delivered under devolution came from two main sources: transferred taxes (mainly motor vehicle and death duties) and reserved taxes collected by the centre from Northern Ireland on a uniform UK basis. The formal arrangement involved the centre deducting a share of reserved taxes to pay for Northern Ireland's Imperial contribution with the 'residue' available to the devolved administration. The idea of an Imperial contribution dated from the Act of Union of 1800 when the Governments of Ireland and Britain united. In its twentieth-century form, it meant that the devolved government's expenditure on services was dependent on the Imperial contribution and the Treasury's fiscal policy. Initial expectations that the residue would provide generous funds to Northern Ireland proved over-optimistic, taking no account of the high costs of services, especially law and order, for which devolved government was responsible, nor the changing economic context of the early 1920s. Northern Ireland could not afford to pay for services for which it was responsible, especially if these were to be on a comparable level to those elsewhere in the United Kingdom, and make a meaningful Imperial contribution. In essence, Northern Ireland would require to be heavily subsidised. From the outset, the new devolved government found itself in constant negotiations over the basic principles of fiscal transfers.

An arbitration committee was set up under Lord Colwyn in 1923 to consider Northern Ireland's Imperial contribution. Devising a formula that was flexible, equitable and which would ensure that Northern Ireland could pay for its services while operating within the terms of the 1920 Act proved impossible. Instead, the arrangement was turned on its head.

Instead of the Imperial contribution being subtracted from the sums raised in Northern Ireland through reserved taxes and the residue being available as expenditure on devolved services, the expenditure needs of devolved services were determined and the residue would be given as an Imperial contribution. From the outset, Northern Ireland's political leaders 'wanted the best of both worlds' (Lawrence 1965: 44) and London acquiesced. In 1924, the Minister of Finance in Northern Ireland stated that 'in all matters of social welfare we should be entitled to the same benefits as in Great Britain ... local autonomy did not necessarily imply any lower social status' (Ibid.: 45).

The result was that by the outbreak of the Second World War, a pattern of government and public policy had been set in which Northern Ireland received significant subsidies from the rest of the UK, it made no real financial contribution to the state as a whole and, as discussed below, rode roughshod over its minority community (Harrison 1939; Berriedale Keith 1940: 199). Sir Wilfred Spender, head of the Northern Ireland Civil Service between 1926 and 1944, privately damned the workings of devolution and referred to it as a 'factory of grievances' (Buckland 1979: 1). Spender's experience led him to believe that integration made more sense.

Lawrence notes that the Second World War was a 'turning point in Ulster's evolution' (Lawrence 1965: 63). The strategic importance of Northern Ireland was recognised by both Conservative Prime Minister Winston Churchill and Labour Home Secretary Herbert Morrison in the wartime coalition government. Northern Ireland had earned its place as a full part of the United Kingdom. R.J. Lawrence wrote that, 'war bound Great Britain and Northern Ireland together in indissoluble union'. The possibility that any government in London might press Belfast to come to terms with Dublin (as after the First World War) had grown remote with the years. It was now 'non-existent' (Ibid.: 64). Despite this, at one point in the war, London negotiated with Dublin, behind Stormont's back, with the key British negotiator proposing that 'There should be a declaration of a united Ireland in principle, the constitutional and other practical details of the Union to be worked out in due course' (quoted in Bowman 1989: 228). Nonetheless, the war demonstrated Ireland's strategic significance which proved important for Unionists in the years ahead.

The war was a turning point in another respect. The welfare state would have considerable implications for devolution. The public policy context in which Stormont operated changed considerably but the demands of its leaders remained broadly the same. The welfare state which elsewhere proved important in the continuing reproduction of loyalty, which all states require, created new tensions in Northern Ireland. It offered opportunities to develop loyalties amongst the minority community in Northern Ireland but these were squandered because Stormont never outgrew its origins and Carson's Diceyan advice to the Ulster Unionist Council in 1921 was not taken to heart.

Parliamentary sovereignty and Stormont

In 1923, the Speaker of the House of Commons ruled that no question could be asked on 'transferred matters' (Hadfield 1992: 3). Many scholars have written about the conventions regarding what could be raised at Westminster and the manner in which London turned a blind eye to Northern Ireland's politics. Calvert refers to Westminster's non-interference in Northern Ireland affairs and quotes a Northern Ireland Minister in 1967 stating that these were not 'laws' but 'something more than a convention' (Calvert 1968: 87). The correct view, he maintained, was that 'Westminster would be justified if it could be established that the organs of government in Northern Ireland were pursuing a course calculated to interfere with religious equality. Such a course would be unconstitutional and would lay the foundation for action by Westminster. One or two isolated interferences with religious liberty, however, would be inadequate to establish this basis' (Ibid.: 92). The problem is that what might be deemed 'isolated interference' by one person would be seen as the violation of significant rights by another.

Questions were asked in Westminster in 1948 after Herbert Morrison, Lord President of the Council, told Geoffrey Bing MP that it was wrong to describe Stormont as 'subordinate' (TNA HO 45/22028). As a former Home Secretary, and one who had (and would again) expressed himself forcefully on Northern Ireland matters, it is interesting that Morrison should have got this wrong. A letter drafted by a civil servant and sent from Morrison to Bing stated:

> Suggestions have from time to time been made to the Home Office that it is open to the Government or Parliament of the United Kingdom to overrule the Government or Parliament of Northern Ireland in respect of some matter which the Government of Ireland Act has placed within the jurisdiction of the Government and Parliament of Northern Ireland. Such a suggestion, for example, was made in 1946 about the Act of the NI Parliament relating to local government elections in Northern Ireland. The reply of the Home Office to such suggestions has always been to the effect that while there is power in the United Kingdom Parliament to revoke or amend the Government of Ireland Act, this does not mean that it is open to the United Kingdom Government or the United Kingdom Parliament to intervene whenever the Government or Parliament of Northern Ireland in the exercise of the powers conferred on them does something which the United Kingdom Government or United Kingdom Parliament would not have done had they been responsible. (Ibid.)

This ambiguous statement sums up London's approach well. A

memorandum written by Home Office officials in 1968 on Northern Ireland's constitution aiming to inform debates on Scottish and Welsh devolution, expresses the position with regard to section 75 of the Government of Ireland Act which asserts continued parliamentary sovereignty:

> it has been accepted that the purpose of Section 75 was to preserve the power of the United Kingdom Parliament to terminate or change the constitution of Northern Ireland; successive Governments have taken the view that, so long as Northern Ireland retains its present constitution, it would be wrong for the United Kingdom Government and Parliament to interfere in matters for which responsibility has been delegated to the Northern Ireland Government and Parliament. It should be noted that Section 75 preserves the supreme authority of the Parliament, not the Government, of the United Kingdom, and the United Kingdom could not interfere in transferred matters without legislation passed by virtue of that Section. (TNA T 330/184)

Devolved government in Northern Ireland was the creature of statute and, at least theoretically, was no different from local government. The test came in 1972 when Westminster suspended devolution. Stormont's political leaders argued against suspension but were powerless to prevent it. While Unionists voiced their opposition to the suspension of Stormont, they could not threaten to secede from the UK nor dare undermine their loyalty to it. So long as Westminster had been unwilling to suspend or abolish devolution, Unionist politicians were in a strong position. Parliamentary sovereignty proved less effective in allowing Westminster to put pressure on devolved government, despite Stormont's financial dependence on the centre, than in suspending Stormont's operation. The sovereignty of Parliament may have been the 'dominant characteristic of our political institutions', as Dicey maintained (Dicey 1923: 37) but it proved a blunt instrument.

Parliamentary sovereignty left little scope for judicial activism. Under the customary constitution, the courts could interpret the law passed by Parliament but could not strike laws down as unconstitutional. The courts were neither used in disputes between London and Stormont nor, until later, were they involved in determining whether Stormont's actions were *ultra vires*. Various explanations for this failing have been proposed: 'the unavailability of legal aid until 1965, some unadventurousness by the local legal profession, an unawareness of the opportunities court machinery creates for manipulation of the political process, and a general tendency on the part of the political opposition to dismiss the courts as manifestations of the Unionist establishment' (Palley 1972: 390). The Campaign for Social Justice (CSJ), set up in 1964 to gather information and campaign against discrimination, attempted to take a case of discrimination in housing against a local authority but found that there was no legal method of securing redress against discrimination (Purdie 1990: 98–

99). Another explanation is rooted more in institutional norms. Challenging the actions of a parliament, even a devolved parliament, would have been a departure from the practice of the customary constitution. While Stormont may appear to have had federal qualities, the absence of constitutional case law before the courts, as well as much else besides, suggests that its federal qualities were limited.

Formal machinery and liaison

Existing and new institutions were charged with facilitating unity of government after devolution. Formally, the Home Office was the Whitehall department responsible for devolution. In Sir Frank Newsam's book on the Home Office (Newsam 1954), written when he was Permanent Secretary, Northern Ireland took up just over three pages. The Channel Islands and the Isle of Man combined took up five. Northern Ireland was a place apart. Newsam's discussion consisted of a brief, formal overview concluding with a paragraph that begins to describe how the customary constitution operated and the kind of relations that were a feature of bureaucratic politics:

> Personal contacts which have been established between Home Office officials and their Northern Ireland colleagues have led to mutual understanding and goodwill in the handling of thorny problems, despite occasional differences of opinion. The Northern Ireland Government have attached to the Home Office a responsible member of their Civil Service, so that close liaison may be maintained both with the Home Office and with other Departments of the United Kingdom Government. The Home Office has found this arrangement most helpful. (Newsam 1954: 170)

In 1973, Jim Callaghan reflected on his responsibilities as Home Secretary for Northern Ireland when the 'Troubles' began (Callaghan 1973). His comments are amongst the most frequently quoted on the subject of London's involvement with Stormont (see for example Birrell and Murie 1980: 11; Wichert 1991: 142; Rose 1996: 97). Callaghan recounted that his first Home Office despatch box contained 'not a word about Northern Ireland, although it was the concern of the Home Office' (Callaghan 1973: 1). Much has been made of this anecdote and Callaghan's observation that he was not surprised as the subject rarely came before the Cabinet and Northern Ireland's concerns had 'fallen into a settled routine at the Home Office itself' (Ibid.).

In addition to the Home Office, London's relations with Stormont were formally dealt with by the Governor of Northern Ireland but this was largely an example of the 'dignified' rather than 'effective' part of the constitution (Bagehot 1981 [1867]: 61). Much ritual surrounded the appointment of a Governor (TNA HO 45/20942; PRONI CAB/9T/3/1). In his 1928 study, Quekett noted that the Governor's powers 'are described in general terms'

(Quekett 1928: 35) but ultimately, as the Governor was the centre's presence in Northern Ireland, this provision was an extension of Section 75 of the 1920 Act which asserted parliamentary sovereignty. To all intents and purposes, the Governor was a symbolic presence but, theoretically, had extensive powers bestowed by the authority of the centre.

There was some evidence that the Governor performed a more effective role. A memorandum written by a Home Office official in 1941, when speculation surrounded the governorship of the 76-year-old Duke of Abercorn, insisted that the governorship's functions were 'not only formal':

> They are often spectacular as when, on the sudden death of Lord Craigavon, it fell to the Governor to call for Mr Andrews before he had been elected leader of the party, but in many ways he can play, and does, a useful part behind the scenes. Further it is very desirable that there should be someone in Northern Ireland with a broad outlook in whose house persons of different views in Northern Ireland can meet each other and persons from this country as it were on neutral ground. A non-resident Governor would have to confine himself to giving formal entertainments, at which informal discussion would be practically impossible. The importance of the social functions of the Governor have no doubt been somewhat obscured by the fact that the Duke and Duchess of Abercorn have not in the last few years been in very good health and have not been able to see very much of people. Even as things are, their influence is by no means negligible, due to the fact that they are universally loved and respected.
>
> It is also of course of great value to Whitehall that there should be someone well informed but detached from local politics with whom matters can on occasion be discussed. This aspect also has not been so prominent in the last few years, but at one time it was of considerable importance and is pretty sure to be again. (TNA HO 45/20942)

It depended on the individual holding the post. The Duke of Abercorn commanded some respect in Northern Ireland whereas Lord Erskine, who graduated to the governorship via the Joint Exchequer Board, had little local influence.

Concerns that formal mechanisms for liaison between London and Belfast were absent were periodically expressed at the centre. In early 1963, Henry Brooke (father of Peter Brooke, later Secretary of State for Northern Ireland), the Home Secretary wanted more information about visits to London by Stormont ministers. The review of practice arose in large part because Brooke was a new Home Secretary and had questioned whether his department fulfilled its Northern Ireland responsibilities effectively. A Home Office official noted that there was 'no comprehensive record' of visits (PRONI CAB/9S/47/1). Ministers informed the Home Secretary when they visited Northern Ireland but the traffic tended to be more frequent the other way. Various suggestions were made including more frequent visits to Northern Ireland by Home Office ministers, the appointment of Stormont liaison officers to other departments as well as the Home Office, and that 'some Standing Committee of United Kingdom and Northern Ireland Ministers' be formally appointed. The Home Office view was that more informal meetings would help (Ibid.). Brooke had himself initially favoured more formal machinery for regular meetings between UK and Northern Ireland ministers (Ibid.). One important development was the secondment of staff to Whitehall. Kenneth Bloomfield, later head of the Northern Ireland civil service, for example, spent a little time at the Home Office acquiring experience of Whitehall and studying liaison (Ibid.) but this served more as an induction to his later and more significant experience at the Cabinet Office.

The existence of a separate civil service in Northern Ireland might have been expected to engender centrifugal tendencies but the civil service was dominated by the same mindset found in the political governing class. It was overwhelmingly Protestant, partly because Catholic schools discouraged applications and most Catholics who joined reached a glass ceiling blocking promotion (Shea 1981: 197–198; 177–184). The Northern Ireland Civil Service (NICS) was created in 1921 with civil servants transferred on a voluntary basis from departments in Dublin. It had its own Civil Service Commission charged with recruitment and promotion but, as in so many other respects, the NICS paralleled the home civil service in Britain.

Financing Stormont

The Joint Exchequer Board (JEB) also operated somewhere in the no-man's land between the dignified and efficient parts of the constitution. It had three members, one appointed each by the Treasury and the Ministry of Finance plus a chairman 'appointed by the Crown'. A convention developed, as a Treasury official explained in 1964, that the chairman was a Scot on the grounds that a Scot would be 'sort of neutral between the Governments in Westminster and in Belfast' (TNA T 341/318). Legislation gave the Board responsibility for settling financial matters between the Treasury and the Northern Ireland Government (section 32 of 1920 Act). It never published any reports nor did it meet regularly. Indeed, for significant periods of its history it did not meet at all. Lawrence maintained that it could be 'a buffer between London and Belfast' (Lawrence 1965: 171) but this was rarely, if ever, the case.

The Northern Ireland representative raised three issues at the first meeting of the Board in December 1921: the fairness of Northern Ireland's contribution to its own expenditure; the basis of the contribution; and whether police charges should be deemed military expenses. The Treasury representative resisted opening up discussion on these matters and the Northern Ireland representative had to back down (Follis 1995: 119–120). This set the tone of future relations between the Treasury and the Ministry of Finance and the limitations of the Joint Exchequer Board's field of activity. In the early years, the financial difficulties afflicting devolution ensured that relations between London and Belfast were tense but bilateral negotiations between unequals appears a more accurate description of relations than one suggesting the JEB adjudicated as a powerful intermediary body. The Board was a small body without the resources to intervene effectively, as became evident with the appointment of the Northern Ireland Arbitration Committee (Colwyn Committee) in 1923. It was Colwyn's principles – that the Imperial contribution should be the surplus of revenue over necessary expenditure and *per capita* expenditure should increase *pari passu* with that in Britain – that determined public finances down to 1932 when the figures pointed to a negative contribution (Lawrence 1965: 54–55). At crucial periods when arbitration was necessary, the Board had little or no input.

Developments in the welfare state after 1945 combined with the principle of parity to limit the scope of the Joint Exchequer Board; decisions were taken bilaterally between London and Belfast with the JEB rubber-stamping them. A briefing note, written by a Treasury official in 1952, set out the system. Northern Ireland was credited with the proceeds of taxes and a share of 'reserved' taxes decided by the Treasury and from this was subtracted its expenditure with the balance turned over to the UK Exchequer as an 'Imperial contribution' for national debt, defence etc. In order to prevent taxes in Northern Ireland being reduced at the expense of the Imperial contribution or of social services, there was an understanding that parity in taxation and expenditure would be preserved. Dispute resolution machinery was unnecessary. As the official explained,

> If there were a dispute, it would go before the 'Joint Exchequer Board' – a body consisting of an official from Treasury, an official from N. Ireland Ministry of Finance, and an aged Scottish Judge (Lord Alness who lives in Bournemouth). But it is unthinkable that there should be a dispute of this sort. (TNA T 233/1475)

Agriculture was a significant responsibility from the start. Though transferred to Stormont under the 1920 Act, Northern Ireland received agricultural subsidies directly from London. The Simon Declaration of 1938, when Sir John Simon was Chancellor of the Exchequer, agreed, 'Despite the fact that agriculture in Northern Ireland is a Transferred Service, it is agreed that where agricultural subsidies are granted in Great Britain and circumstances are such as to justify corresponding subsidies in Northern Ireland, no objection will be raised to the cost being borne on the Vote of the Ministry of Agriculture of Great Britain' (Hansard, Commons, 12 May 1938, cols 1708–1709). The reason given at the time was that farmers in Northern Ireland should not be disadvantaged by its remoteness from the market in Britain. This may have been part of the explanation but Northern Ireland's financial situation meant that these subsidies would have stretched Northern Ireland's limited fiscal capacity to the limits.

By the early 1960s, Stormont's financial arrangements bore little resemblance to their statutory basis. Stormont's responsibilities for peace, order and good government under the 1920 Act had widened with the welfare state. By the early 1960s the Imperial contribution had become little more than whatever modest amount Northern Ireland could contribute. A memorandum prepared by the Treasury in 1961 on the financial relations between Britain and Northern Ireland included figures on the Imperial contribution paid by Northern Ireland and the amount that would have been paid had it been based on a crude population basis. The degree of subsidy was significant.

National insurance legislation passed in 1946 provided for equality of benefits and contributions throughout the UK though formally two separate National Insurance Funds operated. As we have seen, these changes also affected Scotland and Wales where the separate National Insurance Commissions established in 1911 were integrated into a uniform system. National Insurance was not self-supporting in the sense that benefits were paid out of contributions. Costs in excess of contributions were provided for by the Exchequers in London and Belfast. As unemployment and ill-health were higher in Northern Ireland, this would create financial problems for Stormont so provision was made to review the operation of the National Insurance Funds periodically and ensure that both payments into the Funds and total balances would be maintained in proportion to each other. In effect, the Northern Ireland National Insurance Fund was subsidised by the British Fund.

In 1949, the Social Services Agreement recognised that equal standards of social service would place an intolerable burden on the Northern Ireland Exchequer. The Agreement relieved Northern Ireland of part of the cost of the National Health Service, National Assistance, Family Allowances and Non-Contributory Old Age Pensions. Stormont would

Table 4.1 Imperial contributions paid by Northern Ireland and amount that would have been paid on strict population basis

	Amount paid £m	Amount due on a population basis £m
1955/56	16	55
1956/57	14	59
1957/58	9.5	55
1958/59	9	56

pay for only 2.5 per cent of the costs, though Northern Ireland's population was 2.7 per cent of the UK's, to take account of its lower taxable
capacity. The UK Exchequer would provide 80 per cent of any expenditure beyond this and the remainder would be met by Stormont. It was
accepted that if the cost of these services was under the 2.5 per cent then
Stormont would contribute 80 per cent of the difference payable to the UK
Exchequer. However, it was not anticipated that this would happen.

A consequence of this dependency was the absence of incentives to gain
any financial independence or seriously address Northern Ireland's weak
economic base. Harold Macmillan, in his diary in March 1955, described
the problem: 'Their industrial problems are not unlike those of Scotland –
but worsened by the fact that they have no coal and even more expensive
freights' (Catterall 2003: 403). There was no absence of enquiries, initiatives, subsidies and demands for action from Stormont politicians. Sir
Basil Brooke relied on his personal contacts with the London establishment (Mulholland 2000: 21) to gain economic support for Northern
Ireland's ailing economy. In 1961, a working party on Northern Ireland's
economy under Sir Robert Hall was set up jointly by the Stormont and
Westminster Governments. Instead of providing the necessary fillip to the
elderly Premier at a time of economic difficulties, the Hall Report called
for greater economic self-sufficiency combining greater efficiency and
productivity, reduced costs and labour migration (Hall 1962: 11). The
report 'fatally damaged' Brooke's leadership (Bew, Gibbon and Patterson
1995: 132). Marc Mulholland has described financial relations between
the Treasury and Stormont: 'The extreme complexity of Northern
Ireland's relationship with the Treasury, the result of a thicket of conventions and, more importantly, an attempt to hide the British subvention,
allowed self-delusion as to Northern Ireland's self-sufficiency to run riot
on the Unionist backbench' (Mulholland 2000: 60). Hall was disillusion-
ing. Brooke was politically damaged and his premiership ended because
Hall exposed that personal contacts in London were no substitute for
successful management of Northern Ireland's economy. The report also
offered an opportunity for Terence O'Neill, Northern Ireland Minister of
Finance and future Prime Minister, to outline an alternative approach.
Instead of reliance on London, O'Neill proposed greater 'self-help' in a
major speech in late November 1962. This represented a different form of
unionism, one that was more devolutionist in outlook.

In 1967, discussions were held between the Treasury and Stormont's
Ministry of Finance as it had become clear that Northern Ireland was
heading into serious deficit but, as one Treasury official noted, 'all the radical
ideas' came from the Treasury. The Treasury suggested 'breaking with parity
and allowing the Northern Ireland Government to direct their finances
according to local requirements instead of following Great Britain's lead'
(TNA T 341/66). This would have allowed Stormont to cut its expenditure

on some services and increase it on others and allow the Treasury to disengage from detailed study of projects but Stormont thought this too radical and that its political implications made it a 'non-starter' (Ibid.). Another idea floated by the Treasury and rejected by Stormont was giving Northern Ireland a straightforward annual grant based on unemployment levels. The idea of abandoning the 'Imperial contribution', long since a fiction anyway, was considered. Treasury officials thought these ideas would place Stormont's finances on a rational footing. It was recognised that there 'could be great difficulties in laying down the rules for calculating the grant; too small a one would not serve its purposes and too large a one would give Northern Ireland freedom to increase expenditure without reference to the Treasury' (Ibid.). The era of the Public Expenditure Survey Committee (PESC), intended to report on the financial implications of policies, had started in Britain in 1961. The Treasury was keen that Stormont should become part of the process. However, in early 1968, the Treasury and Ministry of Finance agreed to suspend discussions. The crisis which afflicted the Labour Government, forcing it to consider major spending cuts, allied with the need for changes in legislation and doubts over Stormont's ability to pursue an independent policy of public expenditure controls, pushed Stormont's finances off the agenda.

Whitehall departments and Stormont's Ministry of Finance had another opportunity to consider relations with Stormont when preparing to give evidence to the Royal Commission on the Constitution. In late 1969, Treasury officials received a draft paper on the financing of devolution prepared by Sir Cecil Bateman of Stormont's Finance Department. A Treasury official commented to his colleagues that what was 'most interesting' was that there was 'no hint in it of any desire by Northern Ireland for more independence, only more money!' (TNA T 341/66). There was no desire to control more taxation, nor any interest in the taxation that Stormont controlled but a 'straight grant from the UK Exchequer ... is quite enough for him' (Ibid.).

Before Stormont was suspended, members of the Royal Commission on the Constitution were interested in how the Stormont system might be improved. Early in 1970, Commissioners and Home Office officials agreed that the 1920 financial settlement was 'nonsense'. The Commissioners had suggested that Stormont's services should be financed through Westminster votes while the officials suggested that this would not be consistent with devolution (Ibid.). The Commissioners were keen to meet with Treasury officials and a Home Office official warned colleagues at the Treasury that the Commissioners thought that 'there was a conspiracy to retain the present system so as to conceal the true character of the "subsidy" to Northern Ireland' (Ibid.). The Home Office conceded that the figures were hard to understand but they were transparent: 'This was not to say that the 1920 system had not to be manoeuvred into giving the right result, mainly by using the Imperial contribution as a balancing factor' (Ibid.). At this stage, two years before Stormont was suspended, it was acknowledged that change was 'no doubt necessary' and that the 1920 system did not work: 'each statutory subvention indeed marked a marginally intolerable strain on the camel's back' (Ibid.). In the event, political events in Northern Ireland meant that the camel's back was never broken.

Ironically, just as Westminster assumed greater responsibility for politics in Northern Ireland, the Treasury was considering making Stormont more financially independent. Whitehall's responses may have appeared contradictory but were provoked by a similar diagnosis. Stormont had become both politically and fiscally irresponsible.

Intergovernmental relations and the welfare state

In his memoirs, John Oliver, Permanent Secretary of Stormont's Ministry of Development for a decade from 1964, listed the variety of institutions and policies that governed relations between Stormont and Whitehall in the era of the welfare state:

> The joint exchequer board; the residuary share of reserved taxation; the imperial contribution; step-by-step; parity; leeway; the re-insurance agreement; the social services agreement; the remoteness grant; the guaranteed price system for agriculture; the Development Programme 1970–75; paragraph 86 in the 1973 white paper on constitutional proposals – all strike a chord in the memory of everyone who follows the course of our public affairs and all reflect the practical arrangements worked on by Ministry of Finance officials since 1921. (Oliver 1978: 39)

These continuously evolving relations create a picture of complex intergovernmentalism but the objective remained consistent: that Northern Ireland broadly followed London's lead in public policy. In 1955, Newark listed the 'more important English Acts of the past twenty-five years' and noted that these had been 'immediately or shortly followed by parallel Northern Ireland legislation' (Newark 1955: 52 n. 1). The key term here is 'parallel' as the legislation passed by Stormont was not entirely a replication of Westminster legislation. This required considerable discussions with the centre, which were often strained.

An example illustrates the nature of parallel policy-making. In 1948, Stormont introduced a Health Services Bill paralleling the 1946 National Health Services Act. In correspondence with the Ministry of Finance, Belfast, a Treasury official wanted to know of 'any departure from the principle of parity of services and expenditure' and suggested consultation between the appropriate ministries as there had been 'little or no contact between your Ministry of Health and the Ministry here' (TNA T 233/170). The reply from the Finance Ministry official expressed surprise at the impression of lack of contact and he quoted the Health Ministry official chiefly concerned:

> There has been frequent close and useful contact between our Ministry and the Ministry of Health in London on the subject of the new Health Service. After a special introduction as the officer directly concerned, I paid four visits to the Ministry in London and discussed many aspects of their legislation and our proposed Bill with a number of Senior Officers. In addition Elwood paid several visits when in London and discussed many of the relevant problems. Our Minister, accompanied by Elwood, had a conference with the Parliamentary Secretary who was deputising for Mr Bevan with whom the appointment had been made. These are all in addition to constant correspondence and other incidental contacts. As a result we are fully satisfied and feel that the Ministry of Health have co-operated exceedingly well in keeping us informed and in assisting us with our scheme as with all aspects of the Health Services. Indeed the relations have been most cordial and we have formed many friendships. (Ibid.)

Parity and leeway were central to discussions and highlight an enduring feature of the policy of shadowing the centre in its policy-making. There were differences in approach due to historic developments. The position of endowments for voluntary hospitals, for example, differed and there was also a difference in the provision of hospital accommodation as Northern Ireland had fewer hospitals to start with. Leeway was the policy of allowing Northern Ireland to 'catch up'; the policy meant that account would be taken when Northern Ireland's historic provision of services lagged behind that of Britain. This inevitably allowed scope for negotiation and intergovernmental skirmishes.

Another example typifying the politics of parity in practice occurred over the issue of rises in prescription charges. In 1956, and again in 1961, announcements were prepared at the centre to increase charges. Conforming with the policy of parity, Belfast was informed in advance but on each occasion the introduction of the increase was delayed by a month as a result of the formal procedures that operated at Stormont. Each chamber at Stormont had to pass affirmative resolutions due to a statutory requirement to consult chemists (Ibid.). The consultation exercise was a sham but was a necessary part of the process.

In these areas of public policy, a broad sense of parity was possible. Though Stormont officials would be invited to witness formal set-piece events, they were often cut out of decision-making, notably on economic policy. Bloomfield recounts his experience accompanying the Finance Minister to London at budget times:

> I would also accompany O'Neill to the Treasury on budget day, and share with him the privilege of learning in advance the main outline of the Budget proposals. It was a very odd experience to sit that afternoon in the Gallery, knowing as very few did what was to come. (Bloomfield 1994: 29)

However, at times when important market sensitive announcements were made at the centre, Stormont would find itself in the dark. In 1952, against a background of serious balance of payments problems, the Chancellor announced increases in the Public Works Loan Board's interest rates with implications for local government finance. Stormont officials only found out when listening to a BBC news bulletin and the Minister only found out by a chance conversation with an official. A senior official at the Finance Ministry wrote to his opposite number at the Treasury complaining about this and earlier lapses in communication. It was claimed that the 'long-standing arrangement between the Treasury and this Ministry under which notification was given to him [the Finance Minister] of changes in economic policy or administration details' had been breached (TNA T 233/808). A similar problem arose when the Chancellor announced changes regarding hire purchase in January 1952. The announcement at Westminster applied to the whole of the United Kingdom though Stormont had responsibility in Northern Ireland. On that occasion, Stormont objected to the centre's encroachment on its jurisdiction (Ibid.). A private note summed up Treasury attitudes well. It reported that 'Sir Wilfred Eady [of the Treasury] feels like apologising, but not too abjectly' (Ibid.). Treasury contempt for officials in Stormont was a recurring theme in relations. During subsequent correspondence, an official in Belfast noted to another at the Treasury that 'it is not the blizzard but rather the sudden squall that rocks the political boat!' (Ibid.).

Consultation between the Treasury and the Northern Ireland Government continued to be discussed. In 1953, the Treasury suggested that a senior Stormont official should visit London every month or six weeks for informal talks. Regular monthly meetings were established. Treasury preparation for these meetings included identifying matters that would be raised. The first of these meetings took place in September 1955. Matters that would be dealt with directly between the Treasury and Finance Ministry were not discussed but instead the focus was on general policy developments. The main items in the first meeting were the employment situation in Northern Ireland, action in the event of a recession and new techniques for the control of investment (Ibid.).

Another feature of relations was that Stormont ministries would sometimes operate as agents of Whitehall departments. Information on the operation of Stormont submitted to the Royal Commission on Scottish Affairs (the Balfour Commission) from different ministries explains these agency arrangements. The Ministry of Commerce in Belfast had rarely acted as agent for the Board of Trade before the war but during and after the war it took on various agency functions. The situation was complicated as 'it is not always possible to draw a rigid dividing line between powers vested in the Northern Ireland Parliament and powers reserved to the Imperial Parliament' (PRONI CAB 9R/42/18).

The experience of devolution from a public policy perspective is fairly predictable in one respect but highly unusual in another. In terms of discussion, negotiations and interpenetration, relations between the centre and devolved area were that these took place within the confines of the principle of parity. Parity was, however, a complex idea especially when issues of leeway so often arose. In many respects relations resembled another example of 'devolution' that existed at this time – the 'administrative devolution' of the Scottish Office – but this was a form of devolution that commentators on Northern Ireland would later describe as 'direct rule'. The Scottish Office operated within similar confines of parity and leeway, even if these terms were not used in Scotland and administrative devolution was, in reality, a form of administrative deconcentration. Stormont operated along these lines in terms of policy-making because of its unusual origins and the policy of successive Unionist governments. Stormont was like the Scottish Office. It lobbied for more resources and ensured that local particularities were taken into account.

Equality of political and social rights

One of Dicey's arguments against home rule was that it would undermine equality of political rights. He had in mind the prospect of inequality of rights emerging between the devolved polity and the rest of the state. From a Diceyan perspective, what was not envisaged were the inequalities within the devolved polity that became a hallmark of the old Stormont system of government. The idea that Stormont created an 'Orange state' (Farrell 1976) has been extensively explored. John Whyte remarked that discussion of the allegations of discrimination was 'almost the only area of Northern Ireland society and politics which had been at all extensively explored' (Whyte 1991: 165). His review of the literature concluded that if a consensus exists then 'it is that the picture is not black, nor white, but grey' (Ibid.: 168). Henry Patterson has called for a 'nuanced reading of the relationship between the [Orange] Order and the Unionist regime' rather than the conventional view of Northern Ireland as an 'Orange state'. He argues that 'while Orange pressure almost always evoked a government response, it was not always one that satisfied Orange militants' (Patterson 2006: 123). However, it is difficult to avoid the conclusion that the principle of equality of rights which was demanded by Unionists across the UK when they opposed Irish home rule was abandoned internally in Northern Ireland.

London failed to intervene, despite such Diceyan clauses in the Government of Ireland Act, 1920 as sections 5 (anti-discrimination provisions) and 75 (sovereignty of Parliament). One occasion when the centre intervened had concerned the 1922 Local Government Bill. Electoral law was retained at Westminster for three years after the establishment of devolution. Local government in Ireland as a whole had been elected using the Single Transferable Vote (STV) under legislation passed in 1919 and this was adopted as the means of electing both the proposed Dublin and Belfast Parliaments under the Government of Ireland Act, 1920. STV, imposed by Westminster, was later incorporated into the Constitution of the Irish Republic but rejected by the Unionist majority in Northern Ireland as soon as it was possible to do so. As Nicholas Mansergh remarked, 'It was a matter affecting the minority and the moral obligation to seek at least their acquiescence had not been respected' (Mansergh 1991: 253). The British Government had backed down when faced with the prospect of the Government in Northern Ireland resigning and forcing a general election. In effect, Northern Ireland had raised the stakes. Winston Churchill, as Colonial Secretary, told the Southern Irish Government, which lobbied against the abolition of STV for local elections, that Westminster's veto of the 1922 Bill could create a 'precedent limiting for the future of Dominion Parliaments' (Hadfield 1989: 50). When it came to *political* rights, the centre engaged in brinkmanship with Stormont but climbed down as intervention would have involved using clause 75. The abolition of STV for elections to Stormont's House of Commons was announced by Lord Craigavon, its Prime Minister at Orange celebrations in 1927 (Mansergh 1991: 254). The stated reasons were those familiarly used by advocates of simple plurality over the single transferable vote. Even with STV, the Unionists were secure in their majority (Ibid.: 256) but the prospect of a split in the Unionist party following STV may have been important (Ibid.: 257). Symbolically, it was rare for Stormont to steer its own course against Westminster's wishes but the preference for simple plurality involved adopting the mother parliament's electoral system.

The Home Office had been more concerned when Stormont passed education legislation in 1925 and 1930 contravening the religious equality clause in the Government of Ireland Act. Lord Londonderry, the first Northern Ireland Education Minister, had been thwarted in his attempts to create a secular education system, in keeping with section 5 of the Government of Ireland Act prohibiting the endowment of any religion. The Catholic Church refused to participate in a committee of inquiry chaired by Robert Lynn, Unionist MP. Catholic fears that reform would undermine Catholic education were mirrored amongst Protestant clergy who also wanted religious instruction as part of the curriculum but feared that Catholic teachers would be appointed in predominantly Catholic areas. Legislation passed in 1925 and 1930 incorporated changes demanded by the United Education Committee of the Protestant Churches (Buckland 1979: 247–265; Hennessy 1997: 40–43). Both the electoral system and education policies 'illustrate not only the myopia of government in Northern Ireland but also the imperial government's unwillingness or inability to correct this myopia' (Buckland 1979: 266). A pattern was established.

Housing and employment also became the focus of grievances amongst Northern Ireland Catholics. In the era of the welfare state, policies existed which might have allowed Stormont to develop its legitimacy amongst the minority community. Instead, such opportunities were used, or considered, to further Protestant ascendancy. Family allowance, a classic example of a universal welfare benefit, was paid to families regardless of wealth or other status. The Northern Ireland Family Allowance Bill of 1956 proposed a lower rate of allowances for children and would have resulted in less money being paid to larger, predominantly Catholic, families. In Unionist circles, it was acknowledged that this would have an adverse impact on Catholic families and it was only dropped when Unionist MPs at Westminster expressed fear of reaction in London (Mulholland 2000: 8–9).

Grievances against discrimination alone cannot explain the rise of the Northern Ireland civil rights movement in the 1960s. The rise of a Catholic middle class, changed expectations, a new context with new models and opportunities for political activism, provocative use of symbols and much else brought protests onto the streets undermining the semblance of legitimacy that Stormont may have possessed. The violence and civil disturbances of October 1968 were investigated by an official enquiry set up by the Governor of Northern Ireland that reported in September 1969. The chapter in the enquiry's report discussing the causes of the disorders made clear that they included real and perceived discrimination (Cameron 1969: ch. 10). Efforts which might have advanced province-building amongst the minority community met with resistance but this was hardly surprising given the rhetoric of Unionism. Prime Minister Craig's boast in 1934 that 'we are a Protestant Parliament and a Protestant State' (Ibid.: 72) could only alienate the minority community. The Diceyan ideal of equality of rights, central to the Unionist case against Irish home rule, was discarded within Northern Ireland.

The problem was that under UK-style devolution, intervention of the kind necessary to protect equal political rights, and indeed social rights later, could only occur through a direct conflict between central and regional government. The absence of a neutral political authority, such as a constitutional court, meant that conflict would take forms that might have been avoided. Conflict was viewed as a political power-struggle rather than a debate on legality or constitutionality. The blurring of the distinction between constitutional politics, requiring broad-based consent for legitimacy, and political disputes was inevitable. Escalation was more likely and entrenched positions difficult to avoid. The political centre would have been unable to protect itself through an intermediary acceptable to both sides with the result that intervention became politically costly and dangerous. But it was less the customary constitution that was at fault than the policies which it permitted.

Devolution as a form of integration

While one scholar of Northern Ireland's intra-communal conflict identified 'three solitudes' in relations between Dublin, Belfast and London, another who studied Stormont's public policies noted the close contact between the centre and Stormont (Lawrence 1965). This apparent contradiction can be explained and highlights what made devolution in Northern Ireland unusual. The layered cake and marble cake metaphors of federalism (Grodzins 1966) capture each of these different interpretations of Northern Ireland's relations with London. The former image of relatively discrete decision-making is relevant as far as formal institutional relations are concerned. The latter image of complex interactions was relevant in terms of bureaucratic politics. Northern Ireland had been created with little thought to mundane public policy matters, matters which affected the everyday lives of people, and no reference to debates on decentralisation. Institutional arrangements to formalise, legitimise and facilitate the necessary intergovernmental relations of an advanced welfare state had simply not been catered for at the outset. Customs and practices were established in the early days of devolution which created a layered cake state mindset. While these conventions operated, another set of conventions developed in the United Kingdom's 'hidden wiring', to borrow Hennessy's phrase (Hennessy 1996). Whitehall developed relations with Stormont and these proved especially important in the era of the welfare state. These suggested the metaphor of the marble cake. This image was more relevant in Northern Ireland than in many other federal or regionalised polities because of the emphasis on remaining part of the UK.

Civil servants who have written memoirs offer important observations on this interaction (Oliver 1978; Bloomfield 1994). From the outset, the intention of Unionist Governments was to shadow the centre. As Quekett noted in 1928,

> The declared ideal of the [Unionist] party at present in the majority is the close union of Northern Ireland with Great Britain, and this ideal constantly inspires the legislative projects and administrative energies of the Government. The economic and industrial forces, moreover, which act upon Northern Ireland, show no signs of setting in a contrary direction. It is true that in many cases, where limited powers of self-government have been granted within the British Empire, there has arisen a demand for greater independence in relation to the Mother Country. But for Northern Ireland as an entity no such demand has seriously been made. The grant of a separate legislature and executive has led rather to uniformity, as between Northern Ireland and Great Britain, in respect of laws and social standards. (Quekett 1928: 71)

A similar observation was made forty years later by Harry Calvert (Calvert 1968: 3). The nature of devolution in Northern Ireland necessitated close contact with the centre. Apart from anything else, Stormont required to know what policies were being planned, introduced and implemented by the centre. As the state's reach into society and the economy developed, contact became more necessary and more intense. That is not to suggest that uniformity of policy-making and implementation occurred. Nonetheless, a detailed knowledge of what London proposed was essential so that any implications for Northern Ireland, which were not accounted for by the centre, could be factored into implementation in Northern Ireland.

Terence O'Neill, Northern Ireland's fourth Premier (1963–69) had been keen that devolution should be established in Scotland. O'Neill was an unusual and unsuccessful reformer and a failure as Premier. He attempted to articulate what devolution meant in a UK context. He initially argued this as early as 1947 (Mulholland 2000: 14). However, his motivation was not diversity of institutions across the UK but rather to create similar institutions across the UK to prevent Northern Ireland looking unusual. His Unionist support for devolution resulted in support for an unusual form of devolution: institutional diversity combined with public policy uniformity. In his autobiography, O'Neill describes how, when appointed Minister for Health at Stormont in 1955, he had considered introducing a measure of rent de-restriction ahead of Westminster. O'Neill quotes the advice of Enoch Powell, the equivalent Minister for England and Wales: 'If ... you go ahead of us in this measure and get into trouble which receives publicity in the British press, then this will make our task difficult. If, however, you follow in our wake when we have blazed the trail, then you can justify your actions without risking your chances or possibly spoiling ours' (O'Neill 1972: 33). In a speech in 1962, O'Neill argued that it was the responsibility of the UK Government to ensure that all areas enjoyed the same levels of prosperity (Mulholland 2000: 21). In May 1970, he addressed a meeting in Edinburgh arguing for Scottish devolution as a means of subverting Scottish nationalism and suggested that this need not involve 'spending more money than the English on a particular service, but doing it more intelligently, or in a way particularly suited to Scotland' (TNA HO 221/161). This was a very limited form of devolution.

The Unionist Government in Northern Ireland was allied with the Conservatives at Westminster. The election of the Attlee Government in 1945 had 'caused consternation among those Unionists for whom the spectre of nationalisation was anathema' (Walker 2004: 104). Prime Minister Brooke warned his Cabinet in Stormont that 'more extreme socialistic measures' would have to be copied if enacted by Westminster (Ibid.: 105). This led to a debate on dominion status for Northern Ireland within the party. Fear of losing working-class Protestant support if the Unionists failed to support the welfare state being created at Westminster, as well as the desire to maintain strong links with London, overcame any anti-welfare sentiment inside the Unionist Party. Nonetheless, some Unionists still harboured anti-welfare attitudes, views which were also prevalent at this time amongst the leadership of the Irish Anti-Partition League who viewed the welfare state as contrary to Catholic principles (Purdie 1986). In 1951, in preparation for a meeting between the Chancellor of the Exchequer and Northern Ireland's Finance Minister, Major Sinclair, Treasury officials were anticipating that Stormont might seek to abandon the principle of parity in social service provision in favour of tax cuts in Northern Ireland. The Treasury view was clear: 'as long as Northern Ireland is politically with us we cannot have double standards in different parts of the United Kingdom' (TNA T 233/1474). In the event, it proved to be only a courtesy visit but the preparations show that any desire for uniformity was not restricted to the Treasury but was strongly supported by Stormont. The following year, however, the Northern Ireland Finance Minister sought to alter two taxes, motor tax and death duties, both under Stormont's control. The Treasury view was expressed in a paper before the meeting describing the proposal as a 'tiresome nuisance' (Ibid.). One concern in the Treasury, expressed in a memo co-authored by William Armstrong (later to head the British civil service) was that 'deviation' from policy in Britain, though within Stormont's powers, should be done 'in such a way as to protect the Chancellor from pressure to follow the Northern Ireland example in this country' (Ibid.). The same point was made regarding death duties which 'must be resisted'. In summing up, the officials noted, 'we dislike both of Major Sinclair's proposals because they give ammunition to those who want to press for similar concessions here, but we cannot suggest that they are against the rules of the game provided they turn out to be reasonable in character, with compensating adjustments elsewhere' (Ibid.).

Conclusion

According to Bulpitt, the period 1926–61 was 'the United Kingdom's *Ancien Régime* and the distinguishing feature of this regime was that it operated as a *Dual Polity*' (1983: 134). The degree of '*political* interpenetration between Centre and periphery was low ... they had little to do with each other, relative, that is, to the situation in the past, the future and to other countries at the same time' (Ibid.: 135). So long as 'political' is taken to mean amongst politicians and excludes civil servants, this observation has some accuracy. Leaving aside the absence of devolved institutions across the state, it is difficult to justify the notion that devolution in Northern Ireland was a form of federalism. Wheare's observation that the Union of South Africa was not federal is worth quoting: 'The principle embodied in the Union is that of the subordination of the regional governments to the general government. Although the provinces are interfered with as little as possible, the powers of supervision are exercised when necessary, and the whole existence of the provinces depends on the good will of the Union Parliament' (Wheare 1963: 30–31). That sums up Stormont's position reasonably well.

Fundamentally, devolved institutions in Northern Ireland were created but without other features of devolved or federal arrangements. Absent from the thinking was any consideration as to relations between the centre and the devolved territory. This was not surprising as devolution *per se* was not the prime motivation. What was on offer lacked what Duchacek described as a 'federal political culture' (Duchacek 1986: 82). Parity was the abnegation of devolutionary thinking but compatible with Diceyan thinking. In one crucial respect Stormont undermined Dicey's watchwords: inequality of rights occurred within Northern Ireland. Stormont insisted on equality of rights across the UK but refused to apply this Diceyan principle within its own jurisdiction.

The old Stormont Parliament was as much a perversion of devolution as majority rule was a perversion of democracy. The inequalities in political rights were certainly a consequence of devolution but arose not between Northern Ireland and the rest of the UK but within Northern Ireland. London's way of handling the situation was almost a form of secession. Charles Taylor's closing remarks in *Reconciling the Solitudes*, his study of Canadian federalism and nationalism, are apposite: 'We are too fluent in the language of universal principles and exclusion, and can only stammer the speech of deep diversity' (Taylor 1993: 200). That may have been part of the Diceyan legacy bequeathed to Canada but at least in Canada efforts to speak the language of deep diversity have long existed.

5

A chaos of areas and bodies: the English dimension

England is perhaps the only great country whose intellectuals are ashamed of their own nationality ... It is a strange fact, but it is unquestioningly true, that almost any English intellectual would feel more ashamed of standing to attention during 'God save the King' than of stealing from a poor box. (Orwell 1941: 48)

There is no English nationalist movement. This is hardly surprising, since England is already governed from its capital city by people who are themselves mostly, though by no means exclusively, English. Indeed, the English tend to use the terms 'England' and 'English' when they mean 'Britain' and 'British', often to the annoyance of the Scots and Welsh. (Kilbrandon 1973: 58, para. 185)

Introduction

England presents the greatest challenge to advocates of devolution in the UK. There is little evidence of support for a separate English Parliament or for regional government in the English regions but devolution to Scotland, Wales and Northern Ireland has implications for England and these implications have been significant in blocking Irish, Welsh and Scottish demands in the past. There are, of course, English regional problems and issues. The functional reach of the state requires some regional tier of government. In other words, the regional questions which face England are those associated with the implications of accommodating the demands of other parts of the UK and the pragmatic issues associated with a developed interventionist welfare state. The need for a regional level of administration, at the very least, followed from increases in the activities of central government in the post-war period, particularly economic and land use planning. Regional tiers of administration have always existed but they existed on an *ad hoc* basis and historically the boundaries for one function have not corresponded with those for another. In large measure, this has made English regionalism less popular than devolution elsewhere, exciting the interest of elites rather than publics. Nonetheless, the issue of English or regional identity has been in the background of political debate throughout the twentieth century.

England and Englishness

The fact that there are far fewer studies of English nationalism and English national identity than Scottish, Irish or Welsh nationalisms does not mean that England and Englishness have been less important. English nationalism conforms with the nationalism which is 'reproduced in a banally mundane way' (Billig 1995: 6). It is a function of the strength of English nationalism, not its weakness, that there has been little attention paid to it by scholars and commentators. It is so pervasive that it is taken for granted. English nationalism has been the nationalism that *need* not speak its name. Yet evidence of it exists in abundance and is widely acknowledged outside England. As the authors of a book on Englishness wrote in its preface in 1986, 'The English do not need nationalism and do not like it. They are so sure of themselves that they need hardly discuss the matter' (Culls and Dodd 1986: Preface). An advisor to the Conservatives in the late 1990s remarked on the problems created for the party as a consequence of its anti-Europeanness: 'pragmatic England, a country whose identity is so profound that it does not need the consolations of obtrusive nationalism, was doubful when Euro-sceptics asserted national identity so vigorously and vulgarly' (Williams 1998: 44).

Politicians in late twentieth-century England have generally been loath to talk about their nationalism. This was not always the case. Stanley Baldwin, Conservative leader from 1923–37, addressed the Royal Society of St George in 1924 'On England and the West'. He began by remarking that, given the occasion, he had, as a public figure, a 'profound thankfulness' that he could use the word England 'without some fellow at the back of the room shouting out "Britain"'. He went on to remark that for him 'England is the country, and the country is England' and explained what this brought to mind:

> The sounds of England, the tinkle of the hammer on the anvil in the country smithy, the corncrake on a dewy morning, the sound of the scythe against the whetstone, and the sight of a plough team coming over the brow of a hill, the sight that has been seen in England since England was a land, and may be seen in England long after the Empire has perished and every works in England has ceased to function, for centuries the one eternal sight of England. (Baldwin 1926: 7)

Even the notion that there was too much diversity in England to allow for the existence of a common sense of nationhood was incorporated into Baldwin's sense of belonging: 'in no nation more that the English is there a diversified individuality. We are a people of individuals, and a people of character' (Ibid.: 5). The romantic notions tied up in Baldwin's England were echoed in a passage in George Orwell's *The Lion and the Unicorn*, written at the height of the Second World War, some of which was repeated by British Prime Minister John Major fifty years later:

> When you come back to England from any foreign country, you have imme-
> diately the sensation of breathing a different air. Even in the first few minutes
> dozens of small things conspire to give you this feeling. The beer is bitterer,
> the coins are heavier, the grass is greener, the advertisements are more
> blatant. The crowds in the big towns, with their mild knobby faces, their bad
> teeth and gentle manners, are different from a European crowd. Then the
> vastness of England swallows you up, and you lose for a while your feeling
> that the whole nation has a single identifiable character. Are there really such
> things as nations? Are we not 46 million individuals, all different? And the
> diversity of it, the chaos! The clatter of clogs in the Lancashire mill towns,
> the to-and-fro of the lorries on the Great North Road, the queues outside the
> Labour Exchanges, the rattle of pin-tables in the Soho pubs, the old maids
> biking to Holy Communion through the mists of autumn mornings – all these
> are not only fragments, but *characteristic* fragments, of the English scene ...
>   Yes, there *is* something distinctive and recognizable in English civilization.
> It is a culture as individual as that of Spain. It is somehow bound up with
> solid breakfasts and gloomy Sundays, smoky towns and winding roads, green
> fields and red pillar-boxes. It has a flavour of its own. Moreover it is contin-
> uous, it stretches into the future and the past, there is something in it that
> persists, as in a living creature. (Orwell 1941: 10–11)

In recent years, English nationalism became more obvious and more discussed as a consequence of perceived threats. Like all nationalisms it responds to an Other. Some of these threats have come from within the UK, some from outside. The prospect of 'ever closer union' with Europe provoked a backlash, as has the establishment of the Scottish Parliament and, to a lesser degree, the Welsh Assembly. This form of English nation-alism is to be found on the left and right of politics. Enoch Powell was its most notable voice in the post-war period. Powell's speech to the Royal Society of St George in 1961, reproduced in the *Daily Telegraph* after his death challenged Kipling's famous words, 'What know they of England, Who only England know?'. His interpretation of the past is significant:

> ... the unity of England, effortless and unconstrained, which accepts the
> unlimited supremacy of Crown in Parliament so naturally as not to be aware
> of it; the homogeneity of England, so profound and embracing that the coun-
> ties and the regions make it a hobby to discover their differences and assert
> their peculiarities; the continuity of England, which has brought this unity
> and this homogeneity about by the slow alchemy of centuries.
>   For the unbroken life of the English nation over a thousand years and more
> is a phenomenon unique in history, the product of a specific set of circum-
> stances like those which in biology are supposed to start by chance a new line
> of evolution. Institutions which elsewhere are recent and artificial creations

appear in England almost as works of nature, spontaneous and unquestioned. (Powell 1998)

Others have indulged in this millenial nationalism. Labour leader Hugh Gaitskell railed against 'the end of Britain as an independent European state ... It means the end of a thousand years of history' in 1962 (Brivati 1997: 414). More recently, John Major warned that the Labour Party would 'vandalize a thousand years of British history' by seeking closer union with Europe (Major 1996). Even though Britain is mentioned, the thinking is unmistakably the pervasive notion of England as an ancient, continuous nation. As a state, Britain did not exist before union with England's neighbours. Most notably, there appears a relationship between the assumption that England has traditionally been 'one and indivisible' and England as a unique, almost non-European state.

Recently, however, the terms 'England' and 'English' have been used more consciously and deliberately as distinct from Britain or the UK. Simon Heffer, Powell's biographer, has taken up the baton in a polemical essay (Heffer 1999). Heffer noted the role of football in promoting an English national identity. The use of the Cross of St George by football fans was like 'bringing a long-forgotten ornament out of a long-closed room. That flag has been somewhere in the collective memory; we all knew it was up in the attic somewhere, but we could not quite remember what it was for, or what its point was' (Ibid.: 33). An English nationalism which is both anti-European and sometimes anti-Scottish is emerging on the right. However, an alternative English nationalism might develop. In the conclusion of his history of Europe, Norman Davies suggested that the Scots 'possess the power to destroy the United Kingdom, and thereby to deflate the English, as no one in Brussels could ever do. They may make Europeans of us yet' (Davies 1996: 1134). More than Scottish, Welsh or Irish nationalism, English nationalism is currently a creature of the political right but has potential to be harnessed for other ends. The distaste, noted by Orwell, which English liberals and socialists have for nationalism, at least so long as it is found outside the Third World or Ireland, has given the right free rein.

England and the Irish Question

Finance and representation were the two throny issues confronting supporters of Irish home rule in the nineteenth century. Prime Minister Gladstone was always suspicious of the financial demands Ireland made on the Treasury (Hammond 1938). In line with his initial support for the removal of Irish representatives from Westminster, he proposed to devolve customs and excise to Ireland but then changed his mind. Determing Ireland's fair share of the Imperial burden, and how Ireland should raise its own revenue, presented problems (Kendle 1989: 47–49). But it was the issue of representation that proved most contentious. Gladstone wrestled with this in each of his home rule bills. In his speech in the Commons on his first home rule bill, Gladstone maintained that there 'cannot be a domestic legislature in Ireland dealing with Irish affairs, and Irish Peers and Representatives sitting in Parliament at Westminster to take part in English and Scotch [*sic*] affairs' (Hansard, Commons, vol. 304, 8 April 1886, col. 1055). His answer was to exclude Irish representatives altogether but this would have resulted in taxation without representation. Decisions affecting Ireland would still be taken in Westminster but without any Irish input. Gladstone's second home rule bill, presented in 1893, included a provision (clause 10) which would have given Ireland seats in the Commons but allowed them to vote only on Imperial affairs and matters that affected Ireland – the 'in-and-out' system. But this was criticised because of difficulties in distinguishing between Imperial and Irish matters. It would also have created considerable problems for parliamentary government with competing majorities for Imperial and non-Imperial affairs. The clause was removed at committee stage and the final version of the bill involved a reduction in the number of Irish MPs at Westminster. This was not so much a solution as a compromise. Irish representation became a proxy for opposing home rule, as it would a century later. Joseph Chamberlain, who left the Liberal Party over his opposition to home rule, conceded this when he agreed that he had used the issue to kill Gladstone's first home rule bill (Hammond 1938: 493).

In responding to a Scottish home rule bill in 1913, A.J. Balfour, the former Conservative Prime Minister, articulated the classic argument against devolution:

A Parliament which really adequately represented England, would be a Parliament which would hardly sit side by side in a position of admitted inferiority to another assembly sitting within these walls. A collision with an Irish Parliament would be bad enough. A collision with a Scottish Parliament is not a desirable thing to think of. But conceive a collision with an English Parliament! I believe that directly you face the question of England's position in your ideal federal system, you will see the utter absurdity of it. To cut up England would be greatly unfair to England, on your principles ... Therefore England will remain as a unit, I presume. A system of four provinces, of which England is one, is so lopsided, so top-heavy, and so unequal a system, that it is impossible that it should retain its equilibrium for any great length of time, and your whole federal system would fall into the grossest absurdity. (Hansard, Commons, 5th series, 30 May 1913, vol. 53, p. 538)

The issue was again addressed after the First World War. Once more the backdrop was Irish home rule and also the perceived need to relieve parliamentary congestion so that on this occasion there were calls for 'home rule all round'. A Speaker's Conference on Devolution was set up following a two-day debate. The debate had been significant not least because unlike previous demands for devolved government, the 'weightiest speeches were made by Englishmen' (Coupland 1954: 320). This was only one of a number of constitutional commissions and special conferences established by the coalition Government between 1916 and 1922. The Speaker's Conference was presided over by House of Commons Speaker T.W. Lowther. Sixteen members of each of the Houses of Parliament were appointed but, as *The Times* noted at the time, its membership was 'undistinguished and unrepresentative' (Tanner 2006a: 247). They agreed that the national components of the UK should form the basis of devolution but, 'with regard to the question whether England should form a unit or should be subdivided, considerable doubt arose, and the Conference decided to see whether any light would be thrown upon this question by an examination of the powers which might appear suitable to be devolved' (Lowther 1920: 3). Ultimately, the Conference agreed that England should be treated as a unit. After considering a list of over a hundred subjects of legislation and administration, the Conference agreed on a list of matters that could be devolved. It also managed to agree on a scheme for financial arrangements between the UK and local exchequers and the division of the judiciary.

It divided on the 'character and composition of the local legislative bodies themselves' (Ibid.: 6). By one vote, it favoured the proposals that became associated with the Speaker over those associated with Murray MacDonald, a Scottish Liberal MP. The Speaker's scheme was more limited, with devolved bodies consisting of Westminster representatives with ultimate power retained at Westminster to block proposals from the devolved bodies. Murray's scheme involved directly elected parliaments in Ireland and Scotland. However, devolution had receded in significance by the time the Conference reported and key figures at Westminster – Lloyd George, Balfour and Curzon – opposed the proposals (Tanner 2006a: 246). Though relieving parliamentary congestion had been one of the motivations behind the establishment of the Conference, the Irish Question had been the main driving force. Irish affairs had taken a distinct turn removing the pressure for change. This proved to be the nearest that devolution all round, dealing with the English problem in a comprehensive way, came to being implemented and even then it was far from reaching the statute book.

Regional policy, regional administration and regional government

The absence of a regionalist movement even remotely comparable to the national movements elsewhere in the UK has meant that English regionalism has been a matter of elite preoccupations. There may well be clear regional cultures in England but these have had only sporadic or very limited political consequences. As the Royal Commission on the Constitution noted, the way in which England is divided up 'depends on the purposes for which the division is made' (Kilbrandon 1973: 65). The distinction between regionalism, regional government and regional administration is particularly relevant in the case of England. Regionalism within England, that is bottom-up social and cultural movements articulating the interests of parts of England, has been politically weak. The cause of elected regional government has failed to become a serious issue. Regional administration, on the other hand, has been a necessary consequence of an interventionist welfare state.

As noted in previous chapters, pressures arising from the growth of government functions have regional implications. Local government had evolved in the nineteenth century but was unable to cope with the demands placed upon it by new acts of parliament, especially those focusing on the cities and large towns. As one classic study of local government in the UK commented, the development of English local government up to the eighteenth century was 'slow and mainly connected with poor relief' but this changed following the Industrial Revolution which 'created in modern times the necessity for increased activity in the sphere of Local Government' and the 'social evolution' – the ravages of diseases, the growth of scientific knowledge and changes in political life (Clarke 1948: 52).

Responses to these new pressures were *ad hoc*. New authorities were created for each new problem. Local government became a 'chaos of areas, bodies, and rates' with a plethora of Town Councils and Vestries, Boards of Guardians, Commissioners of Sewers, Improvement Commissioners, Lighting Inspectors, Turnpike Trustees, Highway Boards, Nuisance Commissioners, Local Boards of Health, River Conservancy Boards, Port Sanitary Authorities, Burial Boards and School Boards (Ibid.: 54). Legislation was passed in the nineteenth century attempting to make local government more rational and to move from the *ad hoc* approach towards an *ad omnia* approach, i.e. from the specific to the general with fewer authorities with more functions. Alongside these developments, there was the related development of central government. The relationship between Parliament and the local authorities was important, especially as subventions or grants were increasingly paid to local authorities to provide services. The nineteenth century was also a period of provincial strength and vitality. Cities other than London produced great leaders who used their local base to launch national careers. London's political dominance was not in doubt but there was, both economically and politically, a more pluralist form of politics in operation in England. As the Royal Commission on the Constitution noted, the need for politicians aspiring to national status to be London-based is a twentieth-century phenomenon (Kilbrandon 1973: 58, para. 186). These changes were slow, evolutionary and marked as often by exceptionalism as by symmetry. The problem was that changes in society and politics were moving faster than the changes in the structure of government. As the twentieth century progressed, larger areas for purposes of administration and government were believed to be required than those provided for in most units of local government. The National Health Service, for example, could not be provided for by local government.

Reforms of local government in England from the nineteenth century seemed to point in the direction of ever-larger units. A prize-winning essay published in 1929, reflecting on reforms in English local government, noted that there was a 'definite line of development: the deliberate adoption of the larger unit' (Ashby 1929: 365). The author insisted that regional government would become a matter of 'paramount importance in the near future' (Ibid.: 368) and listed four principles in the design of such a structure. There should be an equitable combination of urban and rural areas; the structure should anticipate the future needs of the country as a whole with regard to town planning and service provision; there should be an equalisation of the burden of local rates in regions having densely populated industrial townships, wealthy residential districts and depopulated countryside; and there should be a progressive draining of densely populated areas into rural districts and the restoration of contact between 'masses and mother earth' with the consequent opening out of unhealthy areas of the towns (Ibid.: 368). This was an idealistic proposition but it was indicative of a type of not uncommon thinking that was emerging around that time. The need for regional government was part of a wider movement which was tied up with notions of greater state intervention, planning and notions of progress. It was also a response to problems associated with industrialisation and urbanisation.

Regional government was sometimes proposed during discussion of reforming local government, whether this was an overhaul of the entire system or just concerned with one part of England. The Royal Commission on the Local Government of Tyneside which reported in 1937 produced a majority report which recommended a regional council covering an extensive area north and south of the Tyne, including county boroughs and the whole administrative county of Northumberland, and a substantial part of the county borough of Durham, which would have responsibility for public health, mental hospitals, education, public assistance, police, the fire service and highways. A minority report, written by one Commissioner, recommended a greater county borough of Newcastle-on-Tyne to include areas north and south of the Tyne which would nearly double the population and almost treble the acreage of the existing county borough (HMSO 1937a). However, the reaction of many officials was typified in comments made by Sir Gwilym Gibbon, a senior civil servant, that advocates of regional government are 'usually found more among those of academic mind than among men of wide practical experience' (Gibbon 1938: 416–417).

During the First World War, regional offices of central government were established to control food and the distribution of labour. But just as war has been important in creating a strong sense of national identity, war is a 'great centraliser' (Parsons 1988: 49). After the war was over, these offices continued to operate as they were found to be useful in emergency planning to meet housing shortages and administering social services (Kilbrandon 1973: 62, para. 199). Between the two wars, a number of industries went into decline affecting the areas in which they were based. Coal-mining, iron and steel, shipbuilding and cotton were located in Central Scotland, South Wales, West Cumberland, County Durham and Lancashire. Other industries grew, including chemicals, electrical engineering, motor vehicles, aircraft and distributive trades but, for the most part, these did not grow up in the areas which had suffered from industrial decline. Central government's response was to encourage workers to move with their families to the more prosperous areas through the Industrial Transference Board set up for this purpose in 1928. Between 1921 and 1937, 650,000 people were involved in this upheaval (Prestwich and Taylor 1990: 115). It was 'more a labour policy than a regional policy', as one of the leading scholars of regional policy has noted (McCrone 1976: 92). Half a century later, the policy was revived but without government assistance when Employment Minister Norman Tebbit urged the unemployed to 'get on their bikes' to look for work as his father had done in the 1930s. It was not a policy which helped poorer areas. Indeed, it did great harm as those most likely to move, both willing and able to find work elsewhere, were usually young and fit. It was an early and extreme example of a policy designed to take account of regional economic pressures but which further undermined poorer areas and took little account of the views of those living in these areas.

In 1934, the Special Areas Act was passed, designating four special areas: South Wales, North-East England, West Cumberland and Clydeside-North Lanarkshire. Two Commissioners were appointed, one for England and Wales and one for Scotland. However, this proved a 'feeble approach to the problem' (McCrone 1976: 95). Reports produced by the English Commissioner, Sir Malcolm Stewart, highlighted the inadequacies of the legislation. In one report, Stewart remarked that there had been 'no appreciable reduction in the number of those unemployed' (quoted in Ibid.: 100). According to McCrone, the most important factor explaining the failure of the policy was the low level of aggregate demand in the economy as a whole (Ibid.: 102). There had been no attempt to integrate regional and general economic policies, a failure which would be repeated again later. That is not to say that such integration would be easy as the special areas did not exist in isolation from the rest of the economy. So long as there was little control over the latter it would be difficult to assist the special areas. Sir Malcolm Stewart argued that this should be tackled by limits on the congested and more economically prosperous areas into which the population was moving, especially London.

In 1937, the Government appointed a Royal Commission under Sir Montague Barlow to examine the Distribution of Industrial Population. The Barlow Commission reported in 1940, making a number of recommendations in favour of action. It was split on the question of regional government and administration. The majority favoured the creation of a National Board with research, advisory and regulatory functions over the location of industry. Three members of the Commission proposed in addition that regional or divisional bodies should be set up related to the Board. A further three wanted a central government department to take responsibility for the distribution of industry and population and proposed that regional boards, through which the department would act, should be established. Elected regional government found no support in the Commission. The differences which existed were between different models of centralised administration, two of which explicitly proposed regional field administration but emphatically under the control of the centre. However, Barlow did not have much impact after the war. The approach adopted then was based on central demand management.

During the Second World War, England was divided into ten regions, each headed by a Regional Commissioner with extensive powers especially to co-ordinate civil defence. Regional boards were set up consisting of industrialists, trade unionists and central government regional officials. When this structure was dismantled after the war it was because it was seen as an aberration necessitated by the peculiar circumstances of war and because they were unpopular with local authority figures who feared that they would lose power at the expense of the regions. A regional structure for purposes of civil defence and emergencies was maintained but played a minor role in English government.

From 1945, regional offices of different departments were set up according to perceived need in Whitehall. The result was, to borrow Clarke's description of local government development in the previous century, a chaos of areas and bodies. Standardisation was attempted when nine standard regions were created by the Treasury in 1946 with which other central government departments were expected to conform. These nine were based on the ten civil defence regions with some adjustments including the amalgamation of London and the South-East. Nonetheless, the chaos persisted. At its establishment in 1971, the Department of the Environment incorporated thirteen separate regional structures from those departments whose work it had inherited (Kilbrandon 1973: 64, para. 203).

Consensus and expansion

There was remarkable consensus on regional affairs in the early post-war period. This consensus was rooted in inter-war thinking. Hugh Dalton's role as President of the Board of Trade in Churchill's wartime coalition

Government was important in the development of regional policy (Pimlott 1986: 400–407). Dalton was MP for Bishop Auckland in County Durham in the North of England where levels of unemployment had an impact on him (Tomaney 2006: 166). Dalton became interested in the redistribution of resources after visiting the Soviet Union and though repelled by many aspects of the Soviet system, he saw this geographic redistribution as directly relevant to Britain (Pimlott 1986: 211). In a book published in 1935, Dalton wrote that the location of industry needed to be given a high priority: 'Such a policy should guide new industries away from London and its outskirts, and away from the larger cities, to selected smaller towns, to garden cities, both new and old, and into depressed areas. And it should check the present drift from North to South' (quoted in Ibid.: 218). Dalton's thinking in coalition continued to influence the Attlee Government, in which he served for a period as Chancellor of the Exchequer and continued when the Conservatives came back to power in 1951. The Distribution of Industry Act, 1945 was the 'foundation of British regional policy' from 1945 to 1960 (McCrone 1976: 107). This Act replaced the pre-war Special Areas legislation though the boundaries of the areas remained broadly the same as before. The main responsibility for policy was given to the Board of Trade which took over responsibility from the Special Areas Commissioners. It was empowered to build factories in Development Areas, buying land by compulsory purchase if necessary; to make loans with the consent of the Treasury to industrial estate; to make provision for basic public services; and to reclaim derelict land. In addition, the Treasury could provide grants or loans (Ibid.: 110). This was also the period when new towns were developed. Largely a response to urban congestion, they too had a regional development function, though this latter role became more important in the 1960s. It was an era of top-down management.

Minister for the North-East

The degree of consensus was remarkable. Differences of emphasis beween the two main parties might even be explained by the different economic contexts rather than ideological differences (Parsons 1988: 103–104). Relative economic stability and growth in the early to mid 1950s meant that policy instruments created by Labour were thought unnecessary by the Tories. However, the downturn in the economy in the late 1950s resulted in more intervention by the Conservatives. Harold Macmillan was Prime Minister from 1957 to 1963 and had been on his party's left wing with strong sympathies for depressed areas in the 1930s. He had represented Stockton, in the North-East of England, in Parliament during the inter-war depression and this had left its mark. In 1958, the Distribution of Industry Act was supplemented with the passage of the

Distribution of Industry (Industrial Finance) Act which extended the areas and type of industry eligible for assistance and increased the level of assistance. Ted Heath's appointment in 1963 to the office of what had been called the President of the Board of Trade symbolised the change. Heath adopted a new title, 'Secretary of State for Industry, Trade and Regional Development, and President of the Board of Trade'. He used the language of 'growth points' and regionalism and 'for the first, and possibly last time' a British Government attempted to 'integrate the physical and economic aspects of distribution of industry policy within an economic ministry' (Ibid.: 120).

Further developments under the Conservatives before they left office in 1964 have been characterised as the 'regionalisation of policy' (Ibid.: 114). In late 1962, discussions on appointing someone, whether a politician or some 'public figure', responsible for the development of the North-East of England were held at the most senior level in Whitehall against the backdrop of concern about high levels of unemployment. The main ministries involved were Housing and Local Government, Labour, Trade, Transport and the Treasury (TNA T 330/100). However, it was agreed that 'decisions will have to be taken in London' as the key issues could 'only be resolved there', with local authorities to give approval for investment, the choice of 'growth areas' and communications networks. The civil servants' preference was for a 'suitable local man' rather than a Westminster politician who might be called 'the Government's Adviser on North-East Development' (Ibid.). A note to the Prime Minister set out the case in favour of a non-ministerial appointment. However, by early January, the view that a minister should be appointed had gained support and Harold Macmillan sent a minute to Lord Hailsham, the Lord President, inviting him to become Minister for the North-East, with similar oversight responsibilities to the Secretary of State for Scotland, the Home Secretary for Northern Ireland and the Minister of Housing and Local Government for Wales. The first act 'should be to visit the North-East in order to acquire first-hand experience of the local problems and to acquaint yourself with the personalities involved'. The Cabinet could then 'weigh the claims of the North East against the claims of other areas' to reach an 'informed judgement on the proper priorities'. It was to be a temporary post and Macmillan asked Hailsham to consider whether 'some similar action is required' for Merseyside (Ibid.). *The Times* noted that Hailsham already had a wide range of responsibilities. As well as a Cabinet Minister as Lord President of the Council, 'almost tantamount to being a Minister without portfolio who undertakes special tasks', he was Leader of the House of Lords, Minister of Science and a month previously had been given responsibility for co-ordinating sport and recreation (*The Times*, 10 January 1963).

The context of this appointment was wider discussion of regional planning and the machinery of government. Studies were being conducted in various regions – Central Scotland, South-East England, North-West England, the Midlands and Wales – leading to proposals for the Ministry of Housing and Local Government becoming responsible for regional development matters in close collaboration with others, especially the Board of Trade. Regionalism and 'growth points' had become part of the vocabulary of politics, influenced by planning, around this time (Parsons 1988: 134–136).

A White Paper on the North-East was produced against this backdrop. In September, Hailsham reported back to the Prime Minister, listing both positive and negative consequences of bringing his appointment to an end. On the one hand, the appointment was 'on balance popular and its termination would correspondingly be criticised'; the Government would be criticised for the 'incompleteness of our achievement' rather than any plan that emerged; and transfering responsibilities to the Minister of Housing and Local Government raised difficulties given that it already had special responsibility for Wales. On the other hand, Hailsham recognised that this was the 'only natural moment' before an election; there was a need for machinery to deal with these matters; Hailsham did not have permanent staff and as such would likely be 'increasingly defeated by departmental resistances'; the machinery made sense; and 'I would rather go out with a bang than a whimper' (TNA T 330/100). He proposed that the publication of the White Paper was the appropriate time to end the 'arrangement of a Minister with special responsibilities for the North East' (Ibid.). Within a fortnight, Hailsham informed Macmillan that he had discussed these matters in the Cabinet's Economic Policy Committee and was 'surprised by the unanimous dismay and hostility', apart from the President of the Board of Trade, to bringing the office of special minister to an end. Three ministers thought it would be 'politically disastrous' including Sir Keith Joseph, Minister of Housing and Local Local Government, who said his position would be made impossible in the North-East. Hailsham expressed concern that his earlier advice had been wrong. Within a month, Macmillan had resigned on health grounds and Hailsham was making his unsuccessful bid to succeed to the premiership. The consensus would appear to be that his term as Minister for the North-East contributed to increased acceptance of the need for a regional diemnsion to English public policy and government if little else (Tomaney 2006).

In his memoirs, Hailsham acknowledged that there was an 'emotive content' to the appointment (Hailsham 1990: 337). His reputation as a politician prone to gimmickry did not help, especially after he appeared in the North-East wearing a flat cap instead of his usual bowler hat. Neither did his high-flown rhetoric. Describing himself as a 'Minister for the twenty-first century' (Parsons 1988: 116) merely added to suspicions that his main objective was to capture headlines rather than help develop an economically depressed area. His duty was to 'take a sort of Domesday Book or bird's-eye view of the whole area without regard to local-authority boundaries' but with only a 'temporary team of youngish civil servants' to co-ordinate a regional plan (Hailsham 1990: 337–338). When the task was done, the office would disappear. In one respect the office was comparable to the territorial departments. It had a significant symbolic quality. Hailsham was later to complain about the failure of English public opinion to 'harness regional patriotism into coherent regional institututions and policies subject to the sovereignty of Parliament' (Ibid.: 34). In opposition in the 1970s, he argued for a form of federalism (Hogg 1978) but made no effort to pursue this when he was Lord Chancellor from 1979 to 1987.

London

The old London County Council (LCC) was created in 1889 and is generally seen as having contributed to the capital's success in the period leading up to the First World War (Davis 1988). It was the first metropolitan council with a wide range of public responsibilities. The Conservatives would have preferred a more limited territorial remit but their Liberal unionist allies preferred the larger area. Twenty-eight borough councils were later created below the LCC. These bodies replaced smaller parishes and the Metropolitan Board of Works (MBW) which were deemed to be either incompetent or corrupt. The MBW, set up in 1855, had been responsible for providing infrastructure to cope with London's growth including sewage, slum clearance, streets and bridges, the Thames Embankment and fire services. The geographic remit of the LCC was limited to inner London. In 1906, County Hall housed the council's headquarters.

The LCC assumed the MBW's responsibilities but also gained responsibility for city planning, housing and education. Over time, in common with other public institutions, it gained responsibilities both through increasing regulation and powers of intervention in its existing areas of responsibility, and also through additional powers. For the first three decades of the twentieth century it was responsible for the expansion of London's tramways. The main parties contested LCC elections but under different labels: Liberals as Progressives and Conservatives as Moderates, later the Municipal Reform Party. The LCC's first meeting was chaired by the Earl of Rosebery who had, as we have seen, been instrumental in the establishment of the Scotish Office. Amongst the leaders of the LCC was Thomas McKinnon Wood, from 1898–1907. He later became Scottish Secretary, from 1912 to 1916, after becoming a Glasgow MP in the Liberal landslide of 1906. This was still the era when municipal leaders could forge a career on the UK stage.

Labour controlled the LCC from 1934 when Herbert Morrison became leader of the Council until 1940, becoming Home Secretary within six months, while serving as MP for Hackney South. Morrison created an informal leadership, his 'Presidium' (Donoughue and Jones 2001: 191). Housing was given greatest prominence and under his leadership the LCC set out on a massive low-rent council house building scheme with accusations from the Tories that Labour were building council houses in Tory strongholds to undermine Tory support (Ibid.: 199). In 1935, a scheme was introduced by the LCC to introduce a green belt, the 'first attempt since the days of Queen Elizabeth to stop the expansion of London' (Ibid.: 202). This successful initiative led to Morrison being known as 'Mr London' (Pimlott and Rao 2002: 25). Morrison was not averse to fighting with central government across the river from City Hall. He forced the Government to support a new bridge over the Thames in preference to reconditioning an existing one in a dispute that lasted through a number of years in the 1930s.

Inner London was Labour's heartland while the Conservatives prospered in the outer areas, leading them to support a larger territorial authority. In 1957, the Conservative Government set up a Royal Commission on the Government of London, under Sir Edwin Herbert, which reported three years later (Herbert 1960). There was intense debate on how London should be governed with William Robson, an authority on public administration at the London School of Economics, and colleagues arguing for an area-wide London authority while other academics at University College, London proposed a less cohesive 'patchwork quilt' approach (Pimlott and Rao 2002: 25). A factor complicating analysis of London's needs was the rapid growth of the city outwards combined with a decline in its innner core's population.

The Royal Commission recommended the establishment of 52 borough councils and a weaker, strategic authority for Greater London. This was the era of strategic planning but partisan interests had also intruded. The Conservatives passed the London Government Act, 1963 creating the Greater London Council (GLC) and 32 London boroughs. An Inner London Education Authority (ILEA) was also set up with councillors elected in the old LCC innner London area as *ex officio* members. The GLC had reponsibility for strategic planning including main roads and transport, refuse collection, fire and ambulance services and, for a short period, education. Other responsibilities would be shared with the London boroughs which were deemed the primary units of local government. Notably, the GLC preferred to refer to itself as a 'regional' rather than a 'local' authority (Ibid.: 29).

London was always likely to be treated as a special case by virtue both of its size and as the capital city of a highly centralised state. But themes are evident in its evolving politics common to territorial politics throughout the UK. The importance of party politics in influencing its territorial remit and responsibilities, its sometimes difficult relations with the centre and the constant need to take account of both changing population needs and expectations of its populace have been as evident in debates on its structures of government as anywhere else in the UK.

From planning to crisis management

In 1964, Sir Keith Joseph, Conservative Minister for Housing and Local Government, gave a lecture in which he argued: 'Regional plans, yes; regional development, yes; but these do not necessarily involve regional government in the sense of regional representative councils. What they do involve is strong regional arms of central government and a reorganised more effective local government' (Mackintosh 1968: 110). This remained the dominant view. There was an expectation, in some quarters, that regional planning machinery, shortly to be set up by Harold Wilson's Labour Government, might alter that.

Some effort to produce a more rational regional order was attempted in the 1960s under Wilson. This was the era of planning already hinted at under the Conservatives. A new central department was established, the Department of Economic Affairs (DEA), which was to have the job of economic planning. Eight planning regions in England were set up under it, with regional economic planning councils appointed by the Secretary of State. Once more, the main change in the boundaries of the new structure came about in the South-East, with two regions replacing three standard regions. The councils took their members from local government, industry and trade unions and drew up long-term strategies for their regions. Regional economic planning boards of civil servants shadowed the councils. However, the National Plan which was produced by the DEA had little regional input (Parsons 1988: 167).

The Department of Economic Affairs proved unable to cut out a role for itself in British central government, especially one distinct from the Treasury, its main rival, despite (or perhaps because of) the appointment of Deputy Prime Minister George Brown as its first Secretary of State. The department had been seen by Wilson as the 'dynamo of change' (Pimlott 1992: 278). Jim Callaghan, Chancellor of the Exchequer, saw the department as modelled on French indicative planning, a notably centralist, top-down model of economic development (Callaghan 1987: 153). Douglas Jay, Wilson's first President of the Board, was an avowed centraliser and had a different conception of economic development and machinery of government from George Brown. Brown envisaged the regional planning councils and boards evolving into something more than consultative bodies, 'something that could become a new form of regional government' (Brown in Parsons 1988: 156). More than thirty years later, there were echoes of the same tensions in Tony Blair's Cabinet with his Deputy Prime Minister, John Prescott, who had responsibility for regions, being the most ardent supporter of regional government while other senior members were unenthusiastic.

There were many problems with the approach to regional government, administration and policy in the 1960s. The Regional Economic Planning Councils and Boards were responsible for drawing up and overseeing the implementation of regional plans to carry out the National Plan of central government. The failure of the National Plan effectively killed off this experiment. In addition, there was an unwillingness to integrate economic and regional policy. The latter was secondary to the centralist outlook in Whitehall. Those concessions which were made involved a deconcentration of central government efforts to the regions, not redistribution of power. This amounted to field administration, not devolution. A related criticism was voiced by McCrone. The English Regional Councils were expected to represent their regions and fight for their interests, yet they had 'neither money, executive power or electoral legitimacy' (McCrone 1976: 237). They were in a weak position in relation to central government which could ignore them if it wished. McCrone noted that the chairman of the Northern Council had to threaten to resign to attract the attention of central government and that the Southern Council had not been consulted on the issue of London's third airport. The rather 'nebulous advisory role' required reform but 'if it is decided to strengthen them, this may involve making them electorally responsible and perhaps giving them some executive powers. This would put them on the way to being a form of regional Government' (Ibid.). As in so many other respects, the Wilson Governments in the 1960s offered a false dawn as far as regional matters were concerned.

A Royal Commission on Local Government in England, chaired by Lord Redcliffe-Maud, had been established by the Labour Government in 1966 and reported in 1969. A comparable Royal Commission under Lord Wheatley met in Scotland, and the Welsh Office was actively considering local government reform at this time. However, 'resistance to major reorganisation was greater in England' (Alexander 1982: 6). Amongst Redcliffe-Maud's recommendations was a proposal for indirectly elected (chosen from local authorities) provincial councils operating at the level of the Economic Planning Regions to co-ordinate the work of local authorities. The logic behind the recommendation was explained:

> As population, mobility and the involvement of local government in economic questions increase, there will be a growing need for a representative body capable of devising a strategy for the future development of a very large area. Provincial councils are required which can settle the broad economic land use and investment framework for the planning and development policies of operational authorities, they should be rooted in local

government and should work in closest touch with central government. They would replace the present regional economic planning council. (Redcliffe-Maud 1969: para. 238).

It left the issue of whether such councils should also assume the work of over-burdened central government departments to the Royal Commission on the Constitution, set up in the year in which Redcliffe-Maud reported. The report was issued towards the end of the period of Labour rule in the 1960s and its proposals for provincial councils were neither unanimously accepted by the Commissioners nor were they central to its recommendations. Indeed, they were not implemented in the legislation reorganising local government in the 1970s but they were an indication of the direction of some thinking associated with an interventionist welfare state at a time before economic crisis hit the UK.

From disillusion to abandonment

The return of the Conservatives in 1970 brought a different approach to regional questions. Heath's Conservatives resolved not to support 'lame ducks' and maintained that regional problems could not be solved by increasing expenditure. The previous Labour Government's failure to tackle regional problems seemed to have discredited all forms of intervention but the free market rhetoric did not last as the Government was forced to intervene to help ailing industries in some of Britain's poorest areas. One consequence of the U-turns and the later defeat of the Conservatives in elections in 1974 was a reaction against interventionist, including regional, policy amongst right-wing Conservatives. The Industry Act, 1972 introduced a 'whole new apparatus of regional intervention' (Parsons 1988: 181) but this was very much top-down regional policy.

As economic recession hit the UK economy in the mid–late 1970s and the Labour Government signed up to a deal with the International Monetary Fund (IMF) which involved public spending cuts, regional policy initiatives were curtailed and existing policies cut back. Regional policy, which had been part of the Keynesian economic policy agenda, was now under attack under Labour and, with greater vehemence, under the Conservatives. Elected regional government looked at best to be a remote possibility as an active regional policy went into decline.

Conclusion

Unions with the other components of the UK meant that these others were no longer threats to England and thereby were no longer the 'Other' which shaped England's identity. Though the classic descriptions of England and Englishness articulated by a series of twentieth-century politicians and polemicists ranging from Baldwin and Orwell to John

Major may not have resonated with publics in Scotland, Wales and Ireland, these benign descriptions could not mobilise a strong enough sense of Englishness. The 'Other' in twentieth-century England was to be found outside the UK. Two world wars generated a sense of Otherness towards the rest of Europe. After Ireland was removed from Westimister's agenda, though it continued to be a matter of some significance for some of the elite, the prospect that England would be defined in contradistinction to other components of the UK was limited.

A notable part of the rhetoric of Englishness in the twentieth century was the sense of cohesiveness, a refusal to countenance any significant political role for regions within England. Regional government was important in the provision of public services but this developed piecemeal. Occasional calls to recognise economic disparities allowed for the mobilisation of elite opinion but this was rarely linked to the case for elected regional bodies.

However, economic difficulties in parts of England, combined with fears that Scotland might gain a comparative advantage in the 1970s, provoked a wave of regional identity in the North-East, neighbouring Scotland. It proved an almost entirely negative movement, opposed to Scottish devolution, rather than one combining with the Scots and Welsh in arguing for more resources or autonomy. This negative regionalism would make a significant contribution to blocking Scottish and Welsh devolution. But it would also mean that regionalism had a base in the years ahead.

6

The settled will of the Scottish people

There shall be a Scottish parliament.
(Opening clause of the Scotland Act, 1998)

Introduction

At Labour's Scottish conference in March 1994, Labour leader John Smith declared that a Scottish Parliament was the 'settled will of the Scottish people' and would be the 'cornerstone of our plans for democratic renewal' in Britain (*Scotsman*, 12 March 1994). Smith died two months later. His declaration that a parliament was Scotland's 'settled will' became a rallying cry for home rulers. Smith and Labour had moved a great distance in the period he had been in Parliament. As late as 1974, Smith opposed devolution but he became one of its most ardent supporters after becoming Minister for Devolution in the Labour Government in 1976. In 1974, in line with Labour thinking at the time, he had doubted the value of legislative devolution when Scotland already had administrative devolution. Retaining the Scottish Office was more important than an elected parliament. He doubted whether an assembly could be effective without control over trade and industry (*Daily Record*, 31 May 1974; *Scotsman*, 7 November 1974). Smith accepted the change in policy but his party's acceptance of devolution was shallow and electorally expedient. Labour only really embraced devolution in the 1980s after watching the Tories rule Scotland with a diminishing number of MPs while the ranks of Scottish Labour MPs grew. Little of substance changed in Labour's scheme of devolution between 1979 and that which was implemented in 1999 but Labour's level of support for devolution increased significantly.

Hamilton and its aftermath

The Scottish National Party (SNP) was created with the merger of two parties in 1934 but could sustain no electoral progress until the 1960s. Local and parliamentary by-elections in the 1960s saw the SNP finally make electoral headway, culminating in the dramatic by-election victory for the SNP's

Winnie Ewing in Hamilton in 1967. No event in twentieth-century political history provoked Whitehall to examine Scottish politics as intensely as Hamilton (TNA CAB 164/658). As the *Financial Times* noted (14 November 1968) and a Treasury official commented within weeks of the by-election, 'The election of Mrs Ewing has galvanised the Scottish MPs into asking a flood of questions' (TNA T 328/227). Scotland's constitutional status had forced its way onto the agenda as never before.

Prime Minister Wilson set up a committee under Richard Crossman, the Lord President, to 'examine the implications of further devolution for Scotland and Wales, and to report their conclusions to the [Cabinet] Home Affairs Committee' (TNA CAB 165/297). Crossman produced two plans: Plan A to be implemented in the short term and Plan B in the next Parliament (TNA CAB 164/658). The first involved extending administrative devolution (as discussed in earlier chapters) and changes in parliamentary procedure. The idea of a Select Committee on Scottish Affairs – 'this tedious subject' as a Treasury official described it in May 1969 (TNA T 328/358) – emerged against this background. Plan A was largely focused on the Welsh Office though some ideas emerged for extending Scottish administrative devolution. Eventually, two ideas emerged at meetings of the Devolution Committee: a National Assembly for Scotland and a Royal Commission on Scottish Government. Consideration was given to allowing the Scottish Grand Committee – dealing with Scottish affairs in the House of Commons – to meet in Edinburgh, as it had on an experimental basis during the Second World War, but there were practical problems. The idea of a Royal Commission had crystallised by Autumn 1968 and in October Wilson agreed to consider Jim Callaghan's proposal for a Royal Commission to consider the 'whole issue of unitary Government and federalism, including the arrangements with Northern Ireland' (Ibid.). An announcement was made and in April the following year it was officially established. As Henry Drucker and Gordon Brown have written, it was set up because the Labour Government 'wanted an excuse to do nothing in the face of Nationalist success' and so long as the Commission sat it had an 'unimpeachable excuse for taking no action and producing no plans' (Drucker and Brown 1980: 54). The remit was wide but the Commissioners were to interpret it narrowly: 'We have no doubt that the main intention behind our appointment was that we should investigate the case for transferring or devolving responsibility for the exercise of government functions from Parliament and the central government to new institutions of government in the various countries and nations of the United Kingdom' (Kilbrandon 1973: 6–7, para. 13).

Kilbrandon

Lord Crowther was appointed chair of the Royal Commission. Following the return of the Conservatives at the 1970 general election, Crowther told Prime Minister Ted Heath that he had 'no illusions about the reasons for setting up' the Commission and there would be 'no ill feelings' if the Government immediately brought the Commission to an end (TNA PREM 15/74). Crowther also told Heath he thought that devolution had 'gone about as far as was practicable, unless the Government were prepared to contemplate a "Scottish Stormont"' which Crowther did not regard as sensible. In 1972 Crowther died and Lord Kilbrandon, a Scottish judge, took his place. Kilbrandon had very different views on devolution. He not only supported it, but would chair the 'Yes' campaign in the 1979 Scottish devolution referendum and was later sympathetic to Scottish independence.

The Royal Commission published majority and minority reports at the end of October 1973. The minority report or Memorandum of Dissent proposed a system of executive devolution across Britain and was prescient in seeing the importance of the European dimension (Crowther-Hunt and Peacock 1973: 37–49). The main report was signed by all but two Commissioners and set out proposals for devolution to Scotland and Wales, though not for England. What was proposed for Scotland and Wales differed. The Commissioners believed that support for a Scottish Assembly was growing and agreed that an assembly was an 'appropriate means of recognising Scotland's national identity and of giving expression to its national consciousness' (Kilbrandon 1973: 335, para. 1119). Eight of the Commissioners supported legislative devolution. One favoured an assembly with deliberative and advisory functions (Ibid.: 336–337, para. 1123). Legislative devolution had been described in the report as the 'most advanced form of devolution' and was defined as powers being 'transferred to the regions to determine policy on a selected range of subjects, to enact legislation to give effect to that policy and to provide the administrative machinery for its execution, while reserving to Parliament the ultimate power to legislate for the regions on all matters' (Ibid.: 225, para. 734).

The Commissioners supported the continued supremacy of the UK Parliament but anticipated that 'in the ordinary course this power would not be used to legislate' for Scotland in devolved matters (Ibid.: 337, para. 1126). Only prescribed functions would be transferred. The unicameral Assembly would be elected by Single Transferable Vote (STV) for a fixed term of four years. Its financial arrangements would also be very different from those of the old Stormont system. Matters transferred would be 'mainly, but not exclusively' those held by the Scottish Secretary and Lord Advocate covering the 'fields of the environment, education, health, social services, home affairs, legal matters, and agriculture, fisheries and food' (Ibid.: 338, para. 1129). But Scottish Office responsibility for electricity supply, aspects of agriculture, fisheries and food would not be transferred. The report took the view that a 'devolved legislative assembly should have its own separate civil service' (Ibid.: 245, para. 807).

Kilbrandon favoured an Exchequer Board, independent of the Scottish and UK Governments with the Scottish budget timed to fit in with central government's public spending round. The Board would define the total level of expenditure after considering representations from both the Scottish Government and the Treasury. Kilbrandon thought that central government could not be an 'arbiter' as it was 'itself an interested party' (Ibid.: 204, para. 671), and there was a need for some 'constitutional check' on the Treasury as the 'dominant interested party'. A small board with specialist staff was needed as a 'counterweight to the Treasury' which would 'fix the standards by which regional services would be measured, and would decide how those standards should be costed from region to region' (Ibid.: 205, para. 672). This scheme for financing devolution was preferred to giving the Assembly independent revenues, essentially taxation, or a block grant formula based on Scotland's needs. Kilbrandon noted that a needs-based block grant system would either involve detailed measurements of needs for each service or some more arbitrary formula: though they believed that the basic idea of a block grant system was 'sound', they doubted the practicality of one based on detailed needs assessments or the acceptability and workability of an arbitrary formula (Ibid.: 204, para. 669).

The timing of the report proved important. A by-election in Glasgow within a fortnight of the report's publication in late 1973 saw the SNP's Margo MacDonald take a seat from Labour. The SNP leader failed to win a seat in Edinburgh on the same day but this has been almost forgotten in subsequent histories. The Nationalists were making headway with the slogan 'It's Scotland's Oil'. The mix of an advancing SNP, the politics of oil and Kilbrandon's endorsement of devolution set the scene for five years of intense debates in Scotland and London on Scotland's constitutional status.

Whitehall responds to Kilbrandon

Whitehall had provided the Royal Commission with much evidence and various committees of civil servants later pored over the report. The thinking in Whitehall immediately after the report's publication changed little over the next five years. Amongst the numerous papers circulating in Whitehall around this time was one that encapsulated worries about devolution. In a confidential note in late 1973, Sir Douglas Henley of the Treasury set out the Treasury's main concerns:

i.   Central government's requirements for managing the economy had to
     be preserved;
ii. No proposals incompatible with this should be agreed which, he
     maintained, 'limits the scope very substantially';
iii. It was necessary to have fully adequate central control of expenditure,
     including determining the degree of uniformity necessary to maintain
     certain services and the extent of local choice within blocks of spend-
     ing;
iv. Efficiency had to be promoted and not require excessive staffs (TNA
     T 328/1028).

As far as Henley was concerned, Kilbrandon was a 'most unwelcome
distraction from the urgent problems with which we have to deal' (Ibid.).
However, as another Treasury official remarked, 'Horrible as the idea is,
study of legislative devolution for Scotland and Wales can hardly be
avoided' (TNA T 227/4253).

A theme that emerged strongly from these early deliberations was the
need to maintain uniform standards. It was recognised that uniformity of
standards had never existed in many fields to start with and that 'standards' was a difficult concept, but despite this, protecting uniformity of
standards became part of Whitehall's response to devolution. It was also
feared that devolution would inevitably 'generate pressure to increase
whatever allocation may be determined' (TNA T 227/4253). Some Whitehall officials tended to play down existing differences, one questioning the
extent to which Scottish and English education systems differed by noting
that salaries, conditions of service and charges did not vary greatly (Ibid.).

In December 1973, an Official Committee, chaired by Sir John Hunt,
Cabinet Secretary, was set up to consider the Kilbrandon Report. Six
Inter-Departmental Groups of officials with varying remits fed their deliberations into this committee: Co-ordinating and Advisory Machinery;
Political and Parliamentary; Trade and Industry; Social Services; EEC; and
Economic and Financial. The Co-ordinating and Advisory Group was
mainly concerned with proposals for England. The Political and Parliamentary Group thought that North Sea Oil had transformed the Scottish
political scene, believed that the central issue was whether there should be
assemblies at all and saw pressure for change as the only reason for devolution. It considered the establishment of a Scottish Development Agency,
highlighting the body's political rather than economic rationale. The
'guiding principle' of the Trade and Industry Group was the 'economic
unity of the United Kingdom and to secure the benefits of an integrated
market'. Consequently, they felt that the scope for devolution in this area
was 'strictly limited' (Ibid.) but they recognised that 'for political reasons'
there would be a need for a 'trade and industry package'. The Social Services Group drew a distinction between devolving social services to

Scotland and Wales and devolving them to English regional governments. They recognised the need to have a sound system of resource allocation to avoid 'leapfrogging'. The EEC Group followed the main report of the Royal Commission in finding 'rather fewer problems than the other Groups' simply because matters likely to be devolved were thought unlikely to be affected by the EEC (TNA CAB 134/3829).

The Economic and Financial Group recognised that the determination of 'fair shares' would be central to the success of devolution. This group split on the case for an Exchequer Board, with the Treasury and Department of Environment thinking it was unworkable and doubting it would be able to make authoritative decisions. The Scottish and Welsh Offices, Department of Industry and Cabinet Offices considered that an Exchequer Board would be both workable and 'politically indispensable'. In its evidence, the Treasury argued that a board would either have to have a substantial staff or rely on departments to determine spending levels. It noted that if the Board determined levels of spending for Scotland and England then 'it also by subtraction determines the total for England'. The Board would have to be drawn into discussions of the state of the economy, as this was a major consideration in determining levels of spending. It opposed opening up the system of allocating public expenditure to Scotland and Wales (TNA T 227/4253). The Treasury also noted that an objective of domestic spending programmes was providing services to 'common or comparable standards throughout Great Britain', including matters under territorial ministers (TNA T 227/4253). It concluded that there was 'no way of arriving at a demonstrably just formula for allocating resources between the constituent parts of Great Britain'. A population-based formula would fail to take account of 'differing social and economic needs' and an Exchequer Board would 'create additional controversy, by making explicit what is now to a large extent implicit, the factors taken into account in arriving at each region's "share"' (Ibid.).

In July 1974, Hunt produced a paper on the 'Implications of Devolution', summarising the work of his committee, arguing that, with the possible exception of EEC membership, devolution would be the most important constitutional change in 50 years and there was 'reason to think that this is a one-way road … it is at least conceivable that the ultimate consequence would be the break-up of the Union' (Ibid.). This view was found in a paper produced by the Central Policy Review Staff (CPRS), the Cabinet's think tank, in June 1976 discussing 'Strategy and priorities'. It described devolution as the 'most important constitutional issue to face any Government in the last 50 years' and stated that 'the future of the unity of the United Kingdom is at stake' (TNA CAB 129/190/11). The report of the Official Committee went even further by suggesting that these could 'turn out to be the most important decisions in the constitutional field since the abolition of the Irish Parliament in 1800, or even since union with Scotland in 1707'. This theme continued to be heard in Whitehall memoranda throughout the 1970s. Hunt's view that the scope of devolution should be 'strictly limited' would also become common wisdom in Whitehall. He believed there needed to be 'reasonable harmony' in relations between the two levels of government: 'The marriage should stand an occasional row, but constant rows are likely to end in divorce' (Ibid.). Hunt worried that the 'Imperial analogy' might be appropriate: 'once a people with a sense of national identity acquire their own elected assembly, they and not the central authority set the pace of further constitutional advance and there is no turning back, short of military force' (Ibid.). However, he worried that ignoring nationalist pressure might provoke extremism and it was important not to 'offer too little too late', though there was no evidence that 'we are anywhere near' that stage. The conclusion of the Official Committee advising ministers was that devolution 'carries with it dangers which, though unquantifiable, are potentially very serious' and 'might lead to separation'. Nonetheless, the Official Committee believed that on 'practically every ground legislative devolution [rather than Executive devolution] is the preferable option' (Ibid.). It stated that 'North Sea oil is of crucial importance' and that this presented a 'new dimension to the whole question of devolution' since Kilbrandon. Decisions about devolution had to be reached 'in close relation to decisions about oil' (Ibid.).

In his diary, Bernard Donoughue, Wilson's political adviser, described Scottish devolution in July 1974, as 'very boring' and referred to 'Whitehall retreating terrified from devolution' (Donoughue 2005: 164). A fortnight later, he described Cabinet Ministers' reactions to devolution similarly (Ibid.: 169). London politicians, advisers and Whitehall officials for the most part held the view that devolution was an unwanted distraction but one which could probably not be ignored – whatever was to be implemented, however, should be as limited as possible. In late summer 1974, Sir Douglas Henley wrote a note on Kilbrandon stating that Treasury Ministers should be made aware of senior officials' concerns that the Government 'may undertake commitments to measures of devolution for Scotland and Wales without full appreciation of the likely consequences' (TNA T 227/4253). The position of senior Whitehall officials, he wrote, could be summed up in one sentence: 'If the Government's ability to control the economy and to ensure a broadly equitable and acceptable development of the use of resources and the corresponding tax policies is to be maintained, the scope for real devolution of decision-making seems strictly limited' (Ibid.).

At the same time, the political parties and other organisations in Scotland were digesting and responding to Kilbrandon. Just days before Kilbrandon had been published, the Labour Party issued a booklet, 'Scotland and the UK', opposing devolution. It proposed strengthening the

Scottish Affairs Select Committee and the Scottish Grand Committee with
the latter meeting in Scotland during the Parliamentary Recess. Debate
inside the Labour Party became rancorous and ultimately led to Jim
Sillars, Labour MP for South Ayrshire, and John Robertson, MP for
Paisley, breaking away to form a separate Scottish Labour Party in
January 1976 (Drucker n.d.).

An assessment of public opinion in March 1974 by Scottish Office civil
servants recognised the lack of hard evidence but speculated that public
opinion had not crystallised, as there had been no grand debate. It
concluded, 'The main impression within the Scottish Office is that, as the
Commission recorded, many of those who are involved in public life are
in favour of the *status quo*; but there are others, perhaps increasing in
number, who would favour some, generally unspecified, devolution of
responsibilities to Scotland stopping well short of complete separatism.'
The same document noted the greater interest in Kilbrandon in Scotland
than in England and suggested that there was 'resentment in Scotland at
the apathetic, cynical and even facetious reception' given to Kilbrandon in
'some quarters of England' including its 'almost derisory reception by
some English Members of the House of Commons' (NAS SOE 9/338).

Wilson commits to devolution

Labour's adoption of devolution in 1974 resembled support for a Scottish
Office almost a century before. It was symbolically expedient and little
thought went into its public policy implications. According to his senior
policy adviser, Harold Wilson committed his Government to devolution in
1974 'without realising it must have something to do – which meant a
Scottish Executive. Now the PM is desperately trying to torpedo it by
refusing to give them any money to do anything' (Donoughue 2005: 156).
In the event, the Scottish Office was the basis of the proposed assembly's
powers and responsibilities, shorn of some matters.

In June 1974, Edmund Dell, Paymaster General in Wilson's Government, told Douglas Henley of the Treasury that there was no merit in
legislative or executive devolution but that there was a 'real political
problem' which was 'tied up with North Sea oil' (TNA T 227/4253). The
Labour Government's position was less one of embracing devolution than
acknowledging pressure for change. In July, Denis Healey wrote to Wilson
expressing concerns about devolution: 'No way has yet been devised, nor
do I think it is possible to do so, of deciding on block expenditure allocations to Scotland over the years which can satisfactorily be defended as a
reasonable share, without a careful and fairly detailed assessment of the
individual programmes which it is intended to cover, on something like
the present system. This is closely linked with the need to retain a broad
uniformity in standards, in the face of changing needs, in the provision of

a wide range of public services.' He also felt that it would be 'logical also to accept that in time a marginal tax power, confined to such areas as a local sales tax' should follow a substantial measure of devolution (TNA T 328/1031).

A memorandum prepared by a Treasury official in July 1974 outlined the issues for the Chancellor of the Exchequer. Executive devolution was by this stage all but dismissed in view of 'the burden of legislating in different forms for Scotland and Wales and for England; the difficulty of distinguishing policy from execution; the threat of encroachment on local government functions' (TNA T 227/4253). Though legislative devolution was preferred, it too involved difficulties: serious friction between devolved and UK central governments particularly in allocating resources; potentially 'damaging consequences' of varying prescription charges or nurses' pay; the limited nature of devolution in trade and industry where 'aspirations are strongest'; oil policy; the role of Scottish and Welsh Secretaries and Scottish and Welsh MPs at Westminster (Ibid.).

Harold Wilson asked Lord Crowther-Hunt, joint author of the Minority Report of the Royal Commission, who had been appointed a Government Minister, to prepare a scheme of devolution which would give the UK Government 'greater controls over possible Scottish and Welsh Governments and would also provide for greater coordination between these three governments' (TNA T 328/1031). In July 1974, Crowther-Hunt proposed to keep the Secretary of State with a 'very substantial role' (Ibid.). His paper on the subject was headed, 'A restricted scheme of legislative devolution to Scotland' (Ibid.). In response, Nicholas Morrison, Permanent Secretary at the Scottish Office, wrote to Sir John Hunt at the Cabinet Office complaining that the paper had been 'produced without any consultation whatever with the Scottish Office' (Ibid.). Morrison argued that it would make 'complete administrative nonsense' and advised 'in the strongest possible terms against accepting a scheme of this sort' (Ibid.). The Official Committee agreed with Morrison and this form of devolution was rejected for Scotland. The Scottish Office contributed to debates on the form devolution should take, occasionally playing a decisive role, but were never the lead department.

The Government was edging towards a commitment to legislative devolution for Scotland and Wales. During the summer of 1974, as it prepared to issue a White Paper, Wilson was keen to ensure that government and Labour Party policies on devolution should be in line (TNA CAB 129/179). Labour's Home Policy Committee had produced a document in August, 'Bringing Power Back to the People', which stressed that the Labour Movement had 'always recognised that the working classes' strength stems from unity' and that the break-up of the UK would 'only isolate and expose ordinary families to the excesses of big business and market forces'. The paper 'utterly' rejected the idea of an Exchequer

Board, believing that determining 'fair shares' was 'the most fundamental of *political* decisions and cannot be delegated by elected representatives. It must be argued out in Cabinet, with the two Secretaries of State present as of right to speak for Scotland and Wales and approved in the House of Commons' (TNA CAB 129/179; original emphasis).

It has become part of Labour Party folklore that devolution was rejected by a meeting of the Executive of the Labour Party in Scotland in June when most of its members were not in attendance, preferring to watch a Scotland–Yugoslavia football match. By six votes to five, the Executive decided that 'Constitutional tinkering does not make a meaningful contribution to achieving socialist goals' (Harvie 1994: 189). The party in London was 'enraged' (Drucker and Brown 1980: 93) and forced the Scottish party to hold a special conference in August where the trade union block vote was used to ensure that the leadership view prevailed (Ibid.: 94). A private Labour poll was deliberately leaked in advance of the conference showing that Labour would lose thirteen seats to the SNP if it did not change its policy on devolution (Ibid.: 93). Support for devolution was passed overwhelmingly at the special conference, 'a death-bed repentance, inspired by electoral fear and by pressure from London' (Butler and Kavanagh 1975: 34). This allowed the Government to issue a White Paper in September 1974 supporting devolution in principle but skating over many issues. Harold Wilson called a general election the next day, the second to be held in 1974. The two elections in 1974 saw advances for the SNP: they won seven seats in February and added a further four in October, and held second place in 35 of Labour's 41 seats.

The Scotland and Wales Bill and the Scotland Act

The results of the October 1974 general election concentrated minds. Eight days after the election, Permanent Secretaries across Whitehall met to consider a paper on devolution written by Sir John Hunt. An official note summarising the meeting shows the change of mood: 'In the post-Election situation a minimal solution is now out of the question ... the Government's options are being closed all the time' (TNA FCO 49/551). Further SNP advances at Labour's expense were anticipated if the Government appeared to be dragging its feet. The Permanent Secretaries even thought that failure to act might lead to direct action such as rent strikes or the blowing up of pipelines. They were conscious of the need to address Scottish expectations but constrained by a desire to limit devolution. A number of observations are interesting from the perspective of what emerged later. They noted that little thought had been given to resolving constitutional disputes but rejected a 'constitutional tribunal such as the Judicial Committee of the Privy Council' as 'entirely contrary to the spirit of devolution within a unitary state with one sovereign Parliament'. This, they maintained, 'should not be contemplated' (Ibid.). While supporting the preservation of a unified civil service, they believed that a 'split is inevitable'. While seeing few practical problems with regard to the EEC, they were concerned that this would provide the SNP with 'more opportunities to press for full self-government' (Ibid.). They feared a Scottish Constitutional Convention would contain a 'strong SNP element' (Ibid.).

The Permanent Secretaries believed that the reservation of UK powers was important. They felt that the right financial provisions would be enough to limit devolution and that a series of specific reservations would be 'badly received, initially, as a niggling approach; it would make for continuous friction in practice; and the legal view is that the restrictions would be virtually impossible to define in statute' (Ibid.). They recognised problems in retaining the Secretaries of State for Scotland, Northern Ireland and Wales but raised the possibility of one Secretary of State doing the job for all three. The Permanent Secretaries believed that the political climate required a 'stern timetable', with policy settled during 1974–75, legislation introduced in 1975–76, elections in 1976–77 and the assemblies in place 'within the lifetime of the present Parliament'. A referendum on the EEC might lead to pressure for one on devolution but this could be resisted as the EEC was an external matter 'involving an irrevocable decision on international relationships with other States, whereas devolution is an internal matter which would not in any way detract from the continued sovereignty of Parliament' (Ibid.).

In November 1974, Wilson set up a Ministerial Committee on Devolution with Ted Short, Lord President of the Council, in the chair. Its secretariat consisted of John Garlick, Michael Quinlan and J.L. Bantock of the Cabinet Office Constitution Unit (TNA CAB 134/3734). In April 1975, Short produced a paper setting out the main features of the expenditure system. Spending would be determined 'as part of the annual public expenditure review for the United Kingdom as a whole' determined by the 'political judgement of the Government' and voted by Parliament as a 'block grant'. It argued that 'No single formula could be used to produce appropriate shares for Scotland and Wales, and it would tie the hands of the Government unduly to delegate even the task of offering advice on the total to an advisory board' (Ibid.). Under the existing arrangements, supplementary expenditure would be agreed by Parliament. Any such supplementaries agreed for English public services would be 'particularly difficult' (Ibid). The desire to 'avoid a close scrutiny of detailed spending by the assemblies but also to ensure that they cannot overspend without restraint' pointed to a 'formula based on movements in English costs and prices' (Ibid.). The paper drew heavily on work by Garlick, Quinlan and Bantock. It concluded that the main source of finance for the Assemblies 'must be the block grant and that the purpose of any devolved tax powers should be simply to provide the Assemblies with a modest source of

supplementary finance' (Ibid.). The share of spending should be determined as part of the UK's annual public expenditure review and no
account should be taken of the fiscal capacity of Scotland or Wales. A
revenue-based system was unattractive as it meant that decisions on the
allocation of oil revenues – 'whether or not to share the tax; or to divide
the proceeds between different parts of the United Kingdom; and, if they
were divided, the basis of division' – would be 'unavoidable' (Ibid.). The
Constitution Unit recognised that formulae could be used to determine
totals but that it would be 'very difficult to devise adequate criteria for
measuring standards and needs' (Ibid.).

The Government's evolving thinking was evident in a series of discussion and White Papers. The White Paper *Our Changing Democracy*,
published in November 1975, emphasised the political and economic
unity of Britain and was explicit in discussing sovereignty: 'Political unity
means that The Queen in Parliament, representing all the people, must
remain sovereign over their affairs; and that the Government of the day
must bear the main responsibility to parliament for protecting and
furthering the interests of all' (HMSO 1975: 5, para. 19). A single-
chamber assembly was proposed with around 140 members elected by
simple plurality. Elections would be held every four years though the
Secretary of State for Scotland would be empowered to make 'minor
adjustments either way to give a convenient election day' (Ibid.: para. 35).
A Scottish Executive, headed by a Chief Executive, would 'normally be
members of the Assembly, but there would be no rigid rule about this'
(Ibid.: 10, para. 44). The White Paper rejected a separate civil service for
Scotland, maintaining that a unified civil service would help 'consultation
and cooperation' and that it need not lead to 'divided loyalty' (Ibid.: 17,
paras 81–82). Westminster would retain the right to intervene in Assembly business though it was hoped this would happen infrequently. It
opposed any statutory machinery for consultation on European Community matters. The Assembly was to be financed by a block grant 'taking
account both of local needs and of the desirability of some uniformity of
standards and contributions' (Ibid.: 19, para. 94). It rejected tax powers
for the Assembly other than a 'general power to levy a surcharge on local
authority taxation, whether on the rates as at present or on any new
system introduced in the future' (Ibid.: 22, para. 108). This would be
available if the Assembly ran into deficit or wanted to have a higher level
of expenditure. The matters to be devolved included 'local government,
extensive law functions, health, social work, education, housing, physical
planning, the environment, roads and traffic, crofting, most aspects of
forestry and many aspects of transport' (Ibid.: 35, para. 170).

John Mackintosh, political scientist and Labour MP, commented on the
'nervous approach, which wrote so many restrictions and exemptions into
the White Paper' (Mackintosh 1975). He interpreted government state-

ments as suggesting that the White Paper was negotiable and identified 'two crucial issues' that needed to be addressed: the Secretary of State's powers to intervene in the affairs of the Assembly and methods of negotiating or allocating the block grant to 'prevent detailed control by the Treasury' (Ibid.). Mackintosh speculated that some aspects of the White Paper reflected pressure from various interest groups: 'it was probably the fears of the leaders of the legal profession that led to the very unsatisfactory section on responsibility for the Scottish legal system. Similarly, senior academics lobbied hard to get the universities excluded. The spokesmen for Scottish industry pressed their alarms over the devolution of economic powers on the Ministers and civil servants who prepared the White Paper' (Ibid.). The Scottish establishment had had their opportunity to influence matters but now, he maintained, it was the chance of the wider Scottish public.

Professor James McGilvray of Strathclyde University's Fraser of Allander Institute warned that there was a danger that the Assembly would be unable to meet the expectations Scots had of devolution. First, its expenditure would be 'ultimately controlled by the Treasury'. Secondly, its spending powers would affect social and environmental rather than economic functions of government and thirdly 'probably nearer 90 per cent of such expenditures are "ongoing" in the sense that they are determined by UK legislation' and therefore not really devolved. The powers were, he felt, 'similar to those of a major local authority'. The 'key political issue' was the 'firm exclusion of any devolved powers over the formation and implementation of economic policy, by which is meant independent powers over taxation, industrial development policy, manpower policies and economic planning' (McGilvray 1975). The White Paper, he maintained, 'rejects all meaningful forms of economic devolution' with the consequence that the 'economic implications of devolution [will be] negligible' (Ibid.).

The Scotland and Wales Bill was published and received its second reading in December 1976 after the Government conceded that referendums would be held in Scotland and Wales. The Cabinet agreed that simultaneous but separate referendums should be held in Scotland and Wales with the outcome dependent on a simple majority. It would be 'once-and-for-all, not repeatable if the answer is No' and an affirmative vote should lead to devolution's implementation and not be merely advisory. The count should follow the precedent of the EC referendum and be declared by regions and island areas in Scotland and counties in Wales (TNA CAB 129/194/3).

The idea of a referendum on Scottish devolution was a pragmatic response to parliamentary pressure. In February 1977, the Cabinet discussed the idea following a motion supporting a Scottish devolution referendum had been signed by 130 MPs. The Cabinet acknowledged that many of its own backbenchers supported a referendum and that this might facilitate passage of the Bill, but a number of 'powerful objections' to a referendum existed: it would involve 'going over the head of Parliament'; it would involve contentious legislation; Welsh Labour supporters were thought to be opposed; it would be difficult to avoid a proliferation of questions, including questions on independence, or a demand for the referendum to be extended to all parts of the UK; the electorate might 'express ill-considered opinions, including perhaps an uncomfortably large Scottish vote for independence'; and the results would not guarantee solving the parliamentary impasse (TNA CAB 128/61/7).

In February 1977, the Government lost a motion on timetabling for the Bill that effectively killed it dead. Labour had lost its overall majority in the Commons and was particularly vulnerable to backbench rebellions. Twenty-two Labour MPs voted against the Government and a further 15 abstained. At a Cabinet meeting following the defeat, Michael Foot acknowledged that the vote had 'underlined the growing importance of the English dimension' (TNA CAB 128/61/7). Polls showed overwhelming public support for devolution in Scotland and a month later the SNP saw its support jump to nine points clear of Labour and the Conservatives. The Government knew it had to respond.

The Government initially expected to reach an accommodation with the Ulster Unionists but this proved difficult, especially over Unionist demands for tougher security measures. Talks with the Liberals began 'with less expectation', not least because Liberal demands were initially 'unacceptably high' (TNA CAB 128/61/12). This was true as far as devolution was concerned as much as any other issue. Initially, the Liberals had asked for revenue-raising powers for the assemblies, promoted a federal-type arrangement and proportional representation for assembly elections. In discussions between the Liberals and the Labour Government on devolution in March 1977, Liberal leader David Steel identified two unresolved areas: the extent and definition of devolved powers, including the method of policing the settlement, and financing devolution. Steel supported separate bills for Scotland and Wales in part because the Conservatives would be 'gravely embarrassed by a Scotland only Bill and some of their abstentionists might move to support the Bill' (TNA CAB PREM 16/1399). Michael Foot was particularly reluctant to accept separate bills, partly influenced by pro-devolution colleagues in the Welsh Labour Party. By July, the Liberals were no longer insisting on revenue-raising powers and had accepted that a federal-type approach would not command parliamentary support though their support for separate bills for Scotland and Wales was accepted.

Michael Foot had taken charge of devolution from Ted Short and announced that separate bills for Scotland and Wales would be introduced into Parliament. He accepted that separate bills were 'essential' despite representations from Welsh Labour colleagues. This was an 'important component for agreement with the Liberals' and had strong support from Labour in Scotland (TNA CAB 129/197/11). Another White Paper, *Devolution – Financing the Devolved Services* (Cmnd. 6890), which was against revenue-raising powers, was published in July 1977. In November, the Scotland Bill was given its second reading by 307 votes to 263 and a timetable was agreed. The timetable meant there was limited time to debate the Bill in detail, which became a source of complaint, especially as the Committee Stage of the Bill was taken by the full House of Commons. Over 500 of the 638 amendments tabled in the Commons were not debated.

The Government suffered an early defeat when the first clause of the Bill was removed by a coalition of Conservatives, Liberals, Nationalists and anti-devolutionists. The clause had declared that the Bill did not affect 'the unity of the United Kingdom or the supreme authority of Parliament to make laws for the United Kingdom or any part of it'. However, it was only a declaratory clause and did not affect the substance of the Bill, including clauses that retained ultimate power at Westminster. The most notable aspects of the Bill's progress through Parliament were the gradual erosion of powers, and the rejection of amendments that would have further empowered the proposed Assembly or would have broken with the Westminster model of parliamentary democracy. George Cunningham, a Scot representing a London constituency for Labour, tabled the most important amendment passed.

The successful Cunningham amendment provided that if less than 40 per cent of the eligible electorate voted 'Yes' then a motion to repeal the devolution legislation should be laid before Parliament. As Cunningham himself described it many years later, it was a 'delayed-action bomb that later blew up devolution' (Cunningham 1989). Even if supporters secured a majority for devolution in the referendum, the prospect of securing 40 per cent of the eligible electorate was a tall order. On the same day, an amendment was successfully moved by Jo Grimond, Liberal MP for Orkney and Shetland, allowing his constituency to opt out of devolution if a majority there voted against it. Attempts were made in the Commons and Lords to introduce a different electoral system for the Assembly. John Mackintosh and Lord Kilbrandon each led moves to introduce the Additional Member System (AMS) but Mackintosh failed in the Commons and though Kilbrandon was initially successful in the Lords, in the first major defeat for the Government there, his amendment was overturned when the Bill returned to the Commons. The proposed Assembly would be elected using First Past The Post (FPTP). Attempts by Mackintosh to give the Assembly revenue-raising powers and to define its powers by listing those that should be retained rather than those to be devolved were also defeated.

Under the 1978 Act, the Scottish Secretaryship would have continued to exist and have a significant role. John Mackintosh took the view that the office of Scottish Secretary would be unnecessary after devolution but acknowledged the need for mechanisms to communicate Scottish opinion to the Cabinet and Whitehall. He warned that a Conservative minority in the Assembly might get its way through the intervention of a Conservative Secretary of State or through blocking the resources necessary to pursue the preferred policy of the Scottish Assembly (Mackintosh 1976: 11). The Scottish Secretary would have remained responsible for four subjects under the 1978 Act: industrial development, agriculture, electricity and the police. But more significantly, the scope of general oversight powers of the Scottish Secretary was considerable. Taken together, it was a grudging measure of legislative devolution that finally passed through both Houses of Parliament.

The 1979 referendum

The referendum campaign effectively started as soon as the decision to hold a referendum had been conceded. Unusually, there had been no by-election in Scotland during the 1974–79 Parliament until 1978 after the Labour MP for Glasgow Garscadden died. Labour's candidate Donald Dewar had long supported devolution and was an experienced former MP. The SNP had been expected to win the seat but Labour held on in April, the first of three Scottish by-elections that year. Margo MacDonald, the SNP's deputy leader and best-known figure, was defeated by Labour's George Robertson in the second in May. John Mackintosh's death robbed Labour of its most committed supporter of devolution and one of the few politicians able to lead a cross-party campaign but another Labour MP was returned in his place. The three new Labour MPs were each committed devolutionists and represented a break with the past but the failure of the Nationalists removed the electoral threat and, for many Labour members, the reason for devolution. The Conservatives had become more anti-devolution after 1975 when Margaret Thatcher became leader, though officially they maintained a more open mind. Conservative policy was to support the principle of devolution but oppose the measure on offer and support a constitutional convention to discuss these matters, a holding policy on the route to outright opposition (Mitchell 1990: 69–83). By the time the referendum came, the SNP had lost its momentum, and the Labour Government had lost support after a gruelling winter of industrial action, looking weary at the end of a Parliament in which it had lost its parliamentary majority.

As referendum day approached, the gap in the polls narrowed. A small majority voted in favour (51.6 per cent for and 48.4 per cent against) on a turnout of 63.7 per cent. The 40 per cent rule required the Secretary of State to move an Order in Parliament repealing the Scotland Act. The Government was reluctant to do so. There was nothing to prevent the

Government moving repeal but voting for devolution's implementation but the Whips informed Prime Minister Callaghan that he could not rely on Labour backbenchers to support devolution (Callaghan 1987: 560). The Government dared not move the repeal order. The SNP attempted to call Labour's bluff by putting down a no confidence motion, hoping to force Labour to move the repeal of devolution. The Conservatives trumped the SNP motion with one of their own. This motion was successful and forced an election. Shortly after coming to power, Margaret Thatcher's Government successfully repealed the Act.

Firming up the commitment

During the 1980s, the rules of the game were called into question in Scotland. The right of the governing party to make policy for Scotland was challenged. It would be an exaggeration to suggest that a legitimacy crisis emerged but there were signs of a legitimacy problem. As the largest party in Scotland, Labour's attitude was significant. This was predicted in a paper delivered after the 1979 election and later published in revised form (Miller, Brand and Jordan 1981). A survey in Scotland conducted at the time of the 1979 election found that the Conservatives were 'trusted less on Scottish affairs than on any other aspect of government irrespective of whether respondents themselves favoured the status quo, devolution, or independence' (Ibid.: 212). This was not the same as a lack of legitimacy but allied with being in government with a shrinking minority over a long period of time, it was the basis for a developing legitimacy problem.

In 1982, a former Labour Cabinet Minister told a senior Scottish journalist, 'We are certain to lose the next election in England. We will return even more Labour MPs from Scotland, but we will be out of office down here for another ten years. We will have to play the nationalist card in Scotland. We will have to go for an Assembly with substantial economic powers – short of independence, but not much short' (*Scotsman*, 28 July 1982). Labour's rhetoric became more nationalist. One MP accused the Conservative Secretary of State of being 'like a colonial governor ... He has no mandate from the nation' (*Scotsman*, 30 July 1982). Another referred to 'flagrant abuses of our democratic institutions' with reference to the imposition of policy on Scotland (*Scotsman*, 28 September 1982). In February 1983, Gordon Brown, Labour's Scottish Vice-Chairman, joined the voices questioning the legitimacy of Conservative rule of Scotland. According to Brown, the job of the Scottish Secretary should be made 'untenable' in the event of a Conservative victory across the UK if Labour won in Scotland (*Glasgow Herald*, 21 and 28 February 1982). However, these statements have to be set in context. Devolution was far from the top of the political agenda. As Bob McLean, later to convene the Labour home rule pressure group Scottish Labour Action (SLA),

remarked, the 'Scottish dimension was carried along in the slipstream of
the wider reform movement in the Party' (McLean 1991: 40). Nonetheless, there were signs of the commitment firming up. At its 1983 Scottish
conference, Labour supported revenue-raising powers for a Scottish
Assembly, as it was still styled. But equally, there were signs of procrastin-
ation. A party commitment to devolution took four years to appear as a
'white paper'. The details of the tax-raising powers were subject to endless
enquiry by the party.

The promise of direct action never materialised after the 1983 election
but cheap talk – 'no mandate' and making Conservative rule 'untenable'
– had consequences. The language, expectations and understanding of
what was legitimate were changing. Well before the poll tax was introduced in Scotland, the Conservatives were being accused of treating
Scotland as a test-bed. One Labour MP suggested that Scots were 'guinea
pigs' when it came to new policies reducing the powers of local government and privatising the National Health Service and suggested that Mrs
Thatcher had 'no moral mandate' in Scotland (*Glasgow Herald*, 12
September 1983). The term 'no mandate in Scotland' became part of the
rhetoric of Scottish politics. Official Scottish Labour policy changed over
the 1980s. As well as tax-raising powers, Labour agreed to a wider range
of devolved responsibilities and that the proposed body should be called
a Scottish Parliament rather than an Assembly. More important than
changes in powers and responsibilities was the increased priority attached
to the policy. It moved from being caught up in the slipstream to being
central to the mainstream.

Though the SNP lost nine of its eleven seats in 1979 when its vote fell
from 30 per cent to 17 per cent, falling further to 12 per cent in 1983, it
still posed a threat to Labour. In 1987, the SNP won with 14 per cent of
the vote and three new seats but lost the two it had clung onto during its
difficult period between 1979 and 1983. Within months of the 1987 election, the SNP was leading the campaign against the Conservative
Government's poll tax and won the Govan by-election in November 1988
having redefined its aim as 'Independence in Europe'. Labour fear of the
SNP was at its height. Donald Dewar, Labour's Scottish Spokesman, even
started referring to devolution as 'independence in the UK' in 1989
(Mitchell 1998: 490). The policy had not changed substantially but the
context had changed and Labour's level of commitment had firmed up
within a decade of the 1979 referendum.

The evolution of devolution policy

After the 1987 election, Labour introduced a devolution bill in the
Commons. This Scotland Bill was much shorter than the ill-fated Scotland
Act, 1978 but followed its logic in using the responsibilities of the Scot-

tish Office as its starting point. The Scottish Office had gained responsibilities in the intervening period and this was reflected in Labour's 1987 Bill. The logic of devolved responsibilities was historic, owing more to the evolution of the Scottish Office than anything else. The 1987 Bill had, of course, no chance of success as the Conservatives had won that year's general election, but it was a statement of Labour's thinking at the time. But this left a question mark over what Labour should do for the remainder of the Parliament.

A committee of 'prominent Scots' had been set up under the aegis of the cross/non-party Campaign for a Scottish Assembly (CSA) (later renamed Campaign for a Scottish Parliament) after the 1987 election. This 'Constitutional Steering Committee' reported in 1988 under the chairmanship of Sir Robert Grieve, a retired Chief Planner at the Scottish Office (McLean 2005: 104–108). Jim Ross, its secretary and former Scottish Office civil servant in charge of devolution in the late 1970s, drafted its report, *A Claim of Right for Scotland* (CSA 1988). Its critique of the government of Scotland reflected changing constitutional opinion in Scotland. It identified a 'constitutional flaw in the present machinery of Scottish government: it can work only within a limited range of election results' (Ibid.: 3, para. 3.6) It proposed a constitutional convention:

- to agree a scheme for an Assembly or Parliament for Scotland;
- to mobilise Scottish opinion and ensure the approval of the Scottish people for that scheme; and
- to assert the right of the Scottish people to secure the implementation of that scheme (Ibid.: 28).

The idea of a convention had a long pedigree in campaigns for a Scottish Parliament (Mitchell 1996: 113–135). More significant than the idea of a convention was the assertion of popular sovereignty which participants, including 58 of 72 Scottish MPs, signed:

> We, gathered as the Scottish Constitutional Convention, do hereby acknowledge the sovereign right of the Scottish people to determine the form of Government best suited to their needs, and do hereby declare and pledge that in all our actions and deliberations their interests shall be paramount. (Scottish Constitutional Convention 1989: 1)

Within less than a decade, most Scottish MPs had abandoned the idea of parliamentary sovereignty and argued that legitimacy required distinct Scottish institutional expression. The idea's roots lay in the notion of popular sovereignty and reference was made to a legal case that, other than appearing in the *marginalia* of legal textbooks and Scottish nationalist mythology, now took on political significance. *MacCormick v. The Lord Advocate* 1953 was the judicial 'high water mark' for the argument that the Treaty of Union between Scotland and England represented a form of fundamental law (MacCormick 1999: 54) but *politically* the high water mark of this judicial finding came thirty years later. It had been a short step from 'no mandate' to asserting Scottish popular sovereignty. In October 1988, Donald Dewar agreed that Labour would join the Scottish Constitutional Convention having previously ruled it out (McLean 2005: 58, 75). This descision preceded the Govan by-election which saw Jim Sillars, now with the SNP, take the seat. It would not have taken long for Dewar to have worked out that the composition of the Convention was likely to favour Labour overwhelmingly. The by-election only gave Labour more reason to firm up its commitment to devolution.

The Constitutional Convention consisted of Labour, the Liberal Democrats and Greens (though the last withdrew over differences concerning the proposed electoral system), representatives from most local authorities, trade unions, churches and the small business federation and with other bodies observing. The SNP realised the Convention would be dominated by Labour and feared that it would be used to attack independence and so decided not to become involved. The Conservatives were hostile to any form of devolution and never considered participating.

The orthodox view is that the Scottish Parliament established in 1999 was the product of the blueprint produced by the Constitutional Convention. A deeper understanding of devolution shows that its roots lay much further back. Indeed, it could be argued that its roots lay in the establishment of the Scottish Office in 1885. The Parliament's powers and responsibilities broadly mirrored those of the Scottish Office. The Convention may have played a part in agreeing a scheme of devolution amongst its participants but the scheme had already been largely agreed within the Labour Party prior to the Convention's establishment. Some of the most significant issues remained unresolved and were addressed by the incoming Labour Government in 1997: the number of Scottish MPs at Westminster; the future of the Secretary of State; details of the funding arrangements. *Scotland's Parliament*, the White Paper, introduced in July 1997, was explicit in identifying the rationale behind devolution's powers:

> The proposed settlement reflects the changes in The Scottish Office's responsibilities over the past 20 years and the Government's commitment to establish a Scottish Parliament with wide-ranging powers including some matters not currently discharged by The Scottish Office. Among the areas to be devolved, not included in the devolution proposals of the Scotland Act 1978, are economic development, financial and other assistance to industry, universities, training, forestry, certain transport matters, the police and the prosecution system. (Scottish Office 1997: 3)

Donald Dewar confirmed this in Parliament when he compared the 1970s legislation with that being proposed in 1997: 'Unlike in 1978, the full range of the Scottish Office's functions will be devolved' (Hansard, Commons, 24 July 1997, col. 1046).

Where the Convention made a major difference was in its deliberations on the electoral system and issues of representation. An argument that had frequently been deployed against devolution during the referendum in 1979 was that the Assembly would be dominated by the Labour Party, often conflated with the geographical dominance of Glasgow and the central belt. This proved potent in the Highlands and North East of Scotland. Former Conservative Prime Minister Lord Home intervened in the 1979 referendum to recommend a vote against devolution and amongst his reasons included criticism of the electoral system (Mitchell 1990: 91–94). A more proportional system was thought necessary to counteract this argument though, in fact, there was little difference in terms of the geographical spread of representation in the scheme arrived at compared with that of First Past The Post (FPTP). The legitimacy of the scheme was believed to rest heavily on a more proportional system. Not only were the Liberal Democrats keen to abandon FPTP, as enacted in the 1978 legislation, but they were joined by a number of Labour home rulers. At its 1990 Scottish conference, Labour ruled out FPTP as a method for electing the Scottish Parliament and adopted a set of criteria pointing towards the Additional Member System. This decision has been described by one of Labour's supporters as 'pivotal in allowing the Convention to reach consensus' (McLean 2005: 126). As with Labour's U-turn on devolution in the 1970s, it was won on the strength of the trade union block votes against the wishes of a majority of constituency parties. Labour's conversion to AMS was a rational calculation. Though FPTP had converted Labour's minority share of the vote into an overall majority of Scottish seats (in 1992, for example, 39 per cent of the vote gave Labour 68 per cent of Scottish MPs), there was always the danger that FPTP might work to the SNP's advantage. While AMS would make an overall SNP majority very unlikely, it had the same consequences for Labour, ensuring that coalition or minority government would be the norm.

The idea, promoted especially by the trade unions, that the Parliament should aim to have an equal number of women and men, was taken up within the Convention. Though no agreement was reached within the Convention on enforcing it, the Labour Party voted in favour of a mechanism to produce gender equality in its membership of the Parliament. The Liberal Democrats, however, opposed any formal mechanism and only two of their seventeen MSPs were women in 1999. The SNP, outside the Convention, was not immune from this debate and considered mechanisms to ensure more women became elected representatives resulting in the SNP returning 19 men and 16 women in 1999.

The 1997 referendum and first elections

The shift of opinion between the 1979 and 1997 devolution referendums is best explained in terms of legitimacy. A Parliament was deemed the answer to the problem of legitimacy that had arisen in the intervening period of Conservative Governments. Research by campaigners for devolution showed that issues of gender equality and 'new politics' had little appeal. The same research concluded that the best chance of maximising a 'Yes' vote was to 'stress the governance issues – Scottish pride, identity, the intrinsic virtues of taking its own decisions. If voters come to regard the central issues of the referendums to be Scotland's *right to assert its nationhood* and run its own affairs, then the evidence of this survey suggests that both referendum questions should yield a clear "Yes" majority' (Nigel Smith Papers).

Table 6.1   1979 Scottish devolution referendum (Turnout: 63.6%)

	No. of votes	Percentage of votes[a]
YES	1,230,937	51.6
NO	1,153,502	48.8

[a]Parliament decreed that 40% of the electorate had to vote YES for the proposals to go ahead. Failure to achieve this proportion meant that this issue would return to Parliament. The percentage of the electorate voting YES was 32.8%; 30.8% NO. The Labour Government could not command a majority in Parliament, not least because at least 100 Labour MPs opposed devolution.

Table 6.2   1997 Scottish devolution referendum (Turnout: 60.2%)
a. Scottish Parliament

	No. of votes	Percentage of votes
YES	1,775,045	74.3
NO	614,400	25.7

b. Tax-varying powers for Parliament

	No. of Votes	Percentage of Votes
YES	1,512,889	63.5
NO	870,263	36.5

The defeat of all of Scotland's Tory MPs at the 1997 general election meant, in the words of one anti-devolution campaigner, that 'all the generals had been killed'. Coming soon after New Labour's triumph at the polls, the referendum benefited from the Government's honeymoon period. Alex Salmond, SNP leader, was the most formidable advocate of a double 'Yes' vote and, for once, had most of the Scottish media behind him and unusually Labour and the SNP worked together for a common goal. The emphatic victory for devolution and the substantial majority for tax-varying powers would make opposition to devolution in the House of Commons difficult. Indeed, while the Scotland Act, 1978 had been marred by opponents treating the passage of the legislation as part of the referendum campaign and proposing amendments designed to that end rather than to improve the Bill, the 1998 Act would suffer from an opposition that almost dared not criticise the legislation for fear that it lacked the legitimacy to criticise the Bill given the scale of victory for supporters of devolution.

Devolution in practice: unity of government

Labour retained its position as Scotland's largest party in the first elections to the Scottish Parliament against a strong challenge from the SNP. Significantly, the SNP was now firmly in second place. It was easy to forget that the Nationalists had only become Scotland's second party in votes and seats for the first time ever at these elections. There was never much doubt that Labour would form a coalition with the Liberal Democrats; Labour share of seats came nowhere near to an overall majority. Coalition looked set to be the norm. The Additional Member electoral system involved voters having two votes – one for 73 constituency Members of the Scottish Parliament (MSPs), similar to elections to the House of Commons – but another returning 56 regional list MSPs, providing a degree of proportionality. This system ensured that more parties had an opportunity to enter the Parliament. In 2003, seven Green MSPs and six Scottish Socialist Party members were elected along with some independents. The system had ensured that the Parliament would be more representative but it would have the potential to make government more difficult.

The prospect of different parties being in government in London and Edinburgh was always predicted to be the real test of devolution. At least as important was the prospect of a less favourable economic and fiscal context and, of course, the real probability that different parties in government would coincide with economic and fiscal difficulties. In 2007, the SNP became the largest party and formed a minority government in Scotland. The initial reaction from Prime Minister Blair, in his last few weeks in office, conformed with his efforts to prevent Ken Livingstone becoming London Mayor and Rhodri Morgan becoming Welsh First Minister. Blair refused to contact Scotland's new First Minister Alex Salmond. Blair's approach was reminiscent of Margaret Thatcher but his successor Gordon Brown eventually made contact with Salmond. While party political and public policy differences were an inevitable consequence of devolution, the operation of intergovernmental relations in the case of security matters following a terrorist attack on Glasgow airport and the outbreak of foot and mouth disease in the south of England suggested that some of the wilder predictions of breakdown in intergovernmental relations were misguided.

Table 6.3 Results of Scottish Parliament elections, 1999–2007

	Constituency Seats (% vote)	List Seats (% vote)	Total Seats
1999 Labour	53 (38.8)	3 (33.8)	56
2003 Labour	46 (34.6)	4 (29.4)	50
2007 Labour	37 (32.2)	9 (29.2)	46
1999 SNP	7 (28.7)	28 (27.0)	35
2003 SNP	9* (23.8)	18 (20.9)	27
2007 SNP	21 (32.9)	26 (31.0)	47
1999 Cons	0 (15.6)	18 (15.4)	18
2003 Cons	3 (16.6)	15 (15.6)	18
2007 Cons	4* (16.6)	13 (13.9)	17
1999 LibDem	12 (14.2)	5* (12.5)	17
2003 LibDem	13 (15.3)	4 (11.8)	17
2007 LibDem	11 (16.2)	5 (11.3)	16
1999 Others	1 (2.7)	2 (11.2)	3
2003 Others	2 (9.7)	15 (22.3)	17
2007 Others	0 (2.1)	3 (14.6)	3

* Includes Presiding Officer elected after the election

Two competing tendencies have been evident in the New Labour Government that came to power in 1997. On the one hand, there was a 'diffusionist tendency' that looked favourably upon the diffusion of power both upwards (to the EU) and downwards 'to the component countries of the United Kingdom' (MacCormick 1999: 70). There was also the counter-tendency, the 'sovereigntist tendency' which contended that 'final power remains centralized where it has been ever since the emergence of the modern English-and-then-British Constitution, namely in Parliament, with the monarch-in-Parliament' (Ibid.: 71). Devolution involves a case of the diffusion of power alongside the assertion of parliamentary sovereignty. The sovereigntist tendency was evident in Prime Minister Blair's comments during the 1997 general election campaign that, '... as far as we are concerned sovereignty rests with me as an English MP and that's the way it will stay' (*Scotsman*, 4 April 1997). The devolution White Paper stated that 'The UK Parliament is and will remain sovereign in all matters; but as part of Parliament's resolve to modernise the British constitution Westminster will be choosing to exercise that sovereignty by devolving legislative responsibilities to a Scottish

Parliament without in any way diminishing its own power' (Scottish Office 1997: para. 4.2).

Two years before the 1997 general election, Labour argued that the Scottish Secretary would continue to be necessary to 'ensure that Scotland, with Wales and Northern Ireland, retains a voice in the UK Cabinet' (Labour Party 1995: 5). But the heavy-handed references to veto powers in the 1978 Act were dropped from the 1998 Act. Instead, there were a variety of new institutional devices to facilitate communication between London and Edinburgh. Intergovernmental arrangements were decided upon very late in the process. Late at night during the passage of the devolution legislation, the Government announced the intention to establish, 'standing arrangements for the devolved administrations to be involved by the UK Government at ministerial level when they consider reserved matters which impinge on devolved responsibilities' (Hansard, Lords, 28 July 1998, col. 1487). Joint Ministerial Committees (JMCs), consisting of members of the devolved and Westminster governments, concordats between the devolved and central governments and Memoranda of Understanding were agreed but these were explicitly not given justiciable form. While some commentators saw these as representing 'soft law' (Poirier 2001) experience suggests that these have been far less significant than expected. They have no formal legal status and the JMCs have stopped meeting on a regular basis, if they meet at all (Trench 2007b: 160–197). The plenary JMC failed to meet at all between October 2002 and December 2004 even though it was formally required to meet annually (Trench 2007b: 197). Interviews with senior officials suggest that most are aware of concordats agreed between devolved and central government but make no reference to them in their everyday work. In part, these documents are a form of codification of long-existing practice dating from pre-devolution times when Whitehall departments would regularly communicate with the Scottish Office.

Unlike in Northern Ireland where a separate civil service was created after devolution, the civil servants serving the Scottish Executive remain part of the British civil service. It should, however, be noted that a sense of departmental loyalty exists which, in the case of the Scottish Office, was given added potency due to serving a 'national' department of state. In his classic 1973 study, James Kellas refers to the 'full "Scottish" character of the public service in Scotland' (Kellas 1973: 71). The issue of to whom these civil servants will owe ultimate loyalty in the event of conflict between Whitehall and Edinburgh may depend on the nature and subject matter of such a conflict. While it might be surmised that senior officials, still appointed by the Prime Minister, might align with Whitehall in matters with constitutional implications, on matters of everyday public policy they might, as in the past and in any intra-Whitehall disputes, be loyal to the Scottish Government. The issue will be one of perceived legitimacy. Whether civil servants perceive the views of the Scottish Government as more legitimate than the views of colleagues in Whitehall is likely to be influenced by the formal constitutional rules of the game. In other words, civil servants are socialised into operating within a hierarchy of rules and norms with the legal framework of paramount importance. It would be unusual for a civil servant to breach this code. This leads to the conclusion, so far untested, that the unified civil service may prove far more significant in maintaining any notion of unity of government, at least as far as everyday public policy is concerned, than new formal institutions.

In the past, unionist political parties were significant centralising forces (Jones and Keating 1979). Labour and Conservative Parties in Scotland served 'not only to integrate Scotland into the British political system but to centralise the policy process' (Midwinter, Keating and Mitchell 1991: 38). This did not mean they were fully integrated. Mirroring the union state nature of public institutions, power was centralised while both Labour and Conservative Parties had some autonomy and retained symbolic distinctiveness. Scottish manifestos were produced at general elections from 1950 onwards though these largely imitated the parties' British manifestos. Between 1912 and 1965, the Scottish Tories did not use the name Conservative but were called the Scottish Unionist Party (Mitchell 1990; Seawright 1999). Scottish Labour MPs were 'characterised by their deep loyalty to the party' (Hutchison 2001: 95), meaning the Parliamentary Labour Party leadership. Class combined with support for centralised policy-making to make the Labour Party amongst the most significant integrating agents in Scotland.

The new context of devolution continues to affect all parties. Each has had or will have to adapt by emphasising its Scottish credentials. The median Scottish voter in Scottish elections is not to be found in the same place as in UK elections. Successful parties in Scotland have always had to emphasise their Scottishness but that has become more pronounced since devolution. This need not mean an inexorable centrifugal trend but means that the party system operates within a context which encourages divergence. Similar developments are evident amongst interest groups. Again, distinctly Scottish groups or Scottish branches of British groups existed before devolution but these have become more pronounced and more visible since devolution.

New politics?

The rhetoric of 'new politics' fed into debates held within the cross-party Consultative Steering Group (CSG) set up between the referendum and the establishment of the Scottish Parliament. Chaired by future First Minister Henry McLeish, the CSG considered the working practices of the new Parliament. The emphasis, in line with the motives behind the establishment of devolution, focused on issues of representation and legitimacy. Four principles guided the CSG in its deliberations: power sharing between the public, Parliament and Executive); accountability; accessibility; and equality. However, relations between and within the executive branch of government, between Edinburgh and London, and the role of parties were neglected. Expectations that a new political culture would emerge after devolution, especially from the new electoral system, were based on a belief that new institutions would alter Scottish political culture.

While a new consensual politics failed to emerge, other significant changes followed from the AMS system. Proponents of 'new politics' soon discovered that coalition and consensus were not the same. Rooted in adversarial politics, AMS simply operated as an extension of the old system giving rise to a new arena for old partisan conflicts. The origins of the system ensured that, although all MSPs were theoretically equal, debate on the resources available to and the respective roles of constituency and list members became a partisan battleground. Coalition or minority government would be the main outcome of AMS. Having worked together within the Constitutional Convention, Labour and the Liberal Democrats, the largest and fourth parties after 1999, had already established a working relationship. Agreement was reached between the two parties in 1999 on a 'Partnership for Scotland'. Negotiations had focused on one issue, the Liberal Democrats' commitment to abolish student tuition fees. This proved to be the first policy with significant 'spillover' implications, as discussed below. It was also agreed to introduce electoral reform for local government. The nature of the coalition would prove to be a major determinant of policy innovation and divergence. After 2003, a new agreement was reached. After working together for four years, it was more easily agreed and less contentious.

AMS provided opportunities for 'Others' to be elected. Dennis Canavan, a former Labour MP who was denied the opportunity to stand for his party, stood successfully as an Independent in 1999 and 2003. The Greens and Scottish Socialist Party (SSP) each returned a member under the list in 1999. In 2003, the number of Others grew. Canavan was joined as a constituency MSP by Jean Turner, another Independent, fighting a threat to a local hospital. The number of Green MSPs increased to seven, that of the SSP to six and Margo MacDonald, former SNP Member, was returned as an Independent on the Lothian list. The party system had moved from one dominant party plus three others into a multi-party system with a few independents. This too would have implications for the operation of the Parliament and potentially for the formation of an Executive. One SSP MSP elected in 2003 promised that the new rainbow Parliament would bring 'madness and craziness' and 'all sorts of diversity and attitude' (*Scotsman*, 3 May 2003). Gains in terms of representation come at potential costs in terms of effective government.

If 2003 was the year of the 'Others', 2007 saw their decline. The SSP followed the familiar path of hard left parties and experienced a rancorous split. The Greens lost all but two MSPs, Canavan retired and Margo MacDonald was the only Independent to be returned. The party system had been in flux from the outset but what remained consistent was the battle between Labour and the SNP to become Scotland's largest party and a separate battle for third place between the Conservatives and Liberal Democrats. The new electoral system removed Labour's support system and created a more competitive, less predictable party system. This was underscored by an electorate which was far less aligned in terms of party allegiances or class voting.

In a speech in 2001, David Steel, Presiding Officer from 1999 to 2003, set out twelve differences between the Scottish Parliament and Westminster: a fixed term of four years; no annual sessions and legislation continuing through all four years of the Parliament; the AMS electoral system which made coalition almost inevitable; the altered the political architecture of the U-shaped chamber; 'civilised' hours with sittings rarely after 6 pm; a high percentage of women members; Bills scrutinised by relevant committee and evidence taken from interested bodies being debated in the chamber; a Petitions Committee receiving public petitions; a weekly public 'time for reflection' led by different faiths, reflecting their size, instead of Anglican prayers before opening of parliamentary business at Westminster; proceedings webcast; more accessibility for the public; a new modern Parliament building (Steel 2001). The list mixes symbolic and substantive differences. Steel ignored much that has been inherited from Westminster, not least the political theatre of First Minister's Questions. Holyrood is simultaneously the creature of Westminster with a desire to be different. In this respect, it represents part of the historic evolution of Scottish political institutions as much as the Scottish Office.

Devolution and citizenship

A.V. Dicey argued that political rights ought to be uniform across the UK. However, as he was writing in a time when rights were limited, it makes sense to consider the impact of devolution on citizenship incorporating legal, political and social rights (Marshall 1992). In one respect, rights have become more uniform post-devolution. On coming to office, Labour agreed that there should be a reduction in the number of Scottish MPs from 72 to 59. Scotland no longer has the advantage it has had since 1918. Political rights have diverged, however, in the sense that opportunities for Scots to participate in politics have increased. The Scottish

Parliament itself, but also new institutional arrangements for participation including more accessibility to the Parliament and its committees, have opened up decision-making in Scotland.

Insistence on equality of social rights is undermined by devolution as Whitehall officials had warned in the 1970s. However, a number of caveats are necessary. First and foremost, differences in social rights existed before devolution. The provision of education, public health and housing were different in Scotland compared with the rest of Britain. The Scottish Office may have been constrained in its autonomy but it was able to provide different levels of services and, in some cases, different social rights. Funding arrangements were part of the explanation. Levels of public spending were generous in Scotland. Additionally, it was possible to re-prioritise spending levels within the total budget under the old Scottish Office. George Younger, Tory Scottish Secretary, boasted of his use of this power in evidence to the Scottish Affairs Select Committee in 1982 (Mitchell 1990: 99). Nonetheless, devolution offers the prospect of greater inequalities in social rights; it alters matters in a fundamental way. Whereas George Younger was able to reprioritise as a Conservative minister within a Conservative Government, devolution opened up the opportunity for a Scottish Government reprioritising on its own ideological terms rather than those of central government.

Measuring divergence is difficult not least because it existed pre-devolution and devolution coincided with a change of government. It is, however, possible to identify policies which would have been unlikely without devolution, but the main difference has not been divergence so much as the volume of legislation and policy change post-devolution. The lack of peculiarly Scottish legislation pre-devolution was, ironically, partly due to its distinctiveness. Lack of parliamentary time at Westminster meant that even uncontroversial Scottish legislation had to wait its turn, competing not only, as now under devolution, with other Scottish business but with UK business for parliamentary time. That constraint has been eased by Holyrood.

Three policies are worth considering: care for the elderly; higher education tuition fees and the smoking ban. Care for the elderly was the subject of a Royal Commission chaired by Sir Stewart Sutherland in 1997 which reported in 1999. Sutherland recommended that personal care of the elderly should be available according to need and be paid for out of general taxation rather than being means tested. A minority report noted the high cost of such a policy and recommended targeting those most in need. The Scottish Executive under Donald Dewar considered the policy and followed London in rejecting Sutherland's recommendations. However, after Dewar's death, Henry McLeish became First Minister and accepted Sutherland's recommendations. McLeish later admitted that the development of the policy was 'certainly not a textbook example of government at work' (McLeish 2004: 141). The multi-party nature of the Parliament made it easier to reverse the policy when McLeish found that his Labour colleagues were unenthusiastic. Dealings with ministers in London were particularly tense. Amongst those who attempted to put pressure on McLeish to back away from the policy were Prime Minister Blair, Chancellor Gordon Brown, Work and Pensions Secretary Alastair Darling, Health Secretary Alan Milburn and Junior Health Secretary Harriet Harman. However, the main concern, from London's perspective, appears to have been less to do with uniformity of social citizenship rights as the spillover effects of the policy. Again, this was something that civil servants warned about in the 1970s. As McLeish noted in his autobiography, 'It will inevitably become a theme throughout devolution that a policy created north of the border will engage interest groups in England, who will demand parity' (Ibid.: 142). The evidence from this example suggests that the fear, familiarly expressed in much North American literature on social policy, that dispersed authority 'limits the expansion of national systems of social welfare protection' (Swank 2002: 47) fails to take account of other factors. While devolution may create new veto points for conservative interest, it also creates new opportunities for progressive forces. Institutional structures are not determinants of policy, only opportunities. The strength of conservative or progressive political forces cannot be ignored. If conservative forces are dominant across the state while progressive forces are uppermost within the devolved polity then, assuming *ceteris paribus*, there will be pressures for the expansion of social citizenship.

In 1999, the Liberal Democrats included a manifesto commitment to abolish university fees. A compromise was reached with Labour, involving the establishment of a commission to consider the proposal which led to the policy that university students would not pay fees while still at university but that a 'graduate endowment' would be charged after graduation. After the 2003 elections, the coalition agreed not to introduce 'top-up fees', in contrast to the system in England. Though these policies generated a great deal of attention, the extent of divergence has been limited in the short term. The policy may have diverged in principle but university fees across the UK remain a relatively small part of the overall funds going into the sector. However, the prospect of much greater reliance on income from fees in England could open up a significant gap between the systems of higher education in Scotland and England, that would have been inconceivable without devolution.

The smoking ban began as an opposition backbench initiative, dismissed by both the First Minister and his Deputy, but gained wide support amongst health professionals who persuaded the Executive to accept the policy. It was significant in that Scotland led the way; in the past, the Scottish Office managed to pursue policies which differed from those south of the border but rarely broke new ground. The combination of a well-organised lobby and a diligent backbencher forced the Executive to act: the lack of parliamentary time pre-devolution alone would have prevented this kind of initiative. Though the Executive did not gain a reputation for policy leadership in its first eight years, this case showed the potential which devolved government offered.

But, as Keating has noted, while there is 'considerable scope for diversity', the UK Government has 'usually set the agenda, with the devolved administrations obliged to react' (Keating 2005: 215). Barnett had 'reinforced this', most notably in depriving Holyrood of the 'ability to make a fundamental choice in a modern democratic welfare state, about the overall size of public spending and the balance between public and private consumption' (Ibid.). Keating concluded that this 'empties Scottish politics of part of its meaning, reduces the interest in Scottish elections and contributes to the public view that the Scottish Parliament is the lesser influence on public policy even within devolved matters' (Ibid.: 215–216).

Conclusion

Political systems are rarely completely transformed even after revolutions. Scottish devolution is best understood as an important development in a continuous process of challenges to and defence of existing institutions. Its advocates have, understandably, emphasised its novel features but, inevitably, many features reflect institutional arrangements before devolution. This is not to suggest that nothing has changed. Scottish devolution has transformed Scottish politics in significant ways. Changes affecting representation – the electoral system, number of parliamentarians and opportunities for greater participation – have been most significant. Other differences have been less obvious in the early years of devolution when a Labour Government has been in power in London and a fairly compliant Labour–LibDem Administration was in office in Edinburgh. Devolution's most significant impact has been in terms of representative democracy. The lack of legitimacy that marked the years before devolution was restored, and the transition was remarkably smooth. However, there have been intimations of the unintended consequences of devolution in its early years. The Scottish dimension to politics has been enhanced; the SNP now looks more secure than ever before and for the first time has become Scotland's first party. Though the Scottish Office's responsibilities were the basis of devolved government, the crucial added dimension of an elected Parliament has ensured that that policy-making no longer operates within the framework of British Cabinet government but in response to the authoritative choices of a representative Scottish legislature.

7

Devolution is a process: Wales

Devolution is a process, not an event. (Ron Davies)

Introduction

Even more than Scotland, the nature of the union between Wales and the rest of Britain has undergone significant change over a relatively short period of time. A historical overview is essential to understand why Welsh devolution today differs from that which exists in Scotland. What becomes clear is that while Welsh devolution is a pale version of that in Scotland, Welsh institutional development has been more dramatic. Wales demonstrates that while the past shapes the present, it need not dominate the future. Wales has had the advantage of having the Scottish precedent to follow. But the resemblances and precedents should not, in keeping with our understanding of the UK as a state of unions, be seen as the whole story. There is much that has been different and will remain so.

The Welsh language and the constitutional status of Wales

Welsh nationalism was always more radical in its methods than its Scottish equivalent. In 1936, Saunders Lewis, founder of Plaid Cymru and one of the leading twentieth-century Welsh language activists, along with others set fire to a 'Bombing school' (a bombing range for training pilots) in Penyberth in a Welsh-speaking heartland. This 'created a tradition of unconstitutional action' (Davies 2007: 576). That campaign, like others which followed, combined pacifist and nationalist motives in combative, unconstitutional action. It gave rise to a notion of Welsh nationalism as defensive and ethnically-based, which in some forms it was, but at no time was this all there was to Welsh nationalism.

The Welsh language was important in past debates on a Welsh Assembly. National identity had been the great mobiliser of opinion in Scotland where its inclusive nature gave it wide appeal, but it had a mixed effect in Wales. Welsh national identity was intimately related to, though far from synonymous with, the Welsh language. This provided it with an intense commitment but also restricted its appeal. The language became a divisive issue in the 1970s as Plaid became closely associated with its defence (Jones and Jones 2000: 258). There was a territorial dimension to the Welsh language as expressed in the Three Wales Model, derived from a 1979 Welsh survey of public opinion (Balsom 1985). Each of the three 'primary social groupings' Balsom identified had territorial 'enclaves'. *Y Fro Gymraeg* was Welsh-speaking, largely identified politically with Wales and was concentrated in northern and west Wales. Welsh Wales was non-Welsh-speaking, identified with Wales and concentrated in south Wales, while British Wales was non-Welsh-speaking and identified with Britain and was found along the border with England as well as in Pembrokeshire.

The manner in which identity was associated with the Welsh language influenced constitutional preferences and undermined the notion that geographic Wales was a political entity. The gradual development of administrative Wales, over-arching Balsom's Three Wales, played a significant part in allowing the development of Welsh civic nationalism. Many opponents of administrative Wales feared that it would provide a means through which the minority of Welsh speakers would impose their language on the majority while some Welsh speakers feared that it would further dilute the language. Neither fear appears to have had much foundation.

Plaid Cymru (literally the Party of Wales), which had been founded in 1925, emerged as a serious political force in the 1960s in *Y Fro Gymraeg* on the back of Welsh language agitation but failed to make much headway elsewhere. Its main concern was the preservation of the Welsh language and associated communities largely concentrated in north Wales. The party argued in defence of what Saunders Lewis referred to as Welsh civilisation, a particularly Welsh way of life of which the language was a part (McAllister 1998: 506–514). A tension between linguistic, cultural activism and supporting pan-Wales political institutions has run throughout the party's history.

In the 1950s Welsh language activists had campaigned against the Tryweryn reservoir, designed to provide water for Liverpool, which destroyed local Welsh-speaking communities. The project was seen as symbolising central government's contempt for Welsh-speaking communities. Henry Brooke, Minister for Welsh Affairs as well as for Housing and Local Government, supported the dam as the water was, he believed, of no economic use to Wales (Evans 2006: 46). Opposition to the reservoir gave Plaid a campaign issue that helped mobilise support. This had not only been about defending the language but about defending communities that would be submerged.

In a famous radio broadcast in 1962, Saunders Lewis argued that the language ought to be first priority: 'The language is more important than self-government. In my opinion, if any kind of self-government for Wales were obtained before Welsh is admitted and used as an official language in local and national administration in the Welsh-speaking areas of our country, then the language will never achieve official status at all, and its death would be quicker than it will be under the rule of England' (quoted in Butt Philip 1975: 90). Lewis's broadcast galvanised Welsh language activists and contributed to the establishment of the Welsh Language Society (*Cymdeithas yr Iaith Gymraeg*) that year. It engaged in non-violent direct action and pushed the issue of the language up the political agenda. In 1963, Sir Keith Joseph, Conservative Minister for Welsh Affairs, set up an enquiry on the Welsh language under the chairmanship of Sir David Hughes-Parry. This resulted in the Report on the Legal Status of the Welsh Language which recommended parity of status with English (Hughes-Parry 1965). The activities of the Welsh Language Society also opened up political space allowing Plaid Cymru to focus on conventional political activities, notably contesting elections.

London indifference to the language was nothing compared to the hostility to it in many parts of English-speaking Wales. In a debate in the Commons in March 1978, Neil Kinnock, Welsh Labour MP and future party leader, claimed that 'linguistic racialism' operated against non-Welsh-speaking schoolchildren in Welsh-speaking areas, though this claim proved to have no substance (Drower 1984: 51). The 1979 referendum confirmed the importance of the linguistic division. A narrow majority of Welsh speakers voted for devolution while an overwhelming majority of non-Welsh speakers rejected it (Evans and Trystan 1999: 101).

Gwynfor Evans and London reaction

Gwynfor Evans's by-election victory in Carmarthen in 1966, four months after a general election in which Plaid had won only 4.3 per cent of the vote, had a similar impact on Welsh politics as Winnie Ewing's victory in Hamilton would have in Scotland a year later. There was a flurry of Parliamentary Questions on Welsh affairs and Westminster and Whitehall paid more attention to Wales.

In government, Labour was forced to consider supporting devolution, especially after Plaid came close to winning Rhondda West in March 1967. As Duncan Tanner has shown, there were both centralist and decentralist tendencies within Wilson's Labour Government. Tensions had long existed in the Labour Party but these were less focused on the language than the relationship between Welsh nationhood and the machinery of government required to create socialism. As Morgan and Mungham argue, two competing traditions of centralism and devolution have always existed within the Labour Party in Wales. It is commonplace to personify this tension within the Labour Party in the 'two outstanding figures in the

Welsh Labour movement' (Morgan 1989: 2), with Aneurin Bevan representing the centralised state socialist position and Jim Griffiths as the embodiment of Welsh nationhood. This is crude though it contains an element of truth. It was not that Bevan was anti-Welsh but that his conception of being Welsh did not include support for a Welsh Assembly and only latterly did he accept the case for a Welsh Office. In part, Bevan's apparent lack of engagement with the Welsh dimension reflects the nature of politics in his time. As Jones and Jones have argued, the debate inside the Labour Party in Wales was 'fundamentally pragmatic' but 'invoked references to deeper cultural and national allegiances' (Jones and Jones 2000: 242). Labour not only inherited votes from the Liberals in the early twentieth century, but many Liberal values and beliefs, including support for cultural and national diversity. These sometimes sat uneasily alongside Labour's growing support for state centralism. As Morgan and Mungham have written, 'Centralism recommended itself to the labour movement for many reasons, not least because it seemed the surest way to nurture its embryonic power and also seemed the best antidote to parochialism' (Morgan and Mungham 2000: 23). These tensions manifested themselves in debates on a Welsh Office as well as a Welsh Assembly.

The relative weakness of the Welsh dimension in Labour politics in the middle of the twentieth century was reflected in thinking on the meaning of socialism. The perception of a need for a strong centre and equation of equality with uniformity offered little room for a Welsh dimension in terms of public institutions other than cultural bodies. This was expressed in stark terms by Labour figures such as Bevan and Neil Kinnock. Latterly, as Labour's support for socialism dimmed, an opportunity developed for a stronger Welsh dimension, always present but previously in the shadow of Labour centralism.

Labour's programme for government in the 1960s included reform of the machinery of government but this focused mainly on reform of the House of Lords. This reform programme was 'driven by Richard Crossman' (Tanner 2006b: 555) who incorporated pressure for devolved government, reflected in electoral advances by the nationalists in Wales and Scotland, into his thinking. Crossman envisaged British-wide reforms which would have involved English regional government. But while Crossman had some successes in pursuing devolution to Wales and Scotland within this wider context, he came up against strong opposition from Cabinet colleagues and a strong belief that efficient government and redistribution of wealth required strong central government (Ibid.: 576). In the end, Labour could not 'break the hold of its past' and Crossman could 'not overcome entrenched policy orientations, or counter the "national" tensions and rivalries which existed within British territorial management and within "Britishness" itself' (Ibid.: 577).

In February 1968, Welsh Secretary Cledwyn Hughes sent Harold

Wilson a note outlining the case for an elected Council of Wales. He acknowledged the difficulties of introducing such a body but quoted the Secretary of the Welsh Labour Party who had pointed out that there was 'strong, and certainly majority, opinion within the Party for an Elected Council, rather than a nominated Council' (TNA CAB 164/658). Opposition to a nominated Council was due to the large number of nominated bodies already operating in Wales. Hughes warned that the limited support for Welsh nationalism, 'does not mean that there is not a majority which would like to see a greater recognition of the identity of Wales' and that history had 'repeatedly shown how where the comparatively modest national aspirations of a majority have not been met in time, minority parties expressing ... extreme views, have proved able to acquire rapidly a wide support'. Hughes rehearsed the arguments for and against an elected Council. In conclusion, he argued that three possibilities could be announced that year: to 'refuse to make any concessions to Welsh nationalism' (but this would only encourage more demands); to make a 'dramatic expression to Wales by giving it a constitution on the Ulster model'; or to make 'moderate expressions which would take the form of an evolution of existing machinery'. Hughes dismissed the first option and doubted whether the second was the right policy as it would be expensive and would 'involve a reduction in Welsh representation at Westminster which would reduce the Labour Party's chances of majority there'. Hughes saw the third as the 'most attractive option', involving extending the responsibilities of the Welsh Office which he felt was 'necessary anyway', and complementing this with the establishment of an 'elected Council' (Ibid.).

In April 1968, a Cabinet Office official noted that George Thomas, recently appointed Welsh Secretary, took a different view from his predecessor. However, Thomas agreed with Hughes on the need to transfer health, education and agriculture to the Welsh Office. In a letter to Harold Wilson in June, Thomas argued that the 'secret lesson' of Sir Reginald Coupland's 1954 study of Scottish and Welsh nationalism had been to 'never confuse unity with uniformity' (TNA CAB 165/298). Dick Crossman, Lord President of the Privy Council, prepared a note for Harold Wilson after meeting the Welsh and Scottish Secretaries in June 1968. In this note, Crossman acknowledged George Thomas's preference for an indirectly elected regional council over the Welsh Grand Committee meeting in Cardiff. Scottish Secretary Willie Ross objected to an advisory Council for Wales, fearing that it would create a precedent which would be taken up in Scotland. Crossman was concerned that a Welsh Council might 'prejudice the eventual pattern of government in England' (Ibid.). Crossman represented that wing of the Labour Party that believed in reforming the machinery of government. His perspective was drowned out in the need to respond to pressure from Wales and Scotland (Tanner

2006b). Crossman could see the attractions of 'bashing separatism', a view strongly supported by both Welsh and Scottish Secretaries, but was also keen on 'some positive embellishments to show the attractions of unitary UK government' (Ibid.). Crossman's quasi-federal solution, however, had few supporters in Whitehall or the Cabinet. Crossman noted the different histories and institutions of Scotland and Wales and suggested that it would be 'difficult to fit them into the same pattern' and asked, 'Is it really impossible to distinguish them and to give each a pattern of devolution appropriate to its circumstances but demonstrably, and defensibly, not appropriate to the other?' (Ibid.).

Kilbrandon

By 1968, Wilson's Labour Government had drifted towards support for some kind of commission of enquiry into devolution. A Royal Commission was set up the following April and reported in late 1973. Two members of the Commission were, in the words of Gwynfor Evans, 'stalwart Welshmen', both former members of Plaid Cymru (Evans 1996: 189). The opening paragraphs of the chapter on Welsh devolution were notable for the emphasis given to recent developments in administrative devolution in Wales and note was made of the 'deep anxiety that the national identity and interests' were 'subject to a continuous process of erosion' (Kilbrandon 1973: 336, para. 1121). As with Scotland, the Commissioners differed on details but all agreed on the need for a Welsh Assembly though with less support than for the more 'advanced form' advocated for Scotland. Six Commissioners favoured legislative devolution for Wales, two fewer than for Scotland (Ibid.: 336–337, para. 1123). Legislative devolution was defined as transferring powers to determine policies on a selected range of subjects, enact legislation and provide administrative machinery for its execution. The matters proposed for transfer to the Welsh Assembly were largely those of the Welsh Office.

A Memorandum of Dissent, signed by two Commissioners, Lord Crowther-Hunt and Alan Peacock, argued for executive devolution. Crowther-Hunt went on to become Minister of State in the Privy Council Office in 1976, preceding John Smith as 'Minister for Devolution' in Harold Wilson's Labour Government. The main report defined executive devolution thus:

> Parliament and the central government would be responsible for the framework of legislation and major policy on all matters but would, wherever possible, transfer to directly elected regional assemblies the responsibility within that framework for devising specific policies for the regions, for the execution of those policies and for general administration. The regional assemblies, although obliged to implement United Kingdom policies, would be able to exercise a substantial measure of discretion in the way this was

done, developing their own distinctive styles of administration and bringing
the making of decisions nearer to the people affected. (Ibid.: 252, para. 827)

The Memorandum of Dissent criticised the main report in a number of
ways: it had focused 'almost exclusively' on devolution; magnified differences between Scotland, Wales and England; failed to justify or explore
claims of over-centralisation and weakening of democracy; 'seriously
underestimated the likely consequences' of membership of the EEC; and
lacked a comprehensive scheme of reform (Crowther-Hunt and Peacock
1973: vii–viii). The authors argued that it was necessary to work within
four principles:

i.   equality of political rights in all parts of the UK;
ii. reduce excessive burdens on Whitehall and Westminster;
iii. provide opportunities for democratic decision-making; and
iv. provide adequate machinery for redress of individual grievances
     (Ibid.).

From this, they argued for seven democratically elected assemblies and
governments – for Scotland, Wales and five English regions (though they
were flexible on the number of English regions). These would take over
the various 'outposts of central government' as well as various unelected
public bodies, and supervise other bodies such as gas and electricity
boards, flesh out policies legislated for by the Westminster Parliament
within the framework of EEC legislation and have some independent
revenue-raising capacity. Each would have its own civil service (Ibid.:
xvi–xvii).

Two Commissioners – Lord Foot and Sir James Steel – were committed
to all citizens enjoying 'equality of political rights and obligations'
(Kilbrandon 1973: 332, para. 1108). However the main report argued
that while 'equality of democratic rights' was a 'necessary consequence of
political unity', understood as the opportunity to vote, it noted the wide
differences which already existed as a consequence of administrative
devolution and the system of government in Northern Ireland (Ibid: 333:
para. 1109). As far as social citizenship was concerned, Kilbrandon had
argued that social security benefits should be exempt from devolution.
The Scottish Office's functions offered most scope for devolution (Ibid.:
236: para. 773) but it was claimed that the argument for maintaining
uniform standards, which had been used to exempt social security from
devolution, could be applied across a wide range of welfare services
including the health service, school meal charges and student grants.

In preparing its evidence for the Royal Commission on the Constitu-
tion, a Treasury official produced a paper in 1970 comparing Welsh and
Scottish responsibilities. It noted that law and order and education were
Scottish Office responsibilities which had not then been given to the Welsh

Office and that the Welsh Secretary was jointly responsible for agriculture with the Minister for Agriculture. The existence of a separate Scottish legal system and the 'recent creation' of the Welsh Office were seen as 'relevant' (TNA T 328/471). The paper argued that for purposes of demand management there was no need to control detailed financial allocations between functional programmes but that uniformity of standards was important. It was suggested that devolution was 'more likely to be acceptable in those programmes which have a clearly identifiable local output, and where there is not strong national pressure for equalisation of standards' (Ibid.). Equalisation, it was maintained, 'colours the whole expenditure argument' and it was 'very difficult to envisage formulae sensitive and flexible enough to serve this purpose, over a period of years' (Ibid.). Similar points were made in other Treasury papers around this time. The draft of another Treasury paper concluded, 'the big question is whether public opinion in Britain would be willing to accept the growth of a marked divergence in the standards of public services as between Scotland, Wales and England, of a kind which they would not accept as between different parts of England' (TNA HO 221/160).

In preparing its evidence for Kilbrandon in 1970, the Inland Revenue noted that Scotland already had a 'nucleus of a separate tax administration' with nineteen local collection offices as well as an office in East Kilbride collecting pay-as-you-earn tax but that it would be more difficult to give Wales 'substantial independent revenues' as the Revenue had 'no separate organisation for Wales' and 'Wales is far more economically integrated with England' (TNA T 328/471). This view was commonly held throughout Whitehall. In April 1974, a Welsh Office civil servant produced a paper on 'The National Health Services and a Welsh Assembly' arguing that 'improving conditions so as to lessen inequalities, both for the individual and for the deprived areas, could be undertaken only on a national basis' (TNA BD 111/17). The official warned that members of an assembly would be responsive to constituents 'who will be in the main lay people with lay people's prejudices and judgment ... It is a fallacy to think that the patient knows best' (Ibid.). As far as this official was concerned, if an assembly had to be created then the Secretary of State's continuing responsibility for health was essential. The paper was, as another official responded, 'very negative, and sees dangers almost larger than life' and the author was 'firing away at an imaginary target' (Ibid.). But it was not atypical.

In a paper on the 'Implications of Executive Devolution' in February 1974, the Welsh Office noted that Kilbrandon had envisaged the disappearance of the Secretary of State for Wales (Kilbrandon 1973: para. 1169) and questioned how the office could 'long survive the establishment of an elected assembly with substantial (and no doubt ever-widening) functions' (Ibid.). It included a section on 'Maintenance of common standards' where it argued that divergence would soon emerge: 'It is for consideration how far a divergence is tolerable; presumably this toleration would be "written in" or otherwise allowed for in framing the constitution for an elected assembly. In other words, the permitted measure of divergence should be foreseen and allowed for' (Ibid.).

In 1975, the Department of Health and Social Security considered the implications of devolution for social security. A note written in August 1975 argued that a 'uniform social security system depends on uniform rules' (TNA PIN 35/570). This was, they felt, 'common sense' but 'common sense may not be the most marketable of commodities in the first heady days of devolution' (Ibid.).

In February 1974, a paper on education produced by the Social Services Group, one of six Inter-Departmental Groups of officials set up to consider Kilbrandon, noted that the effects of executive devolution would be 'less far-reaching than those of legislative devolution' (Ibid.). Under executive devolution, Westminster would still enact legislation and financial constraints would 'continue to be imposed from the centre' providing a 'check against any major disparity of policies and standards' (Ibid.). It recognised that Wales was well integrated into the English educational system especially as compared with Scotland: 'the flow of pupils, students and teachers across the Scottish border is negligible compared with that between England and Wales' (Ibid.). It warned that Wales could not offer a 'full range of specialist courses' available without the 'system of free trade with England' (Ibid.).

The Social Services Group produced its report in June 1974. It recognised that variations in administrative patterns and differences in the quality of services already existed but it was concerned that devolution would 'result in divergence of policy or of quality of services on a scale likely to cause public disquiet or serious political embarrassment, or likely to result in a "leapfrogging" process between England, Scotland and Wales, with resulting additions to claims on resources' (TNA BD 108/396). It agreed with Kilbrandon that social security was not a suitable matter for devolution 'both because there are strong pressures (as the Commission noted) for uniformity in matters where cash benefits are capable of precise comparison, and because devolution would be uneconomical' (Ibid.). Generally, however, the message was that the policy implications of devolution would be far less than the institutional change involved. A new devolved system would 'obviously be an upheaval, inconvenient and expensive administratively' but 'these difficulties need not amount to an overriding objection in respect of most social services' (Ibid.). It worried that pressures for 'both parity and improvements would tend inevitably to increase the pressure on United Kingdom resources' (Ibid.). It anticipated 'continuing interchange of ideas throughout the United Kingdom and internationally, the normal contacts between professionals and administrators in the social services, and public pressures to avoid falling behind the standards of other regions' which would lead to little difference in the 'end product' under the new system (Ibid.).

The six Inter-Departmental Groups fed into an Official Committee, which produced its report in July 1974. It warned that executive devolution would not be a moderate solution as it would involve elected assemblies with wide-ranging powers with 'formidable difficulties in distinguishing in principle policy from execution and in deciding where the line was to be drawn in any particular case' (TNA CAB 134/3829). It warned that friction with Westminster would be greater under executive devolution as well as between devolved and local governments.

The Official Report concluded that legislative devolution would be preferable to executive devolution, at least as envisaged in the Memorandum of Dissent. It argued that executive devolution could 'probably not be applied to Scotland and Wales alone' as this would place burdens on Westminster to prescribe policy in legislation for England as well as for Scotland and Wales. Westminster legislation would have to prescribe policy for England stating the broad framework and its detailed application as well as policy for executive devolution omitting detailed application and allowing for different applications in Scotland and Wales (TNA CAB 134/3829). Emphasis in the reports of Interdepartmental Groups which fed into the Official Committee was on the Scottish situation but it was recognised that the 'pull of Scotland is a powerful influence on Wales' (Ibid.). But the officials did not have the final say. There was a feeling amongst ministers that the Welsh demand was not as strong as that in Scotland and this was reflected in the scheme that was to be offered.

Welsh devolution 1970s style

Rick Rawlings quotes the Deputy Permanent Secretary at the Welsh Office on how the devolution legislation was drawn up after Labour came to power in 1997 saying, 'we went back to our beloved papers from the 1970s' (Rawlings 2003: 28). For this and for two other reasons – far more information is available and there was almost certainly more debate back then – it makes sense to consider the thinking behind Welsh devolution in the 1960s and 1970s in some detail.

In May 1966, two months before the Carmarthen by-election, Labour's annual conference voted for an elected Welsh Council. In the late 1960s, the Welsh regional office of the Labour Party produced a stream of policy documents on Welsh affairs and in February 1969 a working party was set up to prepare evidence to be submitted to the Royal Commission on the Constitution. This working party produced a document advocating a quasi-federal scheme of devolution: a Welsh Senate with 72 seats with legislative powers and a wide range of responsibilities. However, this proposal was attacked by Welsh Secretary George Thomas and Eirene White MP, Junior Welsh Office Minister and chair of the British Labour Party in 1968–69. The proposals were changed considerably. In its evidence to the Kilbrandon Commission in January 1970, the Welsh party opposed devolution, arguing that legislative devolution would 'reduce the effectiveness of Welsh MPs and the influence of Wales in the UK, and would jeopardise the unity of the country as a whole' (Labour Party in Wales 1970: 11). The party supported an elected Welsh Council as a 'top tier of local government' which would extend democratic control over 'as many as possible of the several nominated committees and statutory boards operating in Wales', to allow for Welsh 'concentration on local problems' and to 'provide a structure of Government that will permit of devolution from the centre' (Ibid.: 12). But Plaid won two seats with 10.7 per cent of the vote in February 1974 and three seats in October with 10.8 per cent. Though Plaid had won fewer votes than it had won in 1970, it was now winning seats. A shift of opinion was discernible amongst Welsh Labour MPs: Welsh Labour was displaying the consequences of the fine balance of opinion in the evolution of its policy and attitudes towards devolution with the natural turnover of Labour MPs resulting in signifi-cant shifts in collective opinion. Nonetheless, in 1974, John Morris was appointed Secretary of State for Wales by Harold Wilson. He had spoken in favour of devolution at Labour's 1968 party conference (Evans 2006: 137). However, Welsh Labour MPs in the 1970s were more hostile than they had been only a few years before.

Amongst the new intake was Neil Kinnock, MP for Bedwellty. Kinnock led a group of six anti-devolution Welsh Labour MPs during the 1974–79 Parliament. Opposition focused upon the case for a referendum which gained support especially within the Welsh Labour Party (Evans 2006: 151). It was difficult to sustain the argument that referendums were alien to the British political tradition given that Harold Wilson had called one in 1975 on European Community membership. Leo Abse moved an amendment supporting a referendum to the first devolution bill which was supported by a large section of the Parliamentary Labour Party, including former Prime Minister Harold Wilson. Anticipating trouble, John Smith, minister in charge of devolution, announced that referendums would be held in Scotland and Wales and that government amendments would be moved accordingly.

Jim Callaghan's Labour Government found itself in an invidious situa-tion. It had promised a measure of Welsh devolution but a considerable number of Labour MPs were hostile, wanted to avoid a general election for fear of defeat and had lost its overall majority in the Commons. The Government relied heavily on MPs from the smaller parties for the passage of its devolution legislation right through to the enactment of the Wales Act (James and Lindley 1983: 40). Initially, the Labour Government had drafted a single Scotland and Wales Bill but this had fallen when a guillotine motion, providing a timetable for amendments, was defeated in the Commons in February 1977. The defeat on the guillotine led the Labour Government to form a pact with the Liberals: both parties faced the prospect of losing seats at a general election.

Labour may have been lukewarm at best but the civil service in Whitehall was hostile. Time and again officials recorded their antipathy to Welsh devolution, even more so than Scottish devolution. Barbara Castle recorded her impression in her diary that officials were 'deeply alarmed at the whole business' (Castle 1980: 497). It was a 'horrible' idea, according to one Treasury official in November 1973 (TNA T 227 4253). There may have been a reluctant acceptance of the need to legislate for Welsh devolution, though even this was not always the case, but arguments were constantly made to ensure that it was a minimal form. Problems did not have to be invented but there often appeared to be little effort to find solutions.

The civil service itself would be directly affected by devolution; a paper produced within the civil service noted a number of consequences. First it was thought that a devolved government would likely insist on having its own separate civil service, as Kilbrandon had recommended. Secondly, while uniform conditions of service, salaries, grading and recruitment were seen as necessary, it was recognised that these could not be imposed on devolved government against its will. Thirdly, there was fear that devolution would adversely affect career prospects, though more so in Wales than Scotland, with repercussions for the quality of the senior civil service. However, it was accepted that devolution might have the opposite effect and that the guarantee of a career in Wales might make the civil service more attractive to Welsh candidates. Fourthly, it was believed that devolution would involve additional manpower resources (TNA BD 108/397).

Though separate bills were introduced, debates on the Welsh Bill often echoed those on the Scotland Bill: clause 1 asserting the unity of the United Kingdom and the supremacy of Parliament was removed; proportional representation was rejected; and the 40 per cent threshold in the referendum was inserted. Separate bills for Scotland and Wales were presented in Autumn 1977. This recognised the different forms of devolution proposed and allowed more time to debate Welsh devolution. In their discussion of the passage of the Wales Act, 1978, James and Lindley suggest altering the famous entry in *Encyclopaedia Britannica*, 'For Wales see England' to 'For Wales see Scotland' (James and Lindley 1983: 45) but this was not quite correct. As with the Scotland and Wales Bill, the Government did not treat devolution as a matter of confidence in the government (Jordan 1979: 31; James and Lindley 1983: 42), thus giving an amber light to rebels. The Wales Bill was presented for first reading in November 1977, gaining its second reading in the Commons by 295 to

264 votes. At third reading the following May, three fewer MPs supported the Bill. The amendment process proved, as in Scotland, to be as much about setting the tone and contours of the referendum debate as it was about ensuring that the scheme would be effective. Studies of parliamentary procedure in debates on the Scotland and Wales Bill and the Wales Act noted the number of wrecking amendments, running contrary to parliamentary procedure, seeking to make the legislation unworkable (Jordan 1979: 10–12; James and Lindley 1983: 36).

The Wales Act received the Royal Assent in July 1978. Legal opinion was unambiguous about the Act's draftsmanship: the Wales Act, 1978 was a 'legal minefield, unstable, and rich with possibilities of litigation' (Foulkes 1983: 94). The proposed Assembly resembled a local authority in that functions were conferred on and to be exercised by the Assembly; it had executive powers only; it could not pass laws for Wales; there would be no power of general competence in any field. The definition of transferred functions was complex; powers would be transferred by detailing specific sections of acts that gave ministers secondary powers which were to be transferred. This was even more complex than the system proposed for Scotland. There was in the latter case, at least, a body of Scots law which helped draftsmen. These secondary legislative powers would vary depending on the corresponding powers given to ministers by Westminster Acts of Parliament. Any future legislation passed by Westminster conferring powers on a Minister of the Crown would only be given to the Welsh Assembly if the new legislation provided for this. There were 176 Acts of Parliament listed in the Wales Act in which powers were given to ministers which would be transferred to the Assembly. It was a cumbersome, rigid and limited means of transferring power. Added to this were numerous exceptions so that, for example, while ministerial powers conferred under Education Acts from 1944 to 1976 were transferred, exceptions were made regarding teachers' pay and the appointment of the Schools Inspectorate (Ibid.: 70). As David Foulkes remarked,

> The technique was then to examine each relevant Act of Parliament, to 'unhook' from it those ministerial powers which it was desired to transfer to the Assembly and to convey them to the Assembly. The range of powers enjoyed by the Assembly depended therefore on the drafting of the Acts by which they were originally conferred on ministers. That drafting was not of course done with the needs of a devolved Assembly in mind but with the needs of government departmental responsibilities throughout the United Kingdom. If the powers enjoyed by the Assembly were found in practice to be coherent, logical, and suitable to a body with jurisdiction over a part only of the Kingdom, that would have been by chance rather than design. It seems very likely that amending legislation would soon be called for by the Assembly. (Ibid.: 72)

The separation of legislative and administrative responsibility might make sense when devolving functions to an unelected body with a limited range of responsibilities. However, it was bound to create problems for an elected body with a variety of functions striving to govern coherently.

The Assembly's finances would come from a block grant provided by the Secretary of State with the consent of the Treasury. The Assembly would be responsible for determining the Rate Support Grant (RSG) awarded to local authorities in Wales. The Treasury would make assumptions about the RSG in determining the Assembly's block grant but these assumptions would not determine what was actually paid out in the RSG. It was anticipated that the RSG would constitute around fifty per cent of the block grant. This became a controversial issue. The Assembly would be able to increase its budget by reducing the RSG and force the local authorities to increase rates to maintain existing levels of public services. In other words, control of the RSG was a back door form of revenue raising.

While the Assembly would be responsible for a significant amount of money, this power was limited in a number of ways. First, the total amount would be determined by the Treasury. Secondly, it could only spend within the statutory confines of the Wales Act. This was a significant power and, used carefully, could allow for changes in public policy over time. Thirdly, most of the budget would be already spoken for. Statutory obligations alone would account for most of the expenditure. In essence, the Assembly had marginal financial autonomy but it would have democratic legitimacy. This, it was feared, was a recipe for frustration.

The referendum held on St David's Day 1979 followed the 'winter of discontent', a series of industrial relations disputes which damaged the standing of the Government. There was little support for the Wales Act 1978, *per se*. Its protagonists focused on the principle of devolution rather than the details of the scheme on offer. The absence of true believers and lack of support given by prominent Labour MPs in Wales left an impression that its real supporters were to be found amongst Plaid Cymru, adding credence to the 'slippery slope' argument (Davies 2007: 650). Its opponents inside the Labour Party focused on four themes: devolution was a step on the slippery slope to separatism; the cost of the Assembly; over-government; and that Welsh might be imposed on the majority of non-Welsh speakers. There was less consistency in the campaign for devolution than amongst those arguing against it (Jones and Wilford 1983: 119), and the polls showed a dramatic decline in support for devolution over the year leading up to the referendum. Edwards and Tanner show that supporters of devolution failed to mobilise a

Table 7.1 The 1979 and 1997 Welsh devolution referendums

	Yes (%)	No (%)	Turnout (%)
1979	20.3	79.7	58.8
1997	50.3	49.7	50.1

sense of cultural identity as there were at least two competing notions of Welshness, undermining rather than complementing each other. Additionally, they show that Labour failed to convince people that devolution involved delivering better government (Edwards and Tanner 2006: 66–67). When asked to explain why they had rejected devolution, 'No' voters responded that it was too costly (61 per cent), it would create another layer of bureaucracy (43 per cent), and would lead to the break-up of the UK (40 per cent) (Evans 2006: 196).

Wales overwhelmingly rejected devolution. On a turnout of 58.3 per cent, 79.7 per cent of those who voted opposed devolution. The best result for supporters of devolution was 34.4 per cent in Gwynedd in sparsely populated North-West Wales with a high proportion of Welsh speakers. Only 12.1 per cent voted for devolution in Gwent, in South-West Wales on the border with England.

There will be no Welsh defence

In his history of Wales, John Davies quotes a letter from veteran nationalist Saunders Lewis to the *Western Mail* four days before the 1979 referendum: 'May I point out the probable consequences of a No majority. There will follow a general election. There may be a change of government. The first task of the Westminster Parliament will be to reduce and master inflation. In Wales, there are coalmines that work at a loss; there are steelworks that are judged to be superfluous; there are valleys convenient for submersion. And there will be no Welsh defence.' As Davies remarked, 'The implications of that letter would be the chief theme of the history of Wales over the following two decades' (Davies 2007: 652). Labour, the Liberals and Plaid Cymru lost support at the subsequent election. The Conservative Party vote rose from 24 to 32 per cent and its number of MPs increased from eight to eleven. In June 1979, Margaret Thatcher's Conservative Government repealed the Wales Act. In its place, it offered a Select Committee on Welsh Affairs. The Conservatives had come to power in 1979 shortly after the referendum in Wales in which they had campaigned vigorously for a 'No' vote. The party secured its largest post-war swing in that election, largely at the expense of the Liberals and no doubt aided by their opposition to devolution. However, the existence of the Welsh Office meant that when the Conservatives were in power, they had either to appoint ministers from amongst the few Welsh Tory MPs or from outside Wales. The party had flowed with the tide of public opinion in 1979 but the growing disenchantment with Conservative rule manifested itself in increased support for devolution. As in Scotland, devolution arose because of the growing problem of legitimacy founded on the idea of Wales as a political administrative entity.

In September 1979, Home Secretary William Whitelaw went back on a manifesto promise to establish a Welsh television channel. Welsh nationalism was at a low ebb but the campaign for the channel provided a useful fillip. Gwynfor Evans threatened to go on hunger strike starting in October 1980. Just weeks before the hunger strike, the Government backed down. Welsh language broadcasting proved a great success, provoking the comment that it was 'virtually the only kind of employment that was expanding' in the early 1980s (Davies 2007: 656).

The issue which dominated Welsh politics in the first half of the 1980s was the miners' strike. Efforts were made to build an all-Wales campaign. Labour and Plaid worked together better in this campaign than they had in the referendum. Leighton Andrews, future Labour Assembly Member, quoted Kim Howells, National Union of Mineworkers Research Officer and later Labour MP, describing how the 'two halves of the nation came together in mutual support' for the first time since the industrial revolution (Andrews 1999: 47). A Welsh defence was created but it would have little power to stop the closure of pits.

The strike may have contributed to a sense of a Welsh national community but the shift in opinion on devolution really began after the Conservatives' third election victory in 1987. The Welsh Conservative share of the vote fell slightly in 1983 from its high point in 1979 but its number of seats rose to 14. A further slip in share of the vote in 1987 saw its number of Welsh MPs fall to eight. By 1992, its share of the vote had again fallen slightly and it was down to six Welsh seats. The number of Tory councillors in Wales also fell and by 1995 there were only 41 across the whole of Wales. The existence of the Welsh Office, headed by a Tory from outside Wales after 1987, fuelled the notion of a 'democratic deficit'. There may not have been the same talk, as in Scotland, of the Tories lacking a mandate, but Welsh opposition MPs started to act as if this was the case. When William Hague, a Yorkshire Tory MP, became Welsh Secretary in 1995, opposition MPs boycotted his first Welsh Questions session in the Commons. Hague's own side did not help. A number of English Conservative Members took to attending Welsh (and Scottish) Question Time in the Commons, taking up much of the limited time available for scrutinising the Welsh Office.

Devolutionists argued that the array of Welsh quangos, appointed by the Welsh Secretary, contributed to this deficit (Morgan and Roberts 1993). In 1991, the Secretary of State for Wales was responsible for 1,400 appointments to 80 quangos with a combined budget of £1.8 billion (Ibid.: 56). The appointment processes and crises in the Welsh Development Agency (WDA) made quangos particularly controversial in Wales as compared with Scotland. Weak regulation resulted in the WDA, founded in 1976 with its Scottish equivalent, being accused of a series of malpractices (Ibid.: 59–63). The appointments were perceived to have been made on the basis of party political considerations rather than merit

(Ibid.: 57–59). It was as if Wales was returning to the kind of public administration which the Northcote–Trevelyan reforms had been designed to abolish in the nineteenth century.

A Campaign for a Welsh Assembly, modelled on its Scottish equivalent which was set up in 1980, was launched in 1987. But more significant were changing attitudes within the Labour Party. Mirroring developments in Scotland, a number of prominent Labour figures who had opposed devolution in 1979 became converts, including some in local government. Ron Davies, MP for Caerphilly, was amongst those who changed his mind. He later wrote that the re-emergence of devolution onto Labour's agenda was 'fuelled by the impact of successive election losses and facilitated by the pressure for local government reform' (Davies 1999: 4). Support emerged almost surreptitiously: devolution was accepted by the party under the guise of local government reform. Morgan and Mungham describe this as the 'smuggler's road to constitutional change: an elected Wales-wide body was, quite consciously, smuggled into being via the provisions for local government reform in Wales, a stark contrast to Scotland, where an elected parliament was openly demanded as an expression of national identity' (Morgan and Mungham 2000: 86). Devolution was presented as part of 'regional' reform throughout the UK and not as an important policy in its own right. Devolution was not adopted by the party with any great enthusiasm: it was 'a peripheral issue and was presented in largely structural terms; no connection was made between an Assembly and Labour's vision for societal change' (Davies 1999: 5). The deepening of Labour's commitment to Scottish devolution shored up its Welsh commitment.

Ron Davies became Shadow Welsh Secretary after the 1992 election and gave priority to the commitment. Calls for a Constitutional Convention, modelled on that in Scotland, were made by the Liberal Democrats, Wales TUC and Labour MP Peter Hain but rejected by the Welsh Labour Party. Kinnock stood down as party leader and the more sympathetic figure of John Smith was elected. It was a sign of Labour's commitment that the election of Tony Blair, deeply unsympathetic to devolution, following Smith's death in 1994 did not diminish Labour's support for a Welsh Assembly. Pro-devolution Labour members may have been 'unsettled' by Blair's 'modernisation' agenda but this may even have 'cemented support for devolution within Labour' (Andrews 1999: 60).

Ron Davies had proposed an assembly elected by a more proportional electoral system with tax-raising powers, primary law-making powers and taking over all the responsibilities of the Secretary of State for Wales. But anti-devolution sentiment inside Welsh Labour had not been stilled. Llew Smith, Blaenau Gwent's Labour MP, produced a paper which defended the constitutional status quo, arguing that he had 'no fundamental objection' to an English MP running the Welsh Office (Smith 1995). Smith challenged the democratic deficit argument, describing it as following a 'nationalist line' and pointed out that Labour had been in power in the past 'with limited support in England but we have been elected to power because we won the majority in the United Kingdom' (Ibid.).

In 1995, Labour produced 'Shaping the Vision', the culmination of a lengthy, sometimes heated, internal debate (Andrews 1999: 60–62). It proposed an assembly with secondary legislative powers but, in line with the 1978 Act, no primary legislative powers. It suggested that there might be scope for primary powers to reform local government and legislating for the Welsh language. The paper was silent on the number of Welsh MPs at Westminster after devolution. The Secretary of State would be retained and the Assembly would be financed by block grant. The simple plurality electoral system would be used. In broad outline, it resembled the 1978 Act but reflected the changed context. As in Scotland, what had changed most was the level of Labour's commitment to devolution rather than what it was proposing.

Debate continued within Wales but the crucial debates were still those inside the Labour Party. Wales Labour Action, again modelled on its Scottish equivalent, was launched at the National Eisteddfod in 1995, arguing for a more radical scheme that included proportional representation. The following year, Davies succeeded in winning support from the Labour conference to give the Assembly powers to restructure quangos. He emphasised the need to be 'inclusive', which almost became a synonym for support for proportional representation. By the following year's conference he had managed to gain support for the Additional Member electoral system. This would be the single most significant difference with the 1978 Act. It would also ensure support from the Liberal Democrats and Plaid Cymru as well as victory in the referendum.

In John Davies' words, the 'internal rhythms of Plaid Cymru move in parallel with the internal rhythms of the Labour party' (Davies 2007: 655). But in 1979, class and national identity appeared to be at war in Wales. In the 1980s, there was greater synchronisation. Class, nation, Labour and Plaid combined initially in futile defence against the Conservative Government. By the 1990s, defensive posturing had given way to more positive campaigning. While the Welsh public may have perceived the Conservatives as unsympathetic, the Conservatives did institute changes that developed a Welsh identity and supported the language. In 1988, Welsh was recognised as a core school subject. In 1993, the Welsh Language Act was passed giving Welsh the same status as English wherever this was practical and expedient and establishing the Welsh Language Board. It had largely been the work of Sir Wyn Roberts, Conservative Welsh Office Minister (Roberts 2006: 267–273). Dafydd (Lord) Elis-Thomas, former Plaid Cymru MP and leader, was appointed chairman of the Board.

The 1997 general election, referendum and creation of the Assembly

Labour had officially ruled out holding a referendum though many members continued to argue for one. In June 1996, Ron Davies announced that a referendum would be held before devolution legislation was passed. The prospect of a referendum caused more anxiety amongst Welsh supporters of an assembly than amongst Scottish devolutionists. Labour's U-turn on holding a referendum was driven by events in Scotland as opposed to pressure from Wales: in conceding a referendum in Scotland, Labour felt obliged to hold one in Wales. The decision was made in London with little, if any, consultation with Wales (Morgan and Mungham: 105). The commitment was a means of getting through the general election without drawing close attention to devolution. Labour's leadership wanted to neutralise the issue which some commentators believed had helped John Major win the 1992 UK election. Ron Davies, however, was keen to make devolution a central plank in Labour's 1997 general election campaign but had some difficulty ensuring that it emerged from behind the highly centralised Labour campaign (Andrews 1999: 80).

In 1997, the Tory vote in Wales was twice that of Plaid Cymru but Plaid won four seats and the Tories won none. Legislation to hold referendums in Scotland and Wales was passed quickly. It was decided that the Scottish referendum, expected to result in a decisive majority for devolution, should precede that for Wales. *The Times* would later thunder that this was the 'logic of the lemming' (*Times*, 17 September 1997). The logic behind the move was obvious: the Welsh were more likely to support devolution if the Scots had already done so. Labour committed more resources to its campaign in Wales than it did in Scotland. Dave Hill, Labour's chief press officer, described the situation thus: 'Scotland is the majority seat and Wales is the key marginal' (Andrews 1999: 91; Morgan and Mungham: 2000: 108). The result could hardly have been closer. The last council area to declare was Carmarthenshire with the second largest share of the vote for devolution of all, enough to secure a majority of 6,721 out of a total of over 1,112,117 who had voted.

Eighteen years of Conservative rule proved important but unlike the thirteen years of Conservative rule in the 1950s, the existence of the Welsh Office meant that Conservative rule was more easily portrayed as minority rule. Though research suggests that national identity combined with partisan alignment to determine the result of the referendum vote in 1997 (Jones and Trystan 1999), what is understood by national identity, its properties and political dynamic remain unexplained. It appears that it was less Welsh national identity so much as Welsh political identity that allowed supporters of devolution to mobilise opinion in favour of an assembly.

The Government of Wales Act, 1998 was then passed, a compromise with few real friends. Ron Davies, Secretary of State for Wales at the time of its passage, later commented that Labour's leadership was 'not convinced of the case for primary legislative powers' so a compromise was found (McAllister 2005: 499). This 'new and untested set of arrangements' (Rawlings 2003: 5) was the old idea of executive devolution debated in Whitehall in the 1970s. Rawlings identified its four key features. First, core matters would be retained at the centre with powers in a range of 'fields transferred'. Secondly, the 'hallmark of executive devolution' was the split between primary and secondary legislative powers and the 'enumeration of the powers devolved statute by statute'; general secondary legislative competence would not be transferred. Thirdly, joint and concurrent powers with central government were defined, most notably the 'supervisory power of central government' to ensure the implementation of European Community law. Fourthly, executive devolution was a 'moving target' with an 'ongoing allocation of powers' as new statutes were passed by Westminster (Ibid.: 5–6). Rawlings has suggested that this amounted to a form of 'quasi-devolution' (Ibid.: 11). The Assembly Government had to bid for Welsh bills or clauses at Westminster, competing with Whitehall departments as it had no primary legislative powers. Problems would arise when different parties were in power in London and Cardiff. But even without any ideological dimension, the existing arrangements were thought to be flawed. Wales was given 'executive devolution', defined as the 'transfer of various subordinate or secondary law-making powers' as distinct from the 'legislative devolution' given to Scotland, meaning the 'straightforward allocation of primary legislative functions' (Ibid.: 5). The arguments made by civil servants in the 1970s, discussed above, were ignored once more.

Three First Ministers and a political suicide

Ron Davies was a convert to devolution from the South Wales valleys, 'blessedly devoid of any association with Aberystwyth' (Davies 2007: 673) unlike so many nationalists and the earlier generation of Labour devolutionists. His drive and conviction that devolution had to be inclusive proved important. Donald Dewar, his Scottish equivalent, had supported devolution for longer but Dewar avoided being party spokesman during the most difficult period leading up to the establishment of the Scottish Parliament between 1992 and 1997. In Scotland, public support only needed to be expressed. In Wales, it had to be won. Davies had to fight hard for the inclusive agenda he astutely identified as necessary to win support amongst the Welsh public. But the absence of a statue of Davies in Wales is not because he remains alive, unlike the Scottish 'father of the nation', but because of personal affairs which led to his resignation in October 1998 and ended Davies' prospect of becoming

Welsh First Minister. This personal trauma set in motion events that resulted in a political trauma for the Labour Party. A contest to succeed Davies as leader involved the party's leadership in London manipulating the rules in order to ensure that Alun Michael, its preferred candidate, defeated the alternative candidate, Rhodri Morgan.

As sections of the Welsh media enjoyed pointing out, Alun Michael was perceived to have been parachuted into a list seat. His authority within the Assembly and his own party was damaged by accusations that the leadership contest had been rigged. In February 2000, Michael was forced to step down. A dispute between the Treasury and the Assembly over EU funding had provoked a motion of no confidence, though this only reflected a deeper disaffection with Michael's leadership. Rhodri Morgan took his place and adopted a style which appeared more willing to challenge London than his predecessor. In a well-trailed speech in December 2002, Morgan emphasised the 'clear red water' between the Labour Administrations in Cardiff and London (*Western Mail*, 12 December 2002). Even if it was rhetorical, it indicated a shift in the terms of debate which might result in substantive change fuelled by rising expectations in Wales.

Wales may have been lukewarm in its support for devolution but voters showed their dismay with London's interference by returning 17 Plaid Cymru Assembly Members (AMs) in the first elections to the Assembly. The AMS electoral system in Wales was less proportional than that in Scotland (the constituency to list seats ratio was 40:20 in Wales compared with 73:56 in Scotland) and Welsh Labour support was consistently higher than its Scottish equivalent so that Labour was expected to win an overall majority in the Assembly. Plaid not only won seats in its heartlands in Welsh-speaking Wales but also took seats in traditionally rock solid Labour constituencies in the old southern coalfields. Dafydd Wigley, Plaid's leader, described it as a 'quiet earthquake' (Trystan, Jones and Scully 2003). In an unguarded moment, Rhodri Morgan had explained that the electoral system was devised to ensure that Labour would win an overall majority in three out of four elections (Osmond 2005: 7). What Morgan had failed to take account of were changes in partisan allegiances in the context of Welsh, as distinct from UK, elections.

In 2003, exactly half the Assembly were women but turnout was 38 per cent, down 8 per cent from 1999. Plaid's 'quiet earthquake' had subsided. It looked as if Labour's problems in 1999, rather than any devolution effect, had been the cause of Plaid's rise. Labour had re-asserted its position but even in a good year for Labour, the party failed to win an overall majority. Labour was never able to govern with an overall majority and has had to operate either as a minority government or in coalition, with the Liberal Democrats during the first two terms of the National Assembly or with Plaid Cymru since 2007.

In 2007, Labour fell back considerably both in its share of constituency

Table 7.2 Results of Welsh Assembly elections, 1999–2007

	Constituency seats (% vote)	List seats (% vote)	Total no. of seats (% of total Assembly)
1999 Labour	27 (37.6)	1 (35.4)	28 (46.7)
2003 Labour	30 (40.0)	0 (36.6)	30 (50)
2007 Labour	24 (32.2)	2 (29.6)	26 (43.3)
1999 Plaid Cymru	9 (28.4)	8 (30.5)	17 (28.3)
2003 Plaid Cymru	5 (21.2)	7 (19.7)	12 (20)
2007 Plaid Cymru	7 (22.4)	8 (21.0)	15 (25)
1999 Cons	1 (15.8)	8 (16.5)	9 (15)
2003 Cons	1 (19.9)	10 (19.2)	11 (18.3)
2007 Cons	5 (22.4)	7 (21.5)	12 (20)
1999 LibDem	3 (13.5)	3 (12.5)	6 (10)
2003 LibDem	3 (14.1)	3 (12.7)	6 (10)
2007 LibDem	3 (14.8)	3 (11.7)	6 (10)
1999 Others	0 (4.7)	0 (5.1)	0 (0)
2003 Others	1 (4.8)	0 (11.8)	1 (1.7)
2007 Others	1 (8.3)	0 (16.1)	1 (1.7)

and list votes with the Others advancing in terms of votes but unable to translate this into seats. The workings of the electoral system meant that while Labour lost six constituencies, it gained two list seats despite a substantial decrease in share of the list vote. The bias in the electoral system, a kind of safety net for Labour, kicked in. The weeks after the elections saw considerable horse-trading amongst the parties with reports that some anti-Labour coalition might emerge but in the end a Labour–Plaid coalition was agreed. Rhodri Morgan's authority, especially in his own party, was weakened and critics of his 'clear red water' strategy were quick to argue that Labour in Wales needed modernisation in much the same way as Tony Blair had changed the party at the centre. Devolution was proving to be a process changing the party system in Wales.

The Richard Commission

In October 2000, Labour and the Liberal Democrats formed a coalition in the Welsh Assembly. An unstable situation had arisen as a consequence of Labour governing as a minority administration. Alun Michael had been forced to resign as First Secretary in February 2000 and was replaced by Rhodri Morgan but it soon became clear that Morgan's ability to govern Wales was limited by having only 28 of the Assembly's 60 seats. After lengthy negotiations, the coalition was agreed and the Liberal Democrats won two of the nine seats in the Cabinet including the appointment of Mike German, Welsh Liberal Democrat leader, as Deputy First Minister. Additionally, a number of policy commitments were made including the establishment of an independent Commission to examine the Assembly's powers and electoral system. Reform was made more likely given the near unanimity that the existing model of Welsh devolution was inadequate and a consensus existed on at least some aspects of reform. A Commission was set up under Lord Richard, a Labour peer and former Leader of the House of Lords, in July 2002. Five Commissioners were appointed after an open competition and a further four were appointed by the main parties.

The Richard Commission offered a trenchant critique of Welsh devolution. It argued that the establishment of the Assembly as a single corporate body had been a 'key element in its subsequent evolution' (Richard 2004: 48). Assembly Members preferred to see the institution operating as a parliament with a separate government and opposition rather than on the old local authority model and in February 2002 had unanimously resolved to create a split between its executive and parliamentary arms. This created tensions between its legal and practical operation. The Commission argued that the Assembly should make it 'absolutely clear that there is a Welsh Assembly Government responsible for executive acts and decisions, separate from the National Assembly itself but directly answerable and accountable to it' (Ibid.: 79). It noted that the arrangements whereby the Assembly proposed legislation to Westminster resulted in the 'fundamental problem' of 'split accountability – proposals initiated in one representative body and scrutinised and adopted in another' (Ibid.: 180). It maintained that if the Assembly was to have legislative powers then it would be 'desirable, though not essential, to confer tax varying powers' (Ibid.: 212). It recognised that the electoral system created 'two types of Assembly Member' and that this was a 'problem that will not be solved by adjustments to AMS' (Ibid.: 238). First Past The Post would 'reduce the representation of some parties to a level well below their support in Wales' and would 'seriously weaken the capacity for opposition and scrutiny' (Ibid.: 239).

Richard recommended:

–   Wales should have a legislative Assembly;
–   in the interim, the framework delegated powers approach should be expanded with the agreement of the UK Government;
–   tax-varying powers are desirable, though not essential;
–   membership needs to rise to 80 to exercise primary legislative powers;
–   the Assembly should be reconstituted as a separate legislature and executive;
–   the electoral system should be changed to Single Transferable Vote (STV) with the increase in membership;
–   these changes should be introduced by 2001. (Richard 2004)

The Richard Commission produced a more detailed, comprehensive blueprint than anything produced by the Scottish Constitutional Convention. Cardiff appeared to be producing 'some of the most creative thinking in the UK constitution' (Rawlings 2005: 824). The Commission achieved unanimity amongst its members, though its Labour nominee signalled that its recommendations should not be implemented for some time.

In response, the Government issued a White Paper, *Better Governance for Wales* in June 2005. This proposed abandoning the old corporate body model: a separate ministerial authority for Wales would be established, accountable to the Assembly but legally distinct. While it conceded that the Assembly should have increased powers, it set out a three-stage process towards this goal: working within the existing framework but allowing more autonomy to the Assembly; transferring powers, with the consent of the Assembly and Westminster, in areas already devolved through Orders in Council; and granting primary legislative powers, subject to a referendum and two-thirds majority of Assembly Members and a majority at Westminster (Wales Office 2005). Ron Davies may have been right in describing devolution as 'an event, not a process' but the White Paper suggested it could be a slow process. Commentators remarked that it was a 'little depressing, but perhaps not surprising that the post-Richard debate has moved so far (and so rapidly) from the Commission's concern with articulating an optimal solution to the problem of making law for Wales' (Jones and Williams 2005: 652).

It was no surprise that the Government rejected tax powers, STV and a larger Assembly. Most controversially the Government proposed banning 'dual candidacy', the practice of candidates standing in constituencies and on a party's regional list, to tackle the West Clwyd Question (this referred to the return of three defeated constituency candidates as regional list AMs in 2003). A new Government of Wales Bill had its second reading in the Commons in January 2006 and was given Royal Assent in July. The proposal to ban dual candidacies was widely criticised as blatantly partisan. But other aspects of the Bill were given less scrutiny.

Relations with Whitehall were unlikely to be transformed by the new Act. Westminster legislation would continue to have to be considered bill by bill in their application to Wales. It was also unlikely to be the last legislative word on Welsh devolution and led one commentator to ask whether 'it will leave significant items of unfinished business on the table, which will need to be tackled sooner or later' (Trench 2007a). The same commentator has argued that it will create a 'very strong executive' and that the Secretary of State for Wales will remain 'godfather of Wales's devolution arrangements' and that the Act was a compromise that set out to appease anti-devolutionists in the Welsh Labour Party as well as advocates of reform. In terms of powers, the continuing role played by the Secretary of State and relations with Westminster/Whitehall, the Act resembles the Scotland Act, 1978 more than the Scotland Act, 1998. In other words, Wales has not yet caught up with what was proposed for Scotland almost thirty years ago in an era when devolution in Britain was offered grudgingly and with stringent controls.

Conclusion

Wales has travelled far since the 1970s. In 1973, James Kellas argued that Scotland had a political system. He provoked a debate on Scotland's distinct position in the British system of politics and government. It is difficult to imagine any scholar making a similar case about Wales at any stage in the period before 1999. Whether a Welsh political system now exists turns on the meaning of the term, but a stronger case can be made that Wales has a political system today than could be made in 1973 about Scotland. In the introduction, the union of Wales and England was described as conforming more to the unitary state form of state formation than the union state form. That remained true throughout most of the union and even the twentieth century. But in the latter half of the twentieth century significant change occurred. As this chapter has demonstrated, debates are framed in past understandings of constitutional arrangements but this does not mean that the past will always prevent change. The 1997 referendum result illustrates this well. Scotland secured a convincing majority for a devolved parliament with tax-varying powers while Wales had a wafer-thin majority for a much weaker assembly. But the swing compared with that in 1979 was greater in Wales and the constitutional leap was at least as significant. The perception that the Government of Wales lacked legitimacy was augmented by the existence of the Welsh Office, an institution that had developed far more quickly than the slow evolution of the Scottish Office. The Welsh Office provided an all-Wales focus which had not previously existed. In his book *When was Wales?*, written after the 1979 referendum, Gwyn Williams wrote, 'Welsh politics had ceased to exist. Wales had finally disappeared into Britain' (Williams 1991: 297). That could no longer be said after 1998.

8

In search of legitimacy: Northern Ireland since 1972

English policy has achieved no triumph so great as the union between England and Scotland ... English policy has never more nearly failed of attaining any part of its objects than in the union with Ireland. (Dicey 1881: 168)

The British Government reaffirm that they will uphold the democratic wish of a greater number of the people of Northern Ireland on the issue of whether they prefer to support the Union or a sovereign united Ireland. On this basis, they reiterate that they have no selfish strategic or economic interest in Northern Ireland. (*Frameworks for the Future*, February 1995)

One of the nonsenses of Northern Ireland is that direct rule has brought with it some of the least attractive elements of former colonial rule. The locals cannot be trusted, and so there is always an Englishman who is permanent under-secretary to the Secretary of State, another Englishman. (Needham 1998: 69)

Introduction: in search of legitimacy

In retrospect, the imposition of direct rule looks inevitable. There was no consensus in Northern Ireland on the basic rules of constitutional politics. As Richard Rose remarked, the 'chief political institutions' of Northern Ireland were 'institutions of discord' (Rose 1971: 113). Northern Ireland lacked a 'loyal opposition', a *sine qua non* for fully legitimate regimes' (Ibid.: 447). In the conclusion of his study of Northern Ireland, Rose argued, 'Any political solution requires two things that are usually conspicuous by their absence: time and goodwill. When discord has been institutionalized for centuries, as in Northern Ireland ... one may have to wait a very long time indeed for time to heal such wounds. The intensity of discord also implies that force is unlikely to provide a prompt and easy solution ... The immediate question is not how long the problem will last, but what shall be done in the here and now. To do nothing is to make a contribution to discord, as Westminster ... [has] shown. Yet action is full of uncertainty' (Ibid.: 472).

For the first time since 1935, troops were sent to Northern Ireland in

August 1969. Prime Minister Harold Wilson had threatened to impose direct rule in the event of sending in troops but instead he put pressure on James Chichester-Clark, who became Prime Minister of Northern Ireland in May, for further reforms. The Home Office and Stormont had discussed the constitutional implications of troops in Northern Ireland: less than a fortnight before the troops were deployed, Stormont Prime Minister Chichester-Clark wrote to Jim Callaghan, the Home Secretary, objecting to press reports of the prospect that 'British troops' would be sent to Northern Ireland 'as if we were some sort of external territory. The British Army is our Army too' (TNA PREM 13/2843). If troops had to be deployed, he felt, they should come under Stormont's remit of 'peace, order and good government'. Chichester-Clark recognised that the Home Office would want to 'seek methods by which you could feel confident of a proper voice in the "law and order" field' (Ibid.) but he was 'appalled' to discover, following meetings between senior officials from Stormont and the Home Office, that Wilson and Callaghan might consider that the deployment of troops required direct rule. He warned that replacing a 'representative Government, freely and democratically elected as recently as February of this year, would be wholly unacceptable to the great majority of Ulster people' and that the 'people of Northern Ireland are as determined to have their own Government as the people of the South were from 1919 on; and you should seriously consider the history of how Dublin Castle tried to cope with Sinn Fein at that time' (Ibid.). The public records include a note of a telephone conversation between Home Secretary Callaghan and Chichester-Clark in which Callaghan stated that the Government in London had 'no desire to assume responsibility for Northern Ireland affairs' but that he 'felt it right to point out the grave constitutional consequences' of troops policing Northern Ireland (Ibid.). He urged Chichester-Clark to 'make a massive recruiting drive for Roman Catholics to go into the Royal Ulster Constabulary' (Ibid.).

Wilson and Chichester-Clark met, along with respective Cabinet colleagues, and issued the Downing Street Declaration. It affirmed the constitutional position of Northern Ireland and the equality of all its citizens; welcomed reforms in local government franchise, local government areas and allocation of houses; and created an Ombudsman and 'machinery to consider citizens' grievances' against public authorities. The Declaration stated, 'In the context of the commitment of these troops, the Northern Ireland Government have re-affirmed their intention to take into the fullest account at all times the views of Her Majesty's Government in the United Kingdom, especially in relation to matters affecting the status of citizens of that part of the United Kingdom and their equal rights and protection under the law' (HMSO 1969: Cmnd. 4154). Home Secretary Jim Callaghan visited Northern Ireland within a fortnight. Communiqués were issued outlining reforms in the franchise, public employment and housing as well as anti-discrimination measures. From Westminster's perspective, this was enough to allow Stormont to continue to exist. Wilson reported meetings with Chichester-Clark to his Cabinet in early September 1969 and summed up the discussion by emphasising the importance of time: 'We had bought time in which to work out a long-term solution. This might be a long time in coming, and it was unlikely to be achieved within the lifetime of the present Parliament. Meanwhile we should avoid being rushed; and in particular there should be no premature withdrawal of troops' (TNA CAB 128/46).

Stormont staggered on for almost another three years. Chichester-Clark had proposed jumping before being pushed, handing over control of the police authorities to the army but was damaged within the Unionist community by accusations that he was London's poodle. In March 1971, Chichester-Clark resigned after less than two years in office having failed to convince London to deploy more troops. He was succeeded by Brian Faulkner, 'widely viewed as Northern Ireland's last chance to keep itself in devolved government business' (Walker 2004: 190).

In January 1972, Sir Burke Trend, Cabinet Secretary, wrote to Ted Heath, who had become Prime Minister in 1970, setting out the problem: 'should any new initiative be based on the fundamental premises that the Border remains intact and that the Stormont system continues; or should it envisage some basic modification on these assumptions? Hitherto, Ministers have judged that it would not be possible to modify either of them without risking the fall of Mr Faulkner's Government and the inevitable need, as a result, to introduce direct rule' (TNA PREM 15/1000). Trend proposed that Westminster legislate to protect Catholic rights and 'a reasonable share in representation not only in Parliament but in Government' (Ibid.). Sir Alec Douglas Home, Foreign Secretary and former Prime Minister, wrote to Heath in mid March 1972, 'I really dislike Direct Rule for Northern Ireland because I do not believe that they are like the Scots or the Welsh and doubt if they ever will be. The real British interest would I think be served best by pushing them towards a United Ireland rather than tying them closer to the United Kingdom. Our own parliamentary history is one long story of trouble with the Irish' (TNA PREM 15/1004). Reginald Maudling, Home Secretary, warned that the existing arrangements could not last but Home wanted to place a time limit on direct rule if it had to be imposed. The increasing violence in Northern Ireland forced Ted Heath's Government to consider exceptional measures. Even before it was approached by Brian Faulkner to introduce internment without trial, the Cabinet Committee on Northern Ireland had discussed this possibility in March 1971 (Heath 1998: 428).

The Northern Ireland Office

Heath eventually imposed direct rule at the end of March 1972. He appointed Willie Whitelaw to be the first Secretary of State for Northern Ireland. There is a consensus that Whitelaw's seniority and diplomatic skills made him an unmatched Secretary of State who made progress during his brief tenure in this office. However, his sympathetic biographers, with access to a wider range of sources, were more critical than many other accounts of his term as Secretary of State. They described his appointment as a 'category mistake' though concede that 'almost everyone with an intimate knowledge of the terrain was automatically disqualified' (Garnett and Aitken 2003: 112–113).

In November 1971, at the Lord Mayor's London Banquet, Heath had warned hardline Unionists that he would not be held to ransom and that Britain had 'no selfish interest in Northern Ireland' and would not stand in the way of a majority wishing to join the Republic (Heath 1998: 432). The Conservative Party's unionism had started to evaporate. Unionism in Northern Ireland also underwent significant change. As Graham Walker has remarked, direct rule 'reduced overnight the Unionist Party from a party of government with patronage at its disposal, to a body of incoherent and ineffectual protest' (Walker 2004: 212). The Official Unionists changed under direct rule as many middle-class members drifted away. Northern Ireland's 'contented classes' would do well under direct rule, with the growth of the public sector (Patterson 2006: 329), leaving others to participate in its often febrile politics. Its democratic nature – described by an adviser to David Trimble as 'run on the lines of Presbyterian anarchy with a whiff of Anglican arrogance' (quoted in Ibid.: 262) – placed it at the mercy of its activist core. As May's 'law of curvilinear disparity' suggests (May 1973), activists and leaders often diverge ideologically leaving the leadership in an invidious position if too much power is held by the activists inside a party. Faulkner's problems with his party partly stemmed from the ease with which members could call special meetings of the Ulster Unionist Council to hold him to account, a problem which would also inhibit future leaders.

The legislation that finally brought Stormont's rule to an end was a 'temporary provisions' Act. Direct rule from London was never intended to be a solution but, despite sporadic periods of devolved government, became the default option after 1972. Various efforts have been made over the years to reinstitute a reformed measure of devolution. Crucial to each was recognition that success depended on cross-community support. Over time, an Irish dimension too was recognised as a prerequisite for achieving legitimacy.

In 1972, London issued a discussion paper, primarily drafted by Northern Ireland civil servant Kenneth Bloomfield, entitled 'The Future of

Northern Ireland', following discussions attended only by the Official Unionists, Alliance Party and Northern Ireland Labour Party (NILP). The paper repeated the long-standing commitment to the union with majority consent but introduced two new dimensions that would eventually become central to any settlement: new institutions must 'give minority interests a share in the exercise of executive power' and an 'Irish dimension' (Northern Ireland Office 1972: 33–34). When Stormont was prorogued, Prime Minister Heath had promised a plebiscite on Northern Ireland's constitutional status as soon as was practicable. The 'border poll' was held in March 1973, asking electors whether they wished to remain part of the United Kingdom or join the Irish Republic. Nationalist and republican supporters boycotted it, damaging its legitimacy. The overwhelming support for the union merely reflected the known wishes of the majority community. It was envisaged that further border polls would be held but this was to be the only one.

After Stormont was established in 1921, Northern Ireland was represented in the House of Commons by thirteen MPs and, after the abolition of University Members, twelve Members of Parliament. Without devolution, Northern Ireland would have returned around twenty MPs (Hadfield 1989: 46). In 1973, the Kilbrandon Commission made only one recommendation on Northern Ireland and that was that the 'same rules should be applied' to Northern Ireland as applied elsewhere for its number of MPs (Kilbrandon 1973: 402, para. 1338) which would mean an increase to seventeen. The Labour Government's precarious position in the late 1970s, governing without an overall majority, strengthened the Unionist Party's bargaining power and resulted in an additional five Northern Ireland MPs being returned at the 1979 and subsequent elections. This brought Northern Ireland broadly into line with the rest of the UK.

Each attempt to restore reformed devolution proved unsuccessful from the Sunningdale Agreement initiated in 1973–74, through the Constitutional Convention in 1975, all-party talks in 1979–80, to Jim Prior's 'rolling devolution'. Unionist opposition to these initiatives focused on power-sharing and/or the Irish dimension. The crucial difference between Sunningdale and what came later was context. Unionist memories of old-style devolution with majority rule were still fresh. Power-sharing in some shape or form, whether using that term or not, was the objective in all efforts to reconstitute devolution by London. Winning the consent of the minority community became a key objective of central government's strategy in the territorial management of Northern Ireland. This meant the rejection of simple majority rule. It would take time for sections of the Unionist community to accept this. Equally, it would take time for an Irish dimension to be acceptable.

The Northern Ireland Office (NIO) was only partially modelled on existing devolution in Scotland and Wales. Though Welsh Secretaries were appointed representing constituencies outside Wales in the 1980s, efforts were usually made to find some minister with a Welsh base or background. No such effort was made in the case of Northern Ireland. The integrationists within Ulster Unionism saw the Scottish Office as a model for Northern Ireland. In his speech to the Unionist Party conference in 1983, party leader James Molyneaux reflected on the differences between the different territorial department:

> Our sense of oneness with the other parts of the Kingdom tends to highlight the deficiencies in methods of government and administration. One such weakness manifests itself in an accident prone Northern Ireland Office. There is good reason for concluding that this results from the lack of continuity of advice. For the present at any rate, Northern Ireland Ministers must of necessity be birds of passage. On average they remain here for about two years ... It would be premature to envisage Ulstermen occupying Ministerial posts in the Northern Ireland Office but thought must be given to allowing Northern Ireland Civil Servants to play a much larger part in top decision making and administration. It is time we started moving to a pattern resembling the Scottish Office which in 1929 [*sic*] was transplanted from Whitehall to Edinburgh for the purpose of making the Department more responsive to Scottish needs and more closely in touch with Scottish thinking. While the move was not anti-English the percentage of Scots in senior posts increased to the present 80 per cent in certain grades. There is too a healthy movement of Scots outwards to Whitehall Departments giving a Scottish influence throughout the United Kingdom Civil Service and consequently a greater and wider understanding of Scottish affairs. (Molyneaux 1983)

As neither Labour nor the Conservatives operated in Northern Ireland, though the latter did briefly and half-heartedly attempt to build up a base after 1989, ministers appointed to the NIO were invariably from outside the polity. Additionally, there was no prospect of a member of the Northern Ireland Civil Service (NICS) becoming permanent head of the department though it was possible for the head of NICS to become Second Permanent Secretary, as in the case of Kenneth Bloomfield.

The Conservatives only started to organise locally as a result of local pressure and Labour's position was complicated by the existence of the nationalist Social Democratic and Labour Party (SDLP), a fellow member with Labour of the Socialist International. The consequence, according to Richard Needham, the longest-serving NIO Minister, was that those who end up holding ministerial office there do so for one of two reasons, 'as a step on the way up or as a step on the way out', though he was an exception himself (Needham 1998: 122). Jim Prior had implicitly acknowledged this in his early idea, though soon abandoned, to create an Executive consisting of Northern Ireland politicians. NIO Ministers were in the unenviable position of representing constituencies outside Northern Ireland and gaining little political credit for their activities. Direct rule brought unity of government to Northern Ireland but that did not mean that a unified system of government existed across the United Kingdom. Northern Ireland continued to be treated as a place apart. It continued to have special procedures for dealing with legislation and public policy, a separate judicial process and a separate civil service.

In his memoirs of his time as a senior public servant in Northern Ireland, Maurice Hayes remarked that 'One of the effects of single-party government for seventy years, and a civil service that reflected the values and ethos of the dominant party, was a lack of challenge, a lack of intellectual vigour, a willingness to accept traditional attitudes and procedures as immutable ... because of what association with doomed policy initiatives would do to official careers' (Hayes 1995: 183). The NICS had been set up in 1921 and had its own head, staff and recruitment and promotion procedures. The NICS was similar to other Stormont institutions in mimicking Westminster and Whitehall but there had been differences that developed incrementally as a consequence of being a separate service. The civil service provided a great degree of continuity from devolved government to direct rule. The new Northern Ireland Office operated alongside the NICS. The wry comment quoted at the start of an article by Paul Carmichael on the NICS is not without foundation, 'This is a damned funny country. There's one crowd singing "Wrap the Green Flag Round Me" and another crowd sings "Rule Britannia" and there's a lot of bloody civil servants up there in Stormont drawing twenty pounds a week and laughing at the lot of us' (Carmichael 2002: 23). However, the criticisms of the public service in Northern Ireland can be overdone. Indeed, the professionalism of the service and absence of discrimination within it are often overlooked or simply taken for granted.

In his memoirs, Hayes recounted a problem in discussing prison policy with Scottish and Welsh Offices: 'changes in the regime that would make sense in the Northern Ireland context were refused because of the fear of a read-across to English and Scottish prisons, which would bring objections from the Home Office' (Hayes 1995: 260). Another example was concerned with proposals from the NICS for more radical and extensive human rights legislation than existed in the rest of the UK, which was opposed by London on the grounds that it might provoke demands for similar provisions there. This ethos combined with support for parity in public policy. Each was inherited into the system of direct rule. Richard Needham has commented on how policy was decided in Whitehall with little input from Northern Ireland: 'The overall direction of the health service was decided in Whitehall, where I had neither influence nor contacts. I never once discussed the Northern Ireland health service with the Secretary of State for Health during the four years I was minister. We were known condescendingly as "the territorials". My function was to be a regional marketing executive for head offices' hand-me-downs!'

(Needham 1998: 99). This was confirmed by a former senior official in the NICS who gave the example of leading the rest of the UK in seat-belt legislation which provoked protest from Unionists who argued that Northern Ireland was being used as a guinea pig. On the other hand, intimidation of witnesses in terrorist trials led to the introduction of non-jury trials (Diplock Courts) in 1976. Northern Ireland was increasingly becoming a place apart. It may have had less autonomy and no devolved government, but citizens there were experiencing a very different form of politics and sets of rights and obligations from any other part of the UK.

Early efforts to restore reformed devolution

The Royal Commission on the Constitution (Kilbrandon) reported in late 1973 and concluded that home rule had been of 'considerable advantage to Northern Ireland' (Kilbrandon 1973: 380). It recognised defects in the system including those of a 'general kind' and those that 'related to the particular circumstances' (Ibid.: 381). The general defects, according to Kilbrandon, were that Stormont's institutions were 'modelled very closely on those at Westminster'; 'independence of action' was not practicable for some functions; and its financial arrangements precluded independent action (Ibid.). The particular defects were those which 'left a large section of the community always in a minority, without any share in government or any prospect of securing a share in government, and the restrictions placed on the exercise of the devolved functions did not suffice to safeguard the interests of that minority' (Ibid.). This was the thinking behind power-sharing. Successive governments at Westminster sought to reconstitute devolution along lines that met the particular defects identified by Kilbrandon but paid little, if any, attention to the general defects. The latter, particular criticisms would be of most concern over the years in efforts to reconstitute devolution.

The Northern Ireland Assembly Act, 1973 and Northern Ireland Constitution Act, 1973 provided for a 78-member assembly elected by Single Transferable Vote (STV) and created three categories of legislative powers: excepted, reserved and transferred (as in the 1920 Government of Ireland Act) along with a power-sharing executive. Excepted matters remained the responsibility of Westminster and included foreign and defence affairs, anti-terrorism, elections, nationality and 'coinage'. Reserved powers included law and order but these might be transferred over time. All other matters were transferred. The Act reiterated Westminster's legislative sovereignty (section 4(4)) and contained anti-discrimination provisions. STV had been used under the original Government of Ireland Act, 1920 but abolished by Stormont. In one of its last acts in 1972, Stormont reintroduced STV for local government which was carried into effect after its demise. The first elections using a more proportional system for almost fifty years in Northern Ireland took place in May 1973 in 26 new District Councils.

Elections to the Assembly were held in June. The Official Unionists were still the dominant force though, as Whitelaw told Heath: 'an uncomfortably large number of seats had been won by dissident loyalists of one kind and another' (TNA PREM 15/1693). Brian Faulkner, leader of the official Unionists and Prime Minister when Stormont was prorogued, recognised the need to take account of the minority community and had persuaded the Ulster Unionist Council, his party's governing body, to support power-sharing in March 1973. Ian Paisley and other hardline Unionists condemned Faulkner's 'sell-out to Dublin'. The backdrop of violence fuelled polarisation and undermined the prospect of compromises winning cross-community support. Nonetheless, parties supporting the institutions won 52 out of 78 seats, including 24 won by the Official Unionists who no longer commanded the dominant position within Unionism that they had during the Stormont years. As Patterson put it, 'Unionism was driven towards a bitter and fevered fragmentation by the twin threats of Provisional [IRA] violence and British intervention' (Patterson 2006: 225).

Policing, detention and a Council of Ireland proved the 'main stumbling blocks' towards agreement amongst the parties supporting power-sharing (O'Leary, Elliott and Wilford 1988: 35). The combination of Willie Whitelaw's diplomatic skills and some of the participants' willingness to compromise ensured progress but it proved short lived. The power-sharing Executive was brokered by Whitelaw in November 1973. The number of places in the Administration was increased from eleven to fifteen. This was a 'fairly shameless piece of pork-barrelling' with the number of 'posts being created to suit the number of ministers' rather than vice versa (Hayes 1995: 165). The portfolios were not designed with effective government in mind and in some cases ministerial responsibilities had few, if any, public policy functions (Ibid.). Brian Faulkner became Chief Executive and Gerry Fitt, SDLP leader, became Deputy Chief Executive. Five other Unionist members and three other members of the SDLP plus Oliver Napier of the Alliance Party became members of the Executive. In addition, other non-Executive ministers included two other SDLP members, one Unionist and an Alliance member. Heath required Whitelaw's skills elsewhere and in November 1973 he became Secretary of State for Employment to deal with industrial relations problems in Britain. Francis Pym was appointed in his place, a less experienced figure with little understanding of Northern Ireland's problems.

Sunningdale and the Constitutional Convention

In December 1973, an 'unprecedented meeting' (Rose 1975: 30) was held at Sunningdale Civil Service College in England attended by British and Irish Government Ministers and leaders of the three Northern Ireland parties involved in the power-sharing Executive. It was the first time since 1925 that members of the Governments of the UK, Irish Republic and politicians from both parts of Ireland had met together. An agreement was reached to establish a Council of Ireland consisting of ministers from the Republic and Northern Ireland, as well as a consultative assembly and secretariat. It was also agreed that the constitutional status of Northern Ireland could not be changed without majority consent in the polity. In addition, the Agreement covered law and order, judicial matters, extradition and policing matters. Faulkner needed a major concession from Dublin to placate his fellow Unionists and urged Liam Cosgrave, Irish Taoiseach, to scrap Articles 2 and 3 of the Irish Constitution claiming jurisdiction over Northern Ireland. However, Cosgrave could not agree to this without a constitutional amendment requiring a referendum in the Republic. Liberal Unionists, such as Basil McIvor, would complain bitterly that the SDLP's insistence on a Council of Ireland 'wrecked the prospects of an otherwise excellent and hopeful power-sharing arrangement' (McIvor 1998: 104). In the event, Sunningdale proved an 'unmitigated disaster for Faulkner's standing in the Unionist community' (Patterson 2006: 240). As Whitelaw told Garret Fitzgerald, Faulkner was 'perhaps further ahead of his party than was quite good for him' (*Irish News*, 1 January 2004, *Irish Times*, 2 January 2004).

The Northern Ireland power-sharing Executive officially took office on New Year's Day 1974. Three days later, Faulkner's command of his party disappeared when the Ulster Unionist Council called a special meeting that voted against the Council of Ireland and the Sunningdale Agreement. Faulkner had no alternative but to resign as leader of the party but continued as Chief Executive of the Northern Ireland Executive. The Executive's legitimacy was finally destroyed after the February 1974 UK general election. The industrial relations problems, which had removed Whitelaw from Northern Ireland, provoked Heath into calling an election at which Faulkner's pro-Assembly Ulster Unionists failed to win a single seat against a disparate coalition of anti-Assembly Unionists contesting seats under the umbrella of the United Ulster Unionist Coalition (UUUC). Frank Cooper, Permanent Secretary at the Northern Ireland Office, remembered a meeting with a 'somewhat shaken and somewhat fearful' Faulkner after the election (TNA FCO 87/334). The Ulster Workers' Council (UWC) staged a general strike, that finally killed off this early experiment in power-sharing. The UWC was a group of trade unionists who brought in some Unionist politicians to lend legitimacy to the strike, though they prevented the politicians taking control. The UWC had existed since the late 1960s as the Loyalist Association of Workers, with an ideological mixture of Ulster Unionism and Labourism; it had roots in Belfast and had often been in dispute with Unionist political leaders.

In May, the Executive resigned. Faulkner went to the House of Lords but died in a horse riding accident soon afterwards. The Assembly was dissolved in July 1974 and a new Act – the Northern Ireland Act, 1974 – allowed Westminster to legislate for Northern Ireland's devolved matters by Orders in Council, involving a much more perfunctory process of parliamentary procedure than would normally be necessary. Excepted matters would still require primary legislation and apart from fair employment laws, Orders in Council were used for Northern Ireland thereafter. In his posthumously published memoirs, Faulkner maintained that the power-sharing Executive might have been the 'greatest breakthrough in Irish politics this century' (Faulkner 1978: 194). It was fifty years too late and a quarter century too early. Sunningdale and the power-sharing Executive may have failed but for many involved it represented the 'bright spring of reforming liberalism' (Hayes 1995: 161).

One manifestation of the fragmentation of Unionism was support for an independent Northern Ireland, a contradiction in terms of unionism and, indeed, of loyalism. Amongst those giving support for this was future Unionist leader David Trimble (MacDonald 2000: 47). Support for a Unilateral Declaration of Independence (UDI) was found amongst the more militant loyalists with whom Trimble associated at this time, though it had some support amongst nationalists and the left who saw UDI forcing responsibility on Northern Ireland. Trimble contributed to a paper that argued that 'Ulster would be an independent republic within the Commonwealth and we can envisage cross-border co-operation on matters of mutual interest. Indeed it might be possible to expand this into some community of the British Isles for all the people of these islands, English, Scots, Welsh, Ulstermen and Irishmen are in fact independent' (Ibid.: 62). This idea would percolate down the years and find partial expression in the 1998 Belfast Agreement. As late as 1988, Trimble continued to make the case for an independent Northern Ireland (Ibid.: 100).

Efforts to restore devolution persisted. Harold Wilson appointed Merlyn Rees Secretary of State for Northern Ireland after Labour returned to power in February 1974. The Government proposed a Constitutional Convention in July and elections were held using STV the following May. Rees did not expect much from this initiative: 'The realistic estimate must be that the Convention is unlikely to succeed fully. This is not, however, to say that the Convention serves no purpose. It is a demonstrable step forward towards getting Northern Ireland to solve their problems together without always expecting to be bailed out by the British Government. This must inevitably be a process in which progress is interspersed with setbacks' (TNA CAB 134/3921/2). The UUUC won 47 of the 78 seats, a majority in favour of a British-style Cabinet system of government based on the largest party in the Assembly. This was unacceptable to the British Government as it would not command cross-community support.

The Constitutional Convention was dissolved in March 1976 following UUUC refusal to accept SDLP involvement in a new Executive. In September, Merlyn Rees was moved to the Home Office and Roy Mason became Northern Ireland Secretary. Mason told James Callaghan, who had succeeded Wilson as Prime Minister in April 1976, that his 'first priority was security' and then to 'put emphasis on employment' with the 'whole issue of constitutional change put on the back burner' (Mason 1999: 161). The policy of 'Ulsterisation' was pursued with 'crude vigour' (Patterson 2006: 251) and involved reducing the number of troops in the polity and replacing them with local police. In the debate on the no confidence motion, which brought down the Labour Government in 1979, Gerry Fitt warned the Conservatives not to seek a military solution in Northern Ireland as Mason had:

> Every Monday morning at ten o'clock he [Mason] sees the Chief Constable. Every Monday at 1pm we hear on the news that so many IRA men have been caught and so many have been sent to jail. Every Monday the Secretary of State looks for a military solution. But there will be Mondays and Mondays and more Mondays when there will be no military solution and there will be no solution at all until we start to grapple with the political problem of Northern Ireland. (Hansard, Commons, vol. 965, 28 March 1979, col. 520)

In 1976, a report produced by four senior civil servants proposed a heavily subsidised economy with an enlarged role for the state (Patterson 2006: 253). Roy Mason's aim of bringing foreign direct investment into Northern Ireland proved futile. Only 900 jobs were created by British and foreign multinationals investing in Northern Ireland between 1972 and 1976, compared with 11,600 between 1966 and 1971 (Rowthorn 1981: 9). The Troubles were largely to blame (Bradley 1996: 38). This was reflected across Northern Ireland's economy as a whole. There was, however, a 'huge expansion of employment in the service sector' (Rowthorn 1981: 11) and the 'only really dynamic factor in the Northern Irish economy' over the decade to 1981 was in 'public consumption' (Ibid.: 22). A Parliamentary Answer in 1993 gave an indication of the huge subsidy Northern Ireland had received over the period from 1966 (Hansard, Commons, 22 March 1993, col. 497). Though security costs constituted the bulk of increased spending, Northern Ireland had received other substantial financial support from the Treasury.

Conservatives in power

On coming to power, the Conservatives continued with Labour's approach though made more effort to re-establish power-sharing devolved government. Things might have been different had not Airey Neave, Conservative Shadow Northern Ireland Secretary, been murdered by the Irish National Liberation Army (INLA), a terrorist splinter group with a 'potent mixture of hard-left politics and ruthless violence' (English 2003: 177), weeks before the 1979 general election. Neave supported a more integrationist approach, favoured by Unionists such as leader James Molyneaux and Enoch Powell, who had become a Unionist MP in 1974 after a career as a Conservative MP in England. Instead, Humphrey Atkins, the new Conservative Secretary of State, proposed a conference of Northern Ireland's four main parties but the Official Unionists refused to participate: disappointed that an integrationist course was not being followed, they boycotted the proceedings. Following discussions with the SDLP, Alliance Party and Democratic Unionist Party (DUP), the Government issued a White Paper in July 1980, which acknowledged the continuing gulf on power-sharing between the parties.

In 1981, James Prior became the most senior politician since Whitelaw to become Secretary of State for Northern Ireland. Against an unpropitious backdrop of Irish Republican Army (IRA) hunger strikes and loyalist anger following the murder of Unionist MP Robert Bradford, Prior proposed to appoint ministers from Northern Ireland, though not necessarily from amongst members of an elected assembly. The idea of replacing Westminster politicians with representatives from Northern Ireland would have been a significant break with Westminster tradition. This idea was soon dropped and replaced by 'rolling devolution'. Rolling devolution had initially been advocated by Brian Mawhinney, Conservative MP for Peterborough who was originally from Northern Ireland. Under this scheme, an assembly would be set up but would initially only have consultative and scrutinising functions but might, over time, gain responsibilities and functions. Westminster would consider increasing its powers on the request of 55 (70 per cent) of the Assembly's 78 members. This weighted majority would prevent a simple majority of Unionists demanding increased powers for the Assembly. Unionists opposed the weighted majority and implicit power-sharing involved while the SDLP was disappointed that Prior's scheme failed to incorporate an Irish dimension (Murray 1998: 111–112). Sinn Féin decided to contest elections to the Assembly for the first time, hoping to outpoll the SDLP.

Legislation was brought before Parliament in 1982. There was a lack of interest in the measure compared with past constitutional legislation concerning Northern Ireland (O'Leary, Elliott and Wilford 1988: 72–73). A core of about twenty right-wing Conservatives attempted to filibuster the Bill but otherwise interest in the Bill was largely confined to Northern Ireland MPs. The Assembly was elected in October 1982. SDLP and Sinn Féin Members refused to take their seats, the former having won 14 seats and the latter 5. The SDLP were involved in the New Ireland Forum which also included the three main parties in the Republic – Fianna Fáil, Fine Gael and the Irish Labour Party – seeking to agree a way forward for Northern Ireland. SDLP involvement in the Forum was partly an attempt to avoid accusations of abstentionism and the 'criticism that they were guilty of the very sins previously committed by the unionist parties' (Cochrane 1997: 5). The *New Ireland Forum* report, issued in 1984, argued for 'a united Ireland in the form of a sovereign independent state to be achieved peacefully and by consent' (New Ireland Forum 1984 para. 5.1.8). But differences amongst its participants meant there was a 'good deal of ambiguity' in the report (Kenny 1986: 41; Whyte 1991: 139). There were suggestions that Charles Haughey, Fianna Fáil leader, threatened not to sign the report unless it included the statement that the 'particular structure of political unity which the Forum would wish to see established is a unitary state' (Ibid.). The nationalist leadership in Northern Ireland was making its commitment to an Irish dimension clear.

The Assembly operated for three and a half years but it never put down roots. There were three phases to its operation. From November 1982 until May 1984, the SDLP boycotted the Assembly and the Official Unionists were in dispute over the allocation of committee chairmanships and security policy, leaving the Assembly operating in little more than name only. It operated in a low-key but reasonably effective manner between May 1984 and November 1985 though it failed to roll forward as Prior had envisaged. The final phase up to its dissolution in June 1986 was dominated by Unionist opposition to the Anglo-Irish Agreement, an Agreement that was in part the outcome of British Government frustration with the failure of progress with devolved government (O'Leary, Elliott and Wilford 1988: 181–194). As an exercise in rolling devolution it had been a failure but the experience was significant in the long-drawn-out process of institutional learning and development. The committee system that was established may have been statutorily restricted but the idea of a fully functioning committee system took root and would be remembered in the design of later proposals for devolved government.

Parliamentary sovereignty and the Irish dimension

The imposition of direct rule was the most obvious manifestation of parliamentary sovereignty. The limits of this power were also obvious in Westminster's failure to impose a constitutional settlement on Northern Ireland. As Dicey had warned, parliamentary sovereignty was limited by external and internal constraints. Externally, it would be limited when the sovereign's subjects 'will disobey or resist his laws' (Dicey 1923: 74). The border poll suggested that sovereignty rested with the people of Northern Ireland and not Parliament at Westminster. The first attempt to create power-sharing institutions collapsed when a loyalist strike brought down the Government in Northern Ireland. This limitation has been evident throughout Westminster's search for a legitimate form of government for Northern Ireland. Parliament at Westminster could not simply legislate to create devolved government – public opinion in Northern Ireland had to be taken into account.

After 1972, interest in Northern Ireland affairs in the Commons declined with fewer MPs from outside the polity participating in debates and questioning government policy than in the past while simultaneously Northern Ireland's MPs remained focused predominantly on local affairs (Gay and Mitchell 2007: 254–256). Direct rule did not result in Northern Ireland being integrated into mainstream parliamentary business. Northern Ireland continued to be a place apart within Westminster and Whitehall. Some Unionists suspected that the British Government wanted to abandon Northern Ireland. This was not an entirely paranoid suspicion. By the time of direct rule, senior figures on the Conservative benches, including Peter Carrington and Willie Whitelaw, had concluded that Irish unity was the ultimate long-term solution (Patterson 2006: 248). In May 1974, Bernard Donoughue, Harold Wilson's chief political adviser, recorded a discussion in his diary of a committee to consider the 'unmentionable' – British withdrawal from Northern Ireland (Donoughue 2005: 124, 129). But Robert Armstrong, Wilson's private secretary, was 'clearly worried' by the idea of withdrawal and urged abolition of the Council of Ireland (Ibid.: 130–131). Donoughue would later play a role in the lead-up to the Belfast Agreement, warning the Labour Party under Tony Blair of the dangers of repeating errors from this earlier period, from the standpoint of a supporter of the principle of consent (Godson 2004: 267–270; 275–276).

In late 1974, consideration was given to international involvement in Northern Ireland. The perceived merit of even the threat of something like a 'United Nations peace-keeping force including Afro-Asian troops' was that it might 'so alarm the parties as to persuade them to an otherwise unattainable compromise capable of averting international involvement altogether' (TNA CJ 4/492). An international force might 'command more confidence and authority' than the British Government and if unsuccessful, the 'odium of failure' would be shared with others (Ibid.). However, the perceived renunciation of sovereignty over Northern Ireland involved in an international peace-keeping force was unattractive to London (Ibid.). There seems little evidence of any conspiracy either to get rid of Northern Ireland or treat it as a training ground for military tactics. Instead, London was fairly open-minded in pursuit of achieving cross-community legitimacy for a settlement.

The Anglo-Irish Agreement of 1985, agreed by Mrs Thatcher on behalf of the UK Government, for the first time gave the Irish Republic rights to be consulted on Northern Ireland. An Intergovernmental Conference was set up 'concerned with relations between the two parts of the island of Ireland' to meet 'on a regular basis' to discuss political, security and legal matters, including the administration of justice and the promotion of cross-border co-operation (HMSO 1985: Article 2). The Agreement 'traumatised Ulster Unionism' (Walker 2004: 233). Harold McCusker, UUP MP, made an 'electrifying speech' (Cochrane 1997: 28) in the Commons denouncing the Agreement, complaining that Unionists had not been consulted and that the 'document has sold my birthright' (Ibid.). Unionists in Northern Ireland saw it as a threat to their rights as citizens of the UK. Article 2 of the Agreement stated that, 'There is no derogation from the sovereignty of either the Irish Government or the United Kingdom Government, and each retains responsibility for the decisions and administration of government within its own jurisdiction'. Neither this nor the first clause affirming no change in Northern Ireland's status without majority consent appeased Unionists.

In an unusual court case, Chris and Michael McGimpsey, brothers who were members of the UUP, challenged the constitutionality of the Agreement in the Irish High Court and Irish Supreme Court. They argued that the Agreement contradicted various Articles of the Irish Constitution including Articles 2 and 3, which defined the Republic's territorial remit as the whole of the island. The High Court in Dublin accepted the right of two Ulster Unionists to challenge the legality of provisions in the Republic's constitution, despite each being wholeheartedly opposed to the articles. From the Court's perspective, they were citizens of Ireland. However, it found against them on the grounds that the Agreement did 'not involve any unconstitutional fettering of the executive powers of government' (Symmons 1992: 317). This was confirmed by Ireland's Supreme Court (Supreme Court 1990; Symmons 1992: 317). The case highlighted the lack of legal recourse available to Unionists in the United Kingdom. However, a comment made by the Irish Chief Justice that the 'reintegration of the national territory is a constitutional imperative' caused concern amongst Unionists and their supporters. Writing in *The Times*, Conor Cruise O'Brien suggested that Mrs Thatcher's assertion that the Agreement strengthened the Union was 'untenable' and concurred with the view that the reception of the Agreement would have been 'transformed' had it been preceded by a referendum in the Republic leading to the abolition of Articles 2 and 3 of the Constitution (*The Times*, 10 March 1990).

A mass Unionist rally in Belfast in November 1985 attracted between 70,000 and 100,000 protestors (*Guardian*, 25 November 1985). It was marked by violence and vandalism and made many Unionist leaders wary of mass protests again. Unionists demanded a referendum and all Union-ist MPs, apart from Enoch Powell, resigned to fight by-elections in protest. A 'Day of Action' took place in March. There was no doubting the extent of Unionist opposition to the Agreement but the British Government stood firm. In May 1986, integrationists set up a Campaign for Equal Citizenship (CEC), arguing that the Conservative and Labour Parties ought to organise in Northern Ireland. This followed an initiative for equal rights on the left by the Campaign for Labour Representation in Northern Ireland set up in 1977, but dissolved in 1993. A joint UUP/DUP Task Force was set up in 1987 to come up with more constructive propos-als and produced a report in July, which was condemned by the CEC for advocating devolution 'outside' the United Kingdom (Walker 2004: 239). The idea of an independent Northern Ireland again reared its head and again was a symptom of Unionist uncertainties and provoked more intra-Unionist discord.

Loyalist paramilitaries were amongst the first to break out of the culture of besieged Unionism. The Ulster Defence Association (UDA) produced a document that embraced a 'pantheon of modern liberal-demo-cratic theory' including support for power-sharing (Ibid.: 217). John Hume, SDLP leader, welcomed it. Towards the end of 1987, secret meet-ings took place between the UUP, SDLP and the Northern Ireland Office signalling a cooling of Unionist anger. By the end of the 1980s, Unionists realised that campaigns against the Agreement had failed (Cochrane 1997: 265) but equally, the British Government had learned lessons. The Agree-ment was not simply a British Government policy but an international agreement between two states. Mrs Thatcher subsequently felt that the alienation of Unionists had been too high a price to pay, especially given that she felt misled by the Irish Government about the levels of co-operation on security matters (Thatcher 1993: 415). Nonetheless, the Agreement was a significant step in the process towards the Belfast Agreement.

In March 1991, Secretary of State Peter Brooke launched three strands of talks: on relations within Northern Ireland; on relations between the people of the island of Ireland; and on relations between the Governments of the UK and Ireland. It was agreed that these should progress on the basis that 'nothing is agreed until everything is agreed' (Cochrane 1997: 276), a formula that opened up the possibility of dialogue that would otherwise have been difficult. Though the initiative did not make progress as measured by an agreement, it represented another step forward in the process of shaping the agenda. Sir Patrick Mayhew replaced Brooke as Northern Ireland Secretary following the 1992 general election. He too embarked on cross-party talks with similar consequences.

The SDLP and Sinn Féin attempted to find a *modus vivendi* while simul-taneously competing for Catholic votes. In the late 1980s, the SDLP's leader John Hume sought to convince Sinn Fein that the UK Government had no military or economic interests in Northern Ireland. Sinn Féin's willingness to talk with Hume and the SDLP was an 'important step by Sinn Féin towards full involvement in constitutional politics' (Murray 1998: 164). Hume and Gerry Adams, Sinn Féin leader, met in 1993 opening up a dialogue with the prospect of a Republican ceasefire. While London and Dublin welcomed a move towards a peace process they were concerned that Hume was 'upping the ante' and forcing the pace of change (O'Kane 2004: 92–93).

The changing context was evident in the Conservative Party. As Sir Robin Butler, Cabinet Secretary, told Eamonn O'Kane, 'By the time John Major became Prime Minister, really by the time he became an MP [in 1979], the Conservatives were no longer the Conservative and Unionist Party, so he didn't have emotionally in his political background that link with the unionists' (O'Kane 2004: 81). David Trimble never 'quite understood where Major's much-vaunted "Unionism" came from' (Godson 2004: 164). Major's Irish counterpart, Albert Reynolds, was equally unencumbered from the Irish nationalist perspective (Ibid.: 81–82). John Major, in the Downing Street Declaration in 1993, asserted that the British Government had 'no selfish strategic or economic interest in Northern Ireland'. This had been trailed in a number of statements made by Peter Brooke from November 1990 (Walker 2004: 241). It had initially been used in a draft written by Kenneth Bloomfield for Peter Brooke for the Secretary of State's 'Whitbread' speech in November 1990, though the phrase was hardly covered in the media which focused on his comment that it was 'not the aspiration to a sovereign, united Ireland, against which we set our face, but its violent expression' (*Financial Times*, 10 November 1990). The phrase then recurred, as if testing for reaction, over the ensuing period leading to the Downing Street Declaration. In December 1992, Patrick Mayhew, Secretary of State from April 1992 until May 1997, repeated Brooke's comments (*Guardian*, 18 December 1992). It would have been inconceivable for the Government to make this comment about Scotland, Wales or England and it was a departure from Mrs Thatcher's assertion that, 'Northern Ireland is part of the United Kingdom; as much as my constituency is' (Hansard, Commons, vol. 12, 10 November 1981, col. 427). Instrumental unionism had replaced primordial unionism in the Declaration. The Government's primary objective was 'peace, stability and reconciliation'.

John Major and Irish Taoiseach Albert Reynolds issued the Downing Street Declaration in December 1993. It was the culmination of a long process and opened up the possibility of Sinn Féin's involvement in talks so long as the IRA ended its campaign of violence. The Declaration reiterated the British Government's position that it had 'no selfish strategic or economic interest in Northern Ireland'. An IRA ceasefire was announced the following summer, followed by a loyalist ceasefire. By the autumn, the British Government announced it would open talks with Sinn Féin. The peace process had begun formally but it had long been under way, however hesitantly. In February 1995, the London and Dublin Governments published *Frameworks for the Future*, the result of work done since the Downing Street Declaration. It was two documents: one published by the British Government and a second joint London–Dublin document. An assembly was discussed along the lines of Strand One of the negotiations conducted in 1992, as well as North–South institutional relations, and British–Irish institutional relations. It was, again, part of the long process of reiterating the need for and articulating options for these different 'strands'. The ideas had been 'extensively trailed' in the media (Walker 2004: 247). Indeed, they had been extensively trailed in previous public statements and policies over a long number of years.

James Molyneaux, leader of the Official Unionists, resigned in August. His leadership had been called into question for some time. Under Enoch Powell's influence, Molyneaux had advocated integration with the rest of the UK to make Northern Ireland appear less unusual and maintained that his 'inside track' approach, involving contact with Downing Street, paid dividends for Unionism. But, as *The Times* commented, 'even if the British Government was still listening to Mr Molyneaux, it was not heeding him' (*The Times*, 29 August 1995). David Trimble was elected in his place. Trimble was a devolutionist who had, as we have seen, at times advocated an independent Northern Ireland and whose approach was more that of the outsider. Initially, he caused concern amongst more liberal elements within Unionism.

The Peace Process and the Belfast Agreement

In April 1997, Seamus Mallon, Deputy Leader of the SDLP, described the Anglo-Irish Agreement of 1985, Downing Street Declaration of 1993, and the Framework Documents of 1995, which paved the way to the Peace Process as 'Sunningdale for slow learners' (*Irish Times*, 2 April 1997). These developments leading to the Belfast Agreement in 1998 took place against a backdrop of inter-communal violence. Though successive governments denied that the violence affected constitutional policy, violence could hardly have failed to affect public opinion, both in Northern Ireland and in Britain. Negotiating with those involved in violence was contrary to liberal democratic principles but progress required dialogue with militants. Throughout the period of the Troubles, British Government politicians and officials spoke directly with or through intermediaries representative of proscribed organisations. In 1994, Sinn Féin maintained that a 'line of communication has existed between Sinn Féin and the British government for over twenty years. It has not been in

constant use. It has been used in an intensive way during such periods as
the bi-lateral truce of 1974–75 and the Long Kesh hunger strikes of 1980
and 1981. It was re-activated by the British government in mid-1990,
leading to a period of protracted contact and dialogue between Sinn Féin
and the British government' (quoted in English 2003: 267). Ceasefires
occurred in 1974–75 and again in 1994 but neither proved as successful
as that which began in July 1997 when the IRA announced its ceasefire,
followed in October by the Combined Loyalist Military Command ceasefire. Constitutional politics were only one dimension, not necessarily the
most important, of the political divide. Throughout the period of direct
rule, reaching agreement on matters relating to peace and order proved as
contentious as agreeing what constitutes good government. Understand-
able sensitivities surrounded not only what should be done but also the
manner in which agreements should be reached.

An international commission was established to advise on decommissioning, chaired by former American Senator George Mitchell. In January
1996, its report was published, outlining six principles (the Mitchell Principles) which parties should adhere to as the price for entering all-party
talks on the future of Northern Ireland. In February, the IRA ended its
ceasefire and in May Gerry Adams indicated that Sinn Féin would agree
to the Mitchell Principles if others did so too. In a speech in Washington
in March, Patrick Mayhew insisted that three conditions had to be met
before Sinn Féin, the political wing of the IRA, could be allowed into the
process. Not only would the IRA have to be committed to disarming but
agreement would be required on how the decommissioning of its arms
took place as well as evidence that this had begun.

American involvement in Northern Ireland's politics was long standing.
Daniel O'Connell had identified opportunities in involving the Irish American community as far back as the 1820s. Opinion in the United States has
been volatile, often responding in an exaggerated way to events in Northern Ireland. Just as the SDLP and Sinn Féin competed for the support of
Catholics in Northern Ireland, parallel organisations existed trying to
enlist support amongst the US's substantial Irish Catholic community. The
Friends of Ireland had been set up in 1981 with the support of Senators,
senior Congressmen and Governors committed to reconciliation in Northern Ireland (Wilson 1995: 180). The precise impact of this group, which
included Senator Edward Kennedy, is unclear, though there is evidence
that they put pressure on the Reagan Presidency to encourage Margaret
Thatcher to modify her relations with Dublin in the early–mid 1980s
(Ibid.: 243–246). During his campaign for the presidency, Bill Clinton had
bowed to pressure to support granting a visa for entry into the US to
Gerry Adams, Sinn Féin leader, as well as sending a 'peace envoy' to
Northern Ireland (Patterson 2006: 323). The visa granted to Adams infu-
riated Prime Minister John Major but the legitimacy that the US gave to

Adams was matched in the UK when Sinn Féin representatives began openly meeting officials and ministers in 1995. But pressure worked both ways and senior American politicians were influenced by the SDLP and Governments in the Irish Republic as well as the British Government at important moments.

Elections to the Northern Ireland Forum were held at the end of May 1996 though Sinn Fein was excluded from the Forum when it met in June because of IRA violence. A massive IRA bomb exploded in the centre of Manchester five days after the start of talks and in July a heavy police presence was required at Drumcree where, for the second year, Orangemen insisted on marching through a predominantly Catholic area. Decommissioning became the main stumbling block in the all-party talks. In the House of Commons, John Major's Conservatives relied on the votes of Ulster Unionists for crucial government business, making it difficult for Major to take the lead in any initiatives in Northern Ireland. The general election in May 1997 provided Labour under Tony Blair with a clear mandate and opened the way for progress. Blair devoted much time to Northern Ireland. In July, the IRA renewed its ceasefire. Progress was hesitant but in September Sinn Féin signed up to the Mitchell Principles allowing the resumption of the multi-party talks, and Adams led a Sinn Féin delegation to meet Prime Minister Blair in Downing Street in December.

When hope and history rhyme

Mary Holland, veteran *Observer* journalist who had covered Northern Ireland's politics from the 1960s, used Seamus Heaney's words to describe the Belfast Agreement secured on Good Friday 1998. It was, she wrote, the moment when 'hope and history rhyme' (*Observer*, 12 April 1998). Holland avoided the euphoria of sections of the British media, reflecting the more circumspect attitude prevalent in the media in Northern Ireland. She endorsed the view that a 'sea-change in people's attitudes' had occurred but acknowledged that 'there is still a long, long way to travel' (Ibid.). Her interpretation of how the agreement had come about recognised both the impact of 30 years of the 'Troubles' but also the role of politicians: 'We spend so much time reviling our politicians, but at Stormont we saw politics practised as an honourable profession' (Ibid.). But the role of civil servants too should not be ignored. Civil servants in Northern Ireland had contributed over many years to thinking which led to the Agreement and, as Ken Bloomfield acknowledged, much of the momentum came from UK Cabinet Secretary Sir Robert Armstrong, 'the ultimate "insider's insider"' and diplomat David Goodall (Bloomfield 2007: 59).

The Agreement had its opponents amongst Unionists. Nationalists and

Republicans overwhelmingly supported the Agreement. Of 350 delegates at Sinn Féin's special *Ard Fheis* (conference), 331 endorsed the Agreement. But there were deep divisions amongst Unionists. Ian Paisley's Democratic Unionist Party opposed it as did six of the ten Ulster Unionist Party (UUP) MPs, but the Council of the UUP gave its backing. The referendum on the Agreement was held in May 1998. An overwhelming majority of voters supported the Agreement but support amongst Unionists was far less decisive. An exit poll found that 96 per cent of Catholics voted for the Agreement compared with only 55 per cent of Protestants (Elliot and Flackes 1999: 595–596). The Belfast Agreement was a multi-faceted document and devolution was only one part, and amongst its least controversial aspects. Its three 'strands' included democratic institutions for Northern Ireland, a North–South Ministerial Council, and a British–Irish Council and Intergovernmental Conference, but it also included sections on rights, safeguards and equality of opportunity, decommissioning of arms, security, policing and justice, and prisoner release. The three strands were inter-connected, each being a concession to some group. The Agreement would be followed by the passage of the Northern Ireland Act, 1998.

Simultaneously with the referendum on the Agreement, a referendum was held in the Irish Republic that proposed to remove Articles 2 and 3 of its Constitution. Article 2 of the Irish constitution stated 'The national territory consists of the whole island of Ireland, its islands and the territorial seas' and Article 3 stated, 'Pending the re-integration of the national territory, and without prejudice to the right of the Parliament and Government established by this Constitution to exercise jurisdiction over the whole of that territory, the laws enacted by that Parliament shall have the like area and extent of application as the laws of Saorstat Eireann and the like extra-territorial effect'. The referendum in the Republic was symbolically important as it ended the Republic's claim to Northern Ireland. On a turnout of 56 per cent, 94 per cent of voters in the Republic agreed with the constitutional amendment.

Table 8.1 Results of the referendums on the Belfast Agreement, May 1998

	Northern Ireland (%)	Irish Republic (%)
Yes	71.1	94.4
No	28.9	5.6
Turnout	81.1	55.6

The Assembly was first elected in June 1998. Six members were returned in each of 18 constituencies using the single transferable vote (STV). The SDLP won slightly more first preference votes than the Ulster Unionist Party but the UUP came top in the number of seats, with final result being

28 UUP; 24 SDLP; 20 DUP; 18 Sinn Féin; 6 Alliance Party; 5 UK Unionists; 2 Progressive Unionists; 2 NI Women's Coalition; and 3 Other Unionists. Each Member of the Assembly had to declare him or herself a 'Unionist', a 'Nationalist' or 'Other'. This was necessary as cross-community support or parallel consent was required for key measures, including the Executive's Programme for Government and the election of the First and Deputy First Minister, an unusual constitutional construct that combined two offices in one.

This enforced coalition amongst the most divided parties in any part of the United Kingdom did not augur well for collective decision-making however necessary it might have been for the peace process. David Trimble, leader of the UUP, was elected First Minister and Seamus Mallon, Deputy Leader of the SDLP, Deputy First Minister. The Unionist-supporting *Belfast News Letter* commented on the first meeting of the Assembly in July 1998, 'a quick glance around the Assembly chamber yesterday provided the proof that Northern Ireland's landscape has changed forever. Every spectrum of politics in this country was represented. And, joy of joys, there was not a Northern Ireland Minister in sight' (*Belfast News Letter*, 2 July 1998). But the meeting was overshadowed by many outstanding difficulties, most notably decommissioning arms. A deadline to agree an Executive, set for the end of October, was missed, as with so many political deadlines in Northern Ireland. Devolution in Northern Ireland has never looked stable, necessitating parallel arrangements to operate. Direct rule and devolved government have operated in tandem like some corrupted version of Bagehot's dictum on efficient and dignified parts of the constitution: 'every constitution must first *gain* authority, and then *use* authority; it must first win the loyalty and confidence of mankind, and then employ that homage in the work of government' (Bagehot 1981 [1867]: 61). The problem was that devolved government had difficulty gaining authority and was rarely able to use it, while direct rule only used its authority. The Northern Ireland Office, still headed by a politician appointed by the Prime Minister from outside Northern Ireland, continued to have a similar role to that before devolution. Between 1998 and 2007, there were five Secretaries of State. The result was that 'old constitutional certainties can now interact with the new: devolution in Northern Ireland falters, Diceyan orthodoxy fills the void to give effect to the preferred measures of the "new" dispensation' (Anthony and Morison 2005: 157–158). While politics may have come off the street, they were far from conventional for a liberal democracy. Within a short space of time, none of the key institutions was functioning as intended. Halfway through 2001, the advisory Civic Forum was the 'only fully functioning institution' (Wilson and Wilford 2001: 84).

The Executive was finally elected in November 1999 and in addition to Trimble and Mallon, three members each were allocated under the system to both the UUP and SDLP and two each to the DUP and Sinn Féin. The UUP allowed Martin McGuinness of Sinn Féin to become Education Minister to stop Republicans taking charge of Culture, Arts and Leisure, with its responsibility for politically significant public symbols. Sinn Féin's other Ministry was Health, giving the party the two main spending departments. As a study of health policy argued, the system was 'designed to induce parties to take office rather than to produce responsibility for policy' (Greer 2003: 202–203). Agreement on an Executive opened up the possibility of meetings of the North–South Ministerial Council and the British–Irish Council. The DUP, however, boycotted meetings and insisted on rotating its two ministerial posts amongst its Assembly Members. First Minister Trimble refused to allow Sinn Féin Ministers to attend Executive meetings of the North–South Ministerial Council in October 2000. Sinn Féin then boycotted the British–Irish Council. The Executive met relatively rarely. Between July 2001 and mid October 2002, it met only 21 times, about once every three weeks (Wilford and Wilson 2003: 94). Not only was the Executive unable to operate with anything approaching collective responsibility but disputes spilled over into the other institutions. It was envisaged that the Assembly would have an active committee structure and that the committee membership would reflect the Assembly's composition. The chairs and deputy chairs of committees would be drawn from parties that did not hold the relevant ministerial portfolio.

The terminology used in the Government of Ireland Act, 1920 was adopted in the 1998 Act. Transferred matters came under the Assembly, reserved matters might be transferred, and excepted matters were retained at Westminster. However, unlike the 1920 Act which involved no real distinction in practice between excepted and reserved matters, under the 1998 Act the prospect that reserved matters might be devolved was anticipated and the Assembly would have been empowered to legislate under this heading with the consent of the Secretary of State. In addition, ministers in the Northern Ireland Assembly were obliged to accompany any proposed legislation with a statement on its implications for equality and human rights. The Act asserted that parliamentary sovereignty remained unaffected. It differed markedly from that which operated in Scotland and Wales. As Anthony and Morison explained, 'there is much about the Northern Ireland version of devolution that relates to the violent past there and the special circumstances of resolving a complex national issue. In particular there is the constitutionally interesting matter of factoring in the involvement of a number of states, including especially the Republic of Ireland and resolving a number of long-standing quarrels that have assumed constitutional status. However beyond this, devolution in Northern Ireland remains about developing government and delivering more accountable, democratic structures for improving the life of those live there' (Anthony and Morison: 191).

Throughout the turbulent years since the Belfast agreement, the 'bloody civil servants up there at Stormont' have maintained their continuous presence at the heart of government. A memorandum by a senior civil servant leaked in February 2001 referred to the 'emerging difficulties under devolution of the absence of the sorts of conventions about the roles of ministers, officials, the Assembly, Committees, etc, which have been evolved over centuries at Westminster' (Wilson and Wilford 2001: 99). The existence of locally based elected representatives running departments and scrutinising policy-making proved uncomfortable for some.

Consociationalism and its critics

The nature of the Belfast Agreement has been subject to considerable debate both amongst politicians and within the academic community. Brendan O'Leary has described the key features of the Agreement as consociationalist (O'Leary 1999; McGarry and O'Leary 2006a and b). Consociationalism refers to the idea defined by Arend Lijphart (1977) as the institutional arrangements designed to create stable democracy in divided societies with four key elements: cross-community executive power-sharing; proportionality rules applied throughout the relevant governmental and public sectors; community self-government (or autonomy) and equality in cultural life; veto rights for minorities (O'Leary 1999: 67–68). Lijphart himself argued that the 1995 Framework Agreements were consociationalist (Lijphart 1996). Additionally, the Agreement has an 'important external dimension' (Ibid.: 68). Others have described it as having a 'consociational lineage, but with ostensibly confederal arrangements knitted into the pattern' (Wilford and Wilson 2000: 87). This debate, as much discussion of consociationalism (Bogaards 2000), has at times conflated three meanings of consociationalism: a description of the institutional arrangements; an empirical theory seeking to explain the origins and predict the consequences of these arrangements; and as a normative proposition offering the best solution for Northern Ireland.

However, some scholars have argued that these structures have entrenched and polarised communal differences (Taylor 2001; Dixon 2005). Four aspects in particular have been identified as having 'entrenched rather than palliated division': acceptance of the 'either/or constitutional choice of the United Kingdom or a United Ireland'; Single Transferable Vote which encourages candidates on small core votes and discourages cross-communal preference formation; communal registration by Assembly Members; and election of the Executive using a proportional formula (Wilford and Wilson 2003: 100). The Agreement works to 'encourage and reward those who pursue strategic ethno-national group calculations and interests – and to have thereby reinforced and politicised ethno-national group divisions – in ways that run counter to promoting liberal politics' (Taylor 2006: 218). This is done primarily through group designation in the Assembly, Executive formation and the electoral system (Ibid.). Dixon has argued that the Agreement is not consociational as it was 'inspired more by an integrationist approach to power-sharing than a segregationist one' (Dixon 2005: 358). McGarry and O'Leary reject the charge of being 'primordial pessimists' who 'exaggerate the immutable and uni-dimensional nature of social divisions' and underplay the ability of people to 'develop new transcendent identities' (McGarry and O'Leary 2006b: 276) but claim instead that consociational arrangements involve 'reasonable realism' (Ibid.: 254).

In October 2006, in an attempt to restore representative government to Northern Ireland, the UK and Irish Governments negotiated the St Andrews Agreement with the parties in Northern Ireland. This was designed to address some of the deficiencies in the Belfast Agreement and was similar to an earlier agreement issued by the two governments in December 2004. Under this new agreement, Sinn Féin would have to accept the Police Service of Northern Ireland and the DUP would agree to power-sharing with nationalists and Republicans. At its *Ard Fheis* (conference) in January 2007, Sinn Féin voted to back the proposals for policing in Northern Ireland. It was anticipated in the St Andrews Agreement that policing and justice would be devolved within two years. There would be a statutory ministerial code and greater accountability of individual ministers to both the Executive and the Assembly as well as amendments to the various institutions including separating the appointments of First and Deputy First Ministers. While the provisions would require greater coherence in the government of Northern Ireland, this statutorily enforced consensus carried with it the danger of government by the lowest common denominator.

Elections to the Assembly confirm that centrist parties have lost ground under devolution. The DUP and Sinn Féin have replaced the UUP and SDLP as the largest parties of the two communities but both parties have moved significantly to the constitutional centre ground. In 2007, the DUP and Sinn Féin became the largest parties in the Assembly, allowing Ian Paisley to become First Minister alongside Martin McGuinness as Deputy First Minister.

The role of the institutions in the process of creating peace will remain contested though there seems less difficulty in assessing the public policy consequences of these arrangements. In evidence to the Opsahl Inquiry, an independent 'citizens' inquiry' conducted in the early 1990s, Gabriel Scally, a director of public health, argued that the 'Troubles' and the emphasis on constitutional politics had 'created a deficit in a wide range of social policy spheres' (Pollak 1993: 319). This was manifested in the 'public understanding of the major strands of the social policy debate, but

Table 8.2 Northern Ireland Assembly election results 1998–2007

Party	1998 First Preference Votes (%)	Seats	2003 First Preference Votes (%)	Seats	2007 First Preference Votes (%)	Seats
DUP	18.1	10	25.7	30	30.1	36
UUP	21.3	28	22.7	27	14.9	18
SDLP	22	24	16.98	18	15.2	16
SF	17.7	18	23.5	24	26.2	28
Alliance	6.5	6	3.68	6	5.2	7
UKU	45.5	5	0.82	1	1.5	0
PUP	2.6	2	1.16	1	0.6	1
Ind			0.88	1		
NIWC[a]	1.6	2	0.83	0		
Others	5.8	3	3.7	0	3.2	1
Greens					1.7	1
Turnout	69.5		63.1		63.5	

Notes: DUP – Democratic Unionist Party; UUP – Ulster Unionist Party; SDLP – Social Democratic and Labour Party; SF – Sinn Féin; UKU – United Kingdom Unionist; PUP – Progressive Unionist Party; NIWC – Northern Ireland Womens' Coalition.

[a]After losing its seats in 2003, the NIWC was wound up in May 2006.

also in the poorly developed social policies of the major Northern Ireland political parties' (Ibid.). Devolved government has developed government and delivered more accountable, democratic structures as some had hoped, but in a faltering and far from perfect way, though it has been part of the process of bringing peace to Northern Ireland. There is evidence that key public policy decisions took more account of party or communal interests rather than collective needs. The closure of a maternity hospital in south Belfast and its relocation into west Belfast by Sinn Féin's Health Minister provoked particular criticism (Wilford and Wilson 2000: 91). Northern Ireland continued to have the worst hospital waiting lists in western Europe.

The Belfast Agreement has consociational elements and some of those who argued for the agreement were informed by academic debates on peacekeeping, but equally many of those were influenced by experience over many years in Northern Ireland. Its consociational nature was the product of consociational thinking but most significantly historical experience. There were many roads to the Agreement just as many people were involved in its creation.

Conclusion

Devolution in Northern Ireland differs markedly from that which operates in Scotland and Wales. Not only had Northern Ireland prior experience of devolution, albeit of a different type from that envisaged in the Belfast Agreement, but also there was a desire to return to devolution from the moment of direct rule in 1972. This contrasted with the antipathy to devolution for Scotland and Wales throughout most of this time. But devolution was never seen as an end in itself but as part of a complex constitutional structure. If there was concern in London about devolving power to Scotland and Wales, at times it seemed that London could not wait to devolve the penury of responsibility for Northern Ireland back to Stormont.

The 'staccato' form devolution has taken in Northern Ireland (Anthony and Morison 2005: 156) was always likely. The delay of eighteen months between the Belfast Agreement being signed and formal transfer of power as well as its discontinuous operation led to Wilson and Wilford referring to devolution in Northern Ireland as 'an event rather than a process' (Wilson and Wilford 2004: 83). But much has changed – even if Northern Ireland cannot yet be described as a model liberal democracy, 'Northern Ireland is, for the most part, now superficially free of obtrusive "security" presences, the death toll from politically-motivated violence is vastly reduced from its early-1970s peak and unemployment has fallen in line with wider macroeconomic trends. On a more profound level, however, this is a society with pathological features' (Wilford and Wilson 2005: 65). In his Nobel Peace Prize speech, shared in 1998 with John Hume of the SDLP, David Trimble referred to the old Stormont as a 'cold house for Catholics' (Trimble 2001: 62) and his intention of creating a 'pluralist Parliament for a pluralist people' (Trimble 2001: 79). The SDLP view of the Peace Process and attendant institutions as 'Sunningdale for slow learners' might be seen as a criticism of Trimble, as one of those hostile to early efforts to build power-sharing institutions. However, the glib nature of the comment hides significant processes of change. Scholars who disagree profoundly in their interpretation of the Belfast Agreement (for alternative perspectives see O'Leary 1997 and Dixon 2001) are able to agree that it built on past policies, whether these were consistent or contradictory. Context and learning proved important. There was little in the Agreement that cannot be traced back to earlier initiatives and all of the problems that it attempted to address were rooted in the old system of devolution and its legacy.

9

The English Question

England is a state of mind, not a consciously organized political institution.
(Rose 1982: 29)

Introduction

England, maintained Richard Rose, claimed no distinctive institutions of
governance 'though it acquires these, if only by default, when Scotland,
Wales, and Northern Ireland opt out of specific policies' (Rose 1982: 31).
In other words, an English dimension emerges simply because it is what is
left, albeit the largest part of the state, after special provisions are made
for Scotland, Wales and Northern Ireland. Robert Hazell has pointed out
that the English Question has resulted from the programme of devolution
and regionalism since 1997. He described it as a 'portmanteau heading for
a whole series of questions about the government of England' (Hazell
2006: 1). England is the 'gaping hole in the devolution settlement' (Ibid.).
England's place in the union and the government of England, especially its
territorial nature, lie at the heart of the English Question but the ramifi-
cations of devolution in Scotland, Wales and Northern Ireland have
hardly impinged on England and the English public seem blissfully
unaware of or not bothered about devolution elsewhere.

The implications for England of devolved government in other parts of
the United Kingdom have long been discussed. Dicey's first book-length
polemic against Irish home rule, written in 1886, was entitled, 'England's
case against home rule' (Dicey 1886). His opponents conceded that
Dicey's contribution was important. John Morley wrote to Dicey telling
him of his admiration, 'first at the exhaustive completeness with which
you have handled the matter, and second at the faultlessness' (Dicey
Papers, Glasgow University, Ms. Gen. 508 (52–54)). Dicey's central argument was explained in the preface to the book: 'My justification for
publishing my thoughts on Home Rule is that the movement in favour of
the Parliamentary independence of Ireland constitutes, whether its advocates recognise the fact or not, a demand for fundamental alterations in
the whole Constitution of the United Kingdom; and while I may without

presumption consider myself acquainted with the principles of Constitutional Law, I entertain the firmest conviction that any scheme for Home Rule in Ireland involves dangerous if not fatal innovations on the Constitution of Great Britain' (Dicey 1886: Preface). This argument has been at the root of all subsequent debates on devolved government and England's position within the UK.

In 1920, against the background of the Speaker's Conference on Devolution, Ryland Adkins, Liberal MP for Lancashire and member of the Conference, complained that 'there is no amelioration of the fact that measures affecting England only have to take their chance without any special preference in the general ruck of Parliamentary business' (Adkins 1920: 327) and argued that the 'main problem of devolution, allowing for the exceptional case of Ireland, is a problem of devolution to England' (Ibid.: 328). The size of England was, he felt, the 'greatest difficulty' (Ibid.) and while he acknowledged the lack of 'active propaganda' for an English subordinate Parliament, he saw English devolution as a 'solution of hope' but only for 'England as a whole' (Ibid.: 331). Still later, when Scottish home rule agitation was at its height shortly after the Second World War, the *Economist* commented, 'Who knows, home rule for Scotland and Wales might even encourage someone to demand a little freedom for the patient English' (*Economist*, 8 July 1950).

But since 1999, devolution has 'not provided a compelling reason why England should follow a similar path' (Curtice 2006: 138). Nonetheless, the context in which devolution has operated to date has to be taken into account before English acquiescence is equated with complete acceptance of devolution. After all, it would have been a mistake to have interpreted past Scottish and Welsh acquiescence with full legitimacy of the pre-devolution constitutional order. Problems could assume greater salience in a different context. Past debates, even those in a different context, may provide pointers to future problems and possible responses.

An alternative perspective on the English Question is focused on territorial politics within England. In 1994, Perry Anderson remarked that regions then enjoyed an 'unambiguously positive valency': the affirmation of regional loyalties and identities was 'all but universal, and the endorsement of the principle of their political representation an increasingly prominent theme of official discourse in Western Europe' (Anderson 1994: 9–10). This was not always so. As Morgan and Mungham note, 'Perhaps it is a comment on the changing nature of the Labour Party that devolution should have been seen as a "pre-modern" cause at the beginning of the twentieth century but as a quintessentially "modern" cause at the end of it' (Morgan and Mungham 2000: 36). Regions were once viewed as politically unimportant, while regionalist movements were regarded as provincial traditionalists reluctant to accept the modern cosmopolitan view of political, economic and social progress.

Regions and regionalism have a number of dimensions which need to be conceptually unpacked. Regionalism is used to refer to bottom-up social movements, of regional communities acting with some degree of coherence for political and social ends. Regional government and administration refer to the formal or informal structure of political institutions that exist for policy-making, implementation or administration. Regional policy exists to promote regional development and to eradicate or, at least, ameliorate, regional social and economic disparities. These are often conflated and though often difficult to disentangle, they are conceptually distinct. The first has been weak in England and at no time has it been as strong as Scottish, Welsh, Ulster or Irish identity and nationalism in any part of England. English regional government and administration, as we saw in chapter 5, has long been important for the delivery of public services. It has been a consistent necessity, albeit one that might take a number of competing forms, with extensive state intervention and it is this that has been the focus of debate in recent times. Regional policy rose to prominence in the past-war period but declined from the late 1970s.

Kilbrandon and England

As we have seen, the rise of Welsh and Scottish nationalism in the 1960s led to the establishment of the Royal Commission on the Constitution (Kilbrandon). The idea of a Commission exploring the government of Scotland had been considered but instead Harold Wilson decided on a Commission with a wider remit, albeit the territorial constitution. This was an opportunity to view matters across the UK as a whole and to consider England's position within the UK. Kilbrandon's main report noted that there had been 'no corresponding demand for purely English policies or for purely English institutions of government. There is no English nationalist movement. This is hardly surprising, since England is already governed from its capital city by people who are themselves mostly, though by no means exclusively, English. Indeed, the English tend to use the terms "England" and "English" when the mean "Britain" and "British", often to the annoyance of the Scots and Welsh' (Kilbrandon 1973: 58, para. 185). The Commissioners felt there was 'no need' to include basic background information 'about the development of the English nation and the arrangements made for its government' (Ibid.: para. 186) as they had done on the other components of the UK. It did note that in the post-war years there had been a need 'for services to be planned and provided over areas greater than those of local authorities' giving rise to a regional dimension to English politics (Ibid.: 71, para. 225).

Kilbrandon advocated regional government, preferring this term to the term 'provincial' as used in the Redcliffe-Maud report on local government in England (Ibid.: 282). However, Kilbrandon was divided in its recommendations for England. The Commissioners agreed that neither

England nor the English regions should have legislative devolution. There was more support for regional co-ordinating and advisory councils: eight Commissioners favoured such councils with about sixty members, partly nominated by central government, partly elected by local government (Ibid.: paras 1188, 1195–1209). The two Commissioners who wrote the Memorandum of Dissent favoured a scheme of executive devolution to English regions as part of a wider plan for all of Britain but the majority opposed executive devolution to the English regions seeing it as involving 'substantial changes in the role of Parliament and the central government' (Ibid.: para. 1193). They felt that a 'more restrictive attitude to devolution' was necessary across Britain than would be possible if applied to 'selected regions only' (Ibid.). If English regions were given the kind of devolution proposed for Scotland and Wales then 'it would become much more difficult to establish and maintain any clear direction in United Kingdom policies' (Ibid.). What was clear is that the logic behind regional government in England was markedly different from the logic behind devolution for Wales and Scotland. Kilbrandon's recommendations for England were overshadowed by those for Scotland and Wales but were just as much part of the story of the evolution of territorial politics in the UK.

Whitehall's response to Kilbrandon concurred with the main report's recommendations for England in doubting the value of English regional devolution. The Social Services Group, one of six Inter-Departmental Groups of officials set up to consider Kilbrandon, completed its report in June 1974. It maintained that major problems with regional devolution in England would exist in education, health and in each of the other social services. Operational responsibility across many social services was already devolved to local government. A regional level for these services, acting as intermediaries, might be possible but even then 'their position would be weak' as they would lack 'practical experience of providing services and the knowledge central government possessed of the full range of developments throughout the country' (Ibid.). The NHS was then adjusting to a 'radical reorganisation' introduced in April which had placed 'great strains on all who work in it' and the officials could see no case for further reorganisation (TNA BD 108/396).

The Coordinating and Advisory Machinery Group, another of the Inter-Departmental groups, dealt mainly with English devolution. It concluded that Kilbrandon's proposals for English regional advisory councils were 'not wholly impracticable' but that there would be 'very little useful work for them' and they would not satisfy 'any real demand for greater regional influence in government' (TNA CAB 134/3829). It wholly rejected the proposals in the Memorandum of Dissent written by two members of the Royal Commission which, they maintained, would lead to five tiers of authorities in England following the reorganisation of local government, the NHS and the water industry. Instead, they proposed that the work of central government departments might be organised on a regional basis. Another problem they identified with English regional government was determining boundaries. It was impossible to avoid creating a South-East region which would be 'overwhelmingly big in terms of size, wealth and population' and this would still be seen as remote from the public (Ibid.). There was simply no appetite in Whitehall for further regional reforms in England and none for the kind of proposals made in either the majority or minority reports of the Kilbrandon Commission.

The Labour Government elected in 1974 had promised to establish Scottish and Welsh Assemblies and after dealing with its immediate industrial relations problems, renegotiation of membership of the European Community and a referendum on continued EC membership, it set about legislating for devolution. The English dimension was simply side-stepped. In 1975, the Labour Party published a consultation paper, *Devolution and Regional Government in England*, presenting arguments for and against English regional devolution. The following year the Labour Government issued a discussion paper, *Devolution: the English Dimension* (HMSO 1976: Cmd. 5732) after it published legislation for Scottish and Welsh devolution. It was accepted that there was greater desire for change in Scotland and Wales and clearer views as to the nature of the change desired. Despite the prospect of Scotland and Wales continuing to be represented in the Commons after devolution, the Government argued against an English assembly or English regional assemblies.

Regionalism and Parliament

The establishment of regional Economic Planning Boards in 1964–65 with eight economic planning regions in England led to proposals for English regional procedures in Parliament. There were limited opportunities for MPs to raise regional matters in the Commons even with an annual debate on regional affairs held from 1963. In April 1966, Prime Minister Harold Wilson announced in Parliament that all-party regional committees would be considered covering all parts of the country (Hansard, Commons, 21 April 1966, col. 81). Three scholars of public administration proposed the establishment of eight English Regional Committees modelled on the Scottish and Welsh Grand Committees, empowered to debate regional affairs with the possibility of establishing sub-committees as well (Jones, Smith and Wiseman 1967). They believed that there was 'insufficient means by which Members of the House of Commons can participate in the formulation of regional policies' (Ibid.: 409) but acknowledged problems with the idea: there was a danger in the proliferation of Parliamentary committees placing invidious demands on MPs' time and that the field of enquiry undertaken by such committees might overlap with other parliamentary committees.

The idea fed into the deliberations of the Royal Commission on the Constitution. A submission from the Study of Parliament Group of scholars discussed the case for and against Regional Committees. Norman Hunt (later Lord Crowther-Hunt), a member of the Royal Commission on the Constitution, wrote a paper arguing that a strong case could be made for establishing a 'counterpoint to the Scottish and Welsh Offices' in each English region but acknowledged that this was unlikely to happen (NAS SOE 9/70). On the back of reforms designed to strengthen parliamentary accountability, Hunt argued for a reformed Select Committee system in which English regions would have a significant role. Recognising that the Commons was too busy, and likely to become busier with accession to the European Community, he suggested that this should be done in conjunction with reform of the House of Lords. The idea of Regional Select Committees in the Lords was dismissed by Kilbrandon. Kilbrandon could see merit in Regional Committees in the Commons which would take Parliamentary Questions and adjournment debates of local and regional concern and might examine public policy towards the regions (Kilbrandon 1973: 322, paras 1073–1079). The Committees would have both Select and Standing Committee functions. However, the idea was lost amongst Kilbrandon's other proposals.

A Standing Committee for the English Regions was set up in 1975 but, according to Borthwick, it 'almost certainly owed nothing to the academic and Royal Commission recommendations' (Borthwick 1978: 203). It was set up at the same time as a Standing Committee on Northern Ireland and though it may not have flowed directly from debates on devolution, these were part of the backdrop. Early meetings had problems achieving a quorum and argued over procedure. As far as Borthwick was concerned, the issue was whether Parliament should operate on functional or territorial lines (Ibid.: 209). Borthwick argued that the absence of a sense of regional identity amongst English MPs, as compared with Scottish and Welsh identities, hindered the cohesiveness of the Committee. Parliamentary procedures had historically reflected the organisation of central government and had a largely functional basis while acknowledging the UK's components apart from England. This also reflected the attitudes of MPs. In a study of over 2,000 speeches on regional policy in the Commons over nine parliamentary sessions from 1968 to 1976, J.F. McDonald concluded that the English regions 'serve a clearly defined administrative purpose, but the divisions have not been such as to create areas with which MPs can identify. This has resulted in relatively little political activity on a regional basis, confirming the view that political regions do not exist in England ... It is unlikely that there will be successful pressure by MPs for English regional autonomy upon the basis of existing planning regions' (McDonald 1979: 29). Parliamentary procedures were less important than the absence of clearly defined English regions. Hogwood and Lindley (1980: 28) quote an older study of regionalism in England in their analysis of regional boundaries used by government:

> Perhaps the most disturbing thing about England's regional institutions is the fact that geographical boundaries have largely been drawn up *ad hoc*. Regional areas for different services are rarely co-extensive. This is mainly because sociological characteristics (political, social and economic features making a homogeneous region) are usually furthest from the minds of administrators when regional boundaries are being designated. (Smith 1964: 8)

Nothing had changed and nothing would change.

The English backlash

The discussion of Scottish and Welsh devolution provoked a backlash in parts of England which contributed to the development of a sense of English regionalism. The Newcastle *Journal* was early in warning that the north of England must not lose out. In November 1974, it reported a meeting between the Government and north-east MPs, quoting Tom Urwin, chairman of the North-East Labour group, expressing his fear that the North-East would come 'second best' in the allocation of resources. The group thought there was an 'undeniable case' for a Minister for the North (*The Journal*, 7 November 1974). But instead of mobilising support for a Minister for the North, the campaign focused its activities on opposing devolution. Days later, Tony Crosland, Environment Minister who opposed devolution, received a letter from the chairman of the Yorkshire and Humberside Economic Planning Council, 'very strongly' opposed to Scottish and Welsh devolution, which compared the economic and social positions of Yorkshire and Humberside with Scotland and Wales, seeing little difference other than that the latter had Secretaries of State and more MPs than population alone merited (TNA HLG 120/2284).

Some north of England MPs complained that devolution to Scotland would place their region at a disadvantage. As the Government attempted to pass legislation to create Scottish and Welsh Assemblies without an overall majority in the Commons, these MPs were able to exact a high price. Many northern MPs wanted an economic development agency, similar to the Scottish Development Agency created in 1975, but fears that a Scottish Assembly would be an economic success tended to be channelled negatively against Scottish devolution rather than positively in favour of changes for their region. This opposition began when leaders of Tyne and Wear County Council in north-east England started campaigning against the Government's devolution proposals (Guthrie and McLean 1978: 194). They argued that Scotland and Wales were already politically advantaged with greater parliamentary representation and territorial departments. Devolution, they maintained, especially without a reduction in MPs, could not be supported. Economic statistics showed that Scotland received more public spending per head than northern England. 'English backlash' MPs in the North-East, who constituted a high proportion of devolution opponents, consisted of two groups: constitutional opponents who feared that a halfway house would fuel nationalism and lead to the break-up of the UK and the *'quid pro quo school'* who sought concessions for English groups (Ibid.: 195–196). There were both federalists and centralists amongst these northern MPs. While they cohered around what they opposed, they were unable to find common ground on what they supported.

The north-east backlash proved important for a number of reasons. First, the Labour Government's majority was vulnerable and only a handful of dissidents could undermine its authority. Secondly, the views expressed by politicians and media in the North-East was reflected in much thinking both in the Cabinet and Whitehall. A private memorandum on devolution written by Sir Douglas Henley for other Treasury officials in July 1974, included a paragraph on the 'English dimension' which noted, 'The relatively deprived areas of England might well press for similar treatment to that given to Scotland. And with directly elected assemblies in Scotland and Wales English opinion might no longer tolerate their over-representation at Westminster The loss of 20 seats would significantly affect the overall balance of Parliament' (TNA T 227 4253). Thirdly, it was easier to mobilise opposition to a flawed scheme than to unite radically different perspectives around a more positive agenda.

Gains made included both symbolic and substantive concessions. The North-East was included in a visit to the UK of American President Jimmy Carter in 1977, the headquarters of British Shipbuilders was housed in the North-East and a major order from the Central Electricity Generating Board was placed with a North-East firm as well as significant inner-city regeneration support for Newcastle and Gateshead and the establishment of a Northern regional branch of the National Enterprise Board (Guthrie and McLean: 198–199). Scottish nationalism and the prospect of devolution had the effect of creating a northern political identity but it was defensive and its gains proved largely transient. The end result was that neither the Scots and Welsh gained assemblies nor did the English regions benefit greatly. The lesson from this episode would become all too clear after 1979.

The West Lothian Question

The West Lothian Question was named after Tam Dalyell, Labour MP for West Lothian. Dalyell was hostile to devolution and persistently raised the anomaly that would result from MPs being able to vote on all English domestic affairs but unable to vote on similar matters devolved to Scotland and Wales. For Dalyell, devolution and a unitary state were 'mutually exclusive': 'Would it not be more honest to admit that it is impossible to have an Assembly – especially any kind of subordinate Parliament – that is part, though only part of a unitary state?' (Hansard, Commons, vol. 939, 14 November 1977, cols 78–79).

Dalyell's alliterative espousal of the 'West Lothian Question' became his hallmark in the devolution debates in the 1970s. In late 1977, he asked Prime Minister Callaghan, 'Under the new Bill, shall I be able to vote on many matters in relation to West Bromwich but not West Lothian, as I was under the last Bill, and will my right hon. Friend be able to vote on many matters in relation to Carlisle but not Cardiff?' (Hansard, Commons, vol. 938, 3 November 1977, col. 31). The question, he maintained, was 'how long will English constituencies and English Honourable Members tolerate ... at least 119 Honourable Members from Scotland, Wales and Northern Ireland exercising an important, and probably often decisive, effect on British politics while they themselves have no say in the same matters in Scotland, Wales and Northern Ireland?' (Ibid.). It was not a new argument. Dalyell was articulating a Diceyan concern expressed in the late nineteenth century in debates on Irish home rule. As Dicey had pointed out a century before, devolution to any one part of the state involves a 'demand for fundamental alterations in the whole Constitution of the United Kingdom' (Dicey 1886: Preface).

The Cabinet discussed the problem of Scottish and Welsh representation at Westminster in January 1977. A note written by the Cabinet Office's Constitution Unit concluded that the 'theoretical logic of this situation' required an 'in-and-out' voting arrangement in which Scottish and Welsh MPs refrained from voting on English 'domestic' issues (TNA CAB 129/194/5). However, 'no form of "in and out" voting has been identified that would be sufficiently consistent with the basic features of our constitution to be workable and which would also meet the equity objective' (Ibid.). There was difficulty in identifying legislation that had no implications for Scotland as well as the 'more fundamental' difficulty of facing deadlock whenever the party balance in the Commons as a whole differed from that in England. It was felt that it might be possible to 'devise some more sophisticated relationship between the House as a whole and an England-and-Wales committee (eg by limiting the competence of the committee to some specified delay of one or two years rather than allowing it indefinitely to block a measure that the House as a whole were prepared to pass).' But the Constitution Unit felt that this could do little more than 'slightly reduce the sharpness of the potential deadlock' and would 'fail to meet the English equity difficulty' (Ibid.), while it recognised that a reduction in the number of Scottish and Welsh MPs, 'while hardly meeting the logic of the situation', would be a 'significant symbolic gesture towards meeting the problem, would raise none of the constitutional difficulties of "in-and-out" voting and is precedented by Northern Ireland' (Ibid.). However, Michael Foot argued that the issue should be considered by a Speaker's Conference and 'deploy it at a moment selected to give best advantage in relation to the passage of the Bill' (Ibid.). There was strong opposition to reductions in Welsh and Scottish representation in the Commons within the Labour Party and this partisan interest proved a stumbling block in any serious effort to address the issue.

The GLC, Metropolitan Councils and functional regionalism in the 1980s

The overwhelming rejection of devolution in Wales and the tiny majority in its favour in Scotland in 1979 meant that the English Question, as defined in terms of the West Lothian Question, disappeared, but the familiar issues concerned with regional policy, regional government and administration remained. However, regionalism in its various forms became unfashionable under the Conservatives after 1979 (Hogwood 1995: 267; Mawson and Spencer 1997: 159). Regional Economic Planning Councils and Regional Health Authorities were abolished though 'bureaucratic mechanisms at regional level have remained' (Hogwood 1994: 17). But there were a number of factors which conspired to keep regions and regional administration alive. The need for some intermediate level of government between the centre and the individual citizen or localities would not disappear simply because of the 'rolling back of the state', which in many respects involved changes in the functions of the state rather than the complete eradication of a role for the state. The rise of regulatory agencies in place of nationalised industries, for example, meant that new agencies were created, some with a regional apparatus. The European Community's regional policy required at least some regional administrative arrangements, especially following reforms instituted in the 1980s, and gave hope to advocates of regional government.

Mrs Thatcher's attitude to local government when she came to office was captured in a throw-away line in her memoirs. They were overspending 'as usual' (Thatcher 1993: 123). Added to this was her perception that the 'hard left's power was entrenched' in local government (Ibid.: 339). She found these perceived failings in the Metropolitan County Councils (MCCs) and, most notably, the Greater London Council (GLC). In their 1983 manifesto, the Conservatives promised to abolish these authorities, the nearest England had to elected regional government. The Metropolitan Councils and GLC were not without their flaws, though some argued that these were not that they had too much power, but that they lacked power and had unrealistic boundaries (Flynn *et al.* 1985: 32). The abolition of the GLC and Metropolitan Councils was the most politically contentious regional issue in English politics in the 1980s. The decision to get rid of them was hasty and rooted in a 'history of conflicts between the government and the Labour-controlled MCCs and the GLC' (Ibid.: 9). The GLC was based across the Thames from the House of Commons and Ken Livingstone, its leader, proved adept in provoking Conservative politicians with policy initiatives that could be dressed up in popular fashion. The GLC attracted an inordinate amount of media exposure simply because its local nature was equated with national coverage by journalists based in the capital. It offered Labour a popular issue on which to campaign against the Conservatives.

The European dimension became important in the 1980s. The ambiguity of the original objectives of the European Regional Development Fund (ERDF) were that the Fund had 'the capacity to fulfil two roles: the promotion of regional development, and/or the provision of a channel for rebates to certain Member States for contributions to the EEC's budget considered to be excessive' (Cawson 1992: 25–26). The ERDF was established in 1975, partly as a concession to the UK after it joined two years before. But in its early days, it was little more than a means of ensuring that states such as the UK which were net contributors to the EC's budget were financially recompensed. Its value as a regional policy was thus limited. Over time, however, it grew in size and significance. The issue of rebates was central to the politics of European Community membership in the UK in the early 1980s but once this was resolved at the Fontainebleau summit in 1984, progress towards 'ever closer union' became possible. Europe attained centre stage in British politics and its regional dimension was inevitably caught up in its controversies.

Allied with and related to the EC's Single European Act were incremental changes in the ERDF which gave local and regional bodies within member states greater roles in the implementation of the policy and saw alliances formed between regions and local authorities, and the European Commission in Brussels. Margaret Thatcher's increasingly shrill opposition to European integration meant that many Labour local authorities saw a common ally in the European Commission. Jacques Delors, President of the European Commission from 1985 to 1994, was adept in articulating a vision of Europe that incorporated a vague notion of subsidiarity, implying that further integration would only occur alongside substantial devolution of power within member states. Mrs Thatcher's hostility to regional government and European integration was articulated in terms of 'sovereignty' (Thatcher 1993: 690). However, subsidiarity proved fairly elusive and was more significant for its symbolic value than its substance (Mitchell 1992). Nonetheless, it helped mobilise opinion in parts of England for some form of regional administration and government.

Hogwood noted three reasons for expecting a decline in 'administrative regionalism' after 1979. The Conservatives had abolished the Regional Economic Planning Councils, the privatisation programme involved removing public sector utilities and industries which had regional levels, and there was decentralisation to institutions below the region (Hogwood 1995: 267–268). However, there were equally good reasons for expecting the continuation and even an increase in administrative regionalism. Large-scale delivery across a wide range of public services required a regional tier. There was an important 'representational role' for the regional level in providing feedback to Whitehall. Privatisation may have removed utilities and industries from one form of state control but these same utilities and industries required to be regulated and this included having regional offices (Ibid.: 268–269).

New 'integrated regional offices' were established in 1994 bringing together the existing regional offices of the Department of Trade and Industry, the Training, Education and Enterprise Division of the Department of Employment and the Departments of the Environment and Transport. These new offices administered a single integrated budget. However, this was not quite an embryonic structure for regional government. Many aspects of government work were not covered and the regions did not correspond with the territorial organisation. But as Hogwood noted,

> Though far from all-embracing in its coverage of government departments and the regional bodies they sponsor [the plan] would, if fully implemented, represent a greater degree of practical co-ordination of activities and alignment of regional boundaries than was actually achieved under the substantially more ambitious economic planning emphasis of the 1960s. (Ibid: 289–290)

Sandford has suggested that the Government Offices for the Regions (GORs), created by the Major Government, were 'a vital foundation of the current [post-1997] regional agenda' (Sandford 2005: 39) and noted that greater co-ordination at the regional level had been a commitment in the Conservatives' 1992 election manifesto. These Government Offices involved some changes in regional boundaries with London becoming a region, separate from the South-East. An Office for Merseyside was created and there were some boundary changes in the North-West.

New Labour and regionalism

Different views on English regionalism were held by senior members of the Labour Government that took office in 1997. John Prescott, Deputy Prime Minister, had been a long-standing supporter of tackling regional disparities and became the strongest, at times it seemed the only, supporter of regional government in the Cabinet. Prescott had been appointed by Michael Foot, Labour's leader in the early 1980s, to reconcile the party's commitment to devolution with its highly centralised 'alternative economic strategy'. With the help of a working group of academics and others, Prescott had produced Labour's *Alternative Regional Strategy* in September 1982. It proposed the creation of regional assemblies and regional planning boards. Prescott envisaged the assemblies initially consisting of nominees from business, unions and local authorities but ultimately being directly elected. A regional input into public expenditure decision-making was part of the effort to create arrangements to ensure that regional matters fed directly into decision-making in Whitehall. Prescott argued that public spending decisions ought to be broken down territorially as well as by service (Prescott and Pendry 1982). The Alternative Regional Strategy (ARS) was a creature of its time. Labour's lurch to the left had been manifested in its Alternative Economic Strategy (AES) involving interventionist machinery of government and central demand management in a relatively closed economy operating outside the EC. The ARS was an attempt to graft a regional dimension onto the AES. Significantly, when the AES was abandoned as the 1980s progressed, the institutions of the ARS were amongst the few remnants of Labour's leftist phase. The logic of the policy would gradually shift from an emphasis on territorial redistribution to increased efficiency in the regions.

In 1992, Labour's manifesto promised, 'A regional tier of government in the English regions will take over many powers now exercised nationally, such as regional economic planning and transport. These new administrations will later form the basis for elected regional governments' (Labour Party 1992). There was little detail to the proposals. Some senior Labour figures were sympathetic to Prescott's desire to tackle regional inequities, notably John Smith who led the party from 1992–94, but Tony Blair demanded a review on assuming the leadership of the party two years later. As the minister in charge of devolution in the late 1970s, Smith was well aware of the West Lothian Question and could see merit in seeking its solution in some English regional dimension. In July 1995, Bruce Millan, former Scottish Secretary and Regional Affairs European Commissioner, was asked by John Prescott to chair a regional policy commission. Millan produced a report a year later which recommended the establishment of Regional Development Agencies (Millan 1996: 33–36). The Millan Commission envisaged that the RDAs should 'be established separate from regional chambers, but responsible to the chambers and acting as their executive arm in the area of economic development' (Ibid.: 33).

English regional government was one of many policies Blair inherited but found unpalatable on becoming Labour leader. However, unlike so many other policies which were ceremoniously ditched in an effort to rebrand the party, the English regional policy neither had salience nor was seen as beyond repair despite its leftist origins. Jack Straw produced a new policy document, *A New Choice for England* in 1996. This criticised the lack of policy co-ordination and democratic deficit inherent in the structures created by the Conservatives and proposed a process to create regional government involving indirectly elected Regional Chambers consisting of regional associations of local authorities which would scrutinise the Government Offices for the Regions (GORs) and be responsible for European work, economic development, transport and planning. These Regional Chambers would be established 'as rapidly as possible' (Labour Party 1996: 7) and would lead to the establishment of directly elected Regional Assemblies.

In its 1997 manifesto, Labour promised to 'establish Regional Development Agencies to co-ordinate regional economic development, help small business and encourage inward investment' (Labour Party 1997). The manifesto was careful in its support for elected regional government:

> Demand for directly elected regional government so varies across England that it would be wrong to impose a uniform system. In time we will introduce legislation to allow the people, region by region, to decide in a referendum whether they want directly elected regional government. Only where popular consent is established will arrangements be made for elected regional assemblies. This would require a predominantly unitary system of local government, as presently exists in Scotland and Wales, and confirmation by independent auditors that no additional public expenditure overall would be involved. Our plans will not mean adding a new tier of government to the existing English system. (Ibid.).

The twin themes of tackling the democratic deficit in England's regions and making the regions more economically efficient were not deemed mutually reinforcing by all members of the Government. Within six weeks of the election, Prescott published a discussion paper on regional development agencies and set out the Government's proposals six months later (DETR 1997). The RDAs were set up in 1999. These were government bodies designed to bring together existing institutions to create greater strategic coherence in economic development and regeneration at regional level. Regional Chambers were set up in summer 1999, one for each RDA, but the relationship between the Regional Chambers and RDAs envisaged by Millan had been abandoned. Instead, RDAs were accountable to Parliament through ministers. These were central government institutions deriving their authority from Parliament. Their legitimacy would rest on their ability to deliver satisfactory public policy outcomes.

The RDAs were non-representative or non-majoritarian institutions. There has been a growth in work on non-majoritarian institutions and accountability amongst political scientists especially drawing on new institutional economics. In his work on public sector control of bureaucracy, Hood introduced the notion 'interpolable balance' (Hood 1991). The key elements of this are control through a series of balanced methods: clear and narrowly defined objectives; strict procedural requirements; judicial review; professionalism and peer review; transparency; and public participation. Non-majoritarian institutions gain legitimacy through a balance of these forms of control rather than the direct legitimacy derived from directly elected institutions. This appears to have been the unstated approach adopted by the New Labour Government in the development of regional institutions in England. Greater coherence with a view to greater efficiency and efficacy was the priority.

In this respect, there was nothing particularly new about the Government's approach to English regions. The *Modernising Government* White Paper of 1999 was then but the latest in a long line of documents which argued,

> Wherever possible, boundaries should coincide with local authority boundaries at local level, and with Government Office regions' boundaries at the regional level. The Government will work from a presumption that geographical boundaries should be aligned in this way whenever public bodies next review their administrative, managerial or delivery arrangements and structures. (Cabinet Office 1999: 33)

Statements such as this had littered pages of government documents over the years. What was novel were the institutions created to achieve these objectives. Sandford has argued that these informal organisations, the networks of regional bodies, have developed alongside the formal institutions, to represent a 'form of regionalism, if not by stealth, then certainly by default' (Sandford 2006: 175). As he expressed it,

> The visible institutions RDAs, GORs, regional chambers, and the large executive agencies – exist in a bed of indigenous networks. These networks are vital in that they transform what would otherwise be a series of loosely connected central government initiatives into a capacity for strategic thinking that is based *in* the region, with staffs and membership which are interested in regional, not national, planning and needs. (Ibid: 183)

If his analysis is correct, it is the informal institutions that have grown up around the formal bodies which are in the process of region building, creating regional communities at an elite level. Whether an unintended consequence of the creation of formal regional institutions by central government or not, it appears that embedded regionalism of this kind may be emerging.

However, this does not necessarily lead to a regionalist social movement. Nor does it mean that these loose networks will become more significant over time. For every example of an informal political institution becoming formalised, there are numerous instances of this not happening. But as public policy scholars have long noted, policies create interests at least as often as interests create policies. The development of limited regional structures of government do appear to have created embedded regional interests that may prove difficult to get rid off.

North-East referendum

The intention, at least of John Prescott, had been that the Chambers would become directly elected assemblies but early signals suggested that this process might, at best, take some time. While Tomaney and Hetherington referred to the 'quiet regional revolution' and of a 'quiet regionalisation' (Tomaney and Hetherington 2004: 121) in England, by the end of 2004, the process of creating Regional Assemblies had come to an abrupt end when an assembly for the North-East was overwhelmingly rejected in a referendum: 78 per cent voted 'No' in a turnout of 48 per cent. The Queen's Speech in November 2003 had promised legislation to allow referendums to be held in English regions and the following month the Government announced that it would take soundings to determine the strength of support for assemblies. Legislation was passed which permitted referendums but prevented a second referendum within seven years in the event of the rejection of an assembly. The Government's soundings led to a further announcement in June 2003 that referendums would only occur initially in three English regions: the North-East, Yorkshire, and the North-West. These were areas in which most support existed for assemblies. According to research, support for an assembly exceeded opposition in all regions though there was also considerable evidence that the public was barely engaged with the issue and that turnout would be low (Ibid.: 132). In the event, the first and last referendum was held in the North-East and the overwhelming rejection killed the idea dead. Little leadership was provided by the Government so that the North-East's predominantly Labour voters (28 of its 30 seats were Labour held) were given no clear signals from the party how to vote. The Prime Minister's brief appearance during the campaign, despite his parliamentary constituency lying within the region, saw him make his first public reference to elected assemblies (Sandford 2005: 97).

As the referendum in the North-East demonstrated, there is no regionalism in England comparable to Scottish and Welsh nationalism. Though survey research shows that over three-quarters of people in the north-east of England believed that government in London 'looks after some parts of England more than others' and 70 per cent believe that the North-East received a 'little' or 'much less than its fair share of government spending' (Devolution Brief 2005) this did not translate into support for devolution. Research suggests that differences within the North-East remained significant with each community fearing that a regional assembly would be dominated by interests other than their own (Smith 2005). This was similar to what had happened in Wales and, to a much lesser extent, in Scotland in 1979. In other words, in the context of the North-East referendum, the most significant 'Other' was not London but each local community's 'Other' within the North-East – Durham vs. Newcastle vs. Middlesbrough and so on. Regionalism was an elite preoccupation in England.

However, supporters of English regional assemblies took heart from the change in attitudes amongst Welsh voters between 1979 and 1997 and noted that the 'increasing constellation of regional institutions and groupings that grew up under the Blair Governments, like the idea that inspired them, had a long pedigree in the north east' (Tomaney 2006: 172). Nonetheless, the notion of England as 'one and indivisible' inherent in the idea of the unitary state, discussed in the first chapter, continued to retain its power.

Regional policy

While regional government and administration developed under New Labour and regionalism as a bottom-up social movement hardly developed, regional policy became fashionable again after 1997, though not in the form it had taken in the past. The changes in regional policy reflect changes in economic orthodoxies. Old ideas and institutions associated with regional policy from the post-war period were dismantled by Margaret Thatcher's Government. New Labour preferred this Tory inheritance than that of previous Labour Governments. Old spatial Keynesianism, when large sums of money were channelled into weak economies, is long gone, and with it went the associated centralised institutions. Central demand management and its regional policy offspring might crudely be viewed as archetypal top-down policy-making. It was deemed to have redistributive objectives. As Martin and Tyler argued, the main premises of 'spatial Keynesianism' were rejected in the 1980s in the UK (more than in other EC member states) in line with a focus on monetary constraints, supply side economics and free market liberalism (1991: 8). The existence and persistence of markedly higher unemployment in the regions of the UK was re-interpreted in terms of 'institutional rigidities' in those areas. Strong unionisation in the regions experiencing de-industrialisation was deemed to maintain real wages in excess of that warranted by productivity and local labour market conditions, thereby creating unemployment and preventing investment. As a result of the general shift to supply-side economic policies and the demise of Keynesianism (including in its spatial form), the finances allocated to regional policies were progressively cut back.

The emphasis has been on enabling regions to develop. Ed Balls, chief adviser to Gordon Brown after 1997 and later a minister in Brown's

Table 9.1 Whitehall's 'regional turn'

Year	Regional turn	Department
1999	Regional Development Agencies established	DETR
1999	*Modernising Government* White Paper	Cabinet Office
2000	Reaching Out: The Role of Central Government at the Regional and Local Level	Cabinet Office (PIU)
2000	Spending Review 2000 (increases RDA funds)	HMT
2000	*Enterprise, Skills and Innovation* White Paper	DTI
2000	Ed Balls and John Healey publish 'The New Regional Policy' pamphlet	HMT[a]
2001	Productivity in the UK: The Regional Dimension	HMT/DTI
2001	Planning: Delivering a Fundamental Change (Regional Spatial Strategies)	DTLR
2002	Spending Review (Single Pot established; reducing regional economic disparities PSA)	HMT
2002	*Your Region, Your Choice* White Paper	DTLR/Cabinet Office
2003	Our Fire and Rescue Service White Paper	Home Office
2003	McLean Review: Investigating the Flow of Domestic and European Expenditure into the English Regions	ODPM/DTI/HMT
2003	The Haskins Report	DEFRA
2003	The Lambert Review of Business–University Collaboration	HMT
2003	Regional Emphasis Documents	HMT
2003	*Building Safer Communities* White Paper	Home Office
2004	Spending Review and Meeting Regional Priorities: Response to the Regional Emphasis Documents	HMT
2004	Barker Review of Housing Supply	HMT
2004	The Allsopp Review	
2004	Devolved Decision Making: Meeting the Regional Economic Challenge	HMT
2004	The Lyons Report (Independent Review of Public Sector Relocation)	HMT
2004	Spending Review	HMT

Note: [a]The pamphlet was not an official Treasury publication, but Balls was chief economic adviser to HM Treasury and John Healey was a minister there at the time of publication.

Source: Lodge and Mitchell 2006: 111.

Government, argued in 2000, 'Our new regional policy is based on two principles – it aims to strengthen the essential building blocks of growth – innovation, skills, the development of enterprise – by exploiting the indigenous strengths in each region and city. And it is bottom-up not top-down, with national government enabling powerful regional and local initiatives to work by providing the necessary flexibility and resources' (Balls 2000: 12–13). Brown himself distinguished between the 'ambulance work' of the first generation of regional policy which provided assistance to poorer regions, the second generation that sought to create incentives for business and industry to locate in particular regions and this third generation which focused on the need to build capacity in the regions (Brown 2001) which required developing English regional institutions discussed above. There was a gradual 'regional turn' in Whitehall, notably in the Treasury, which had three elements: improved regional data; greater emphasis on tackling regional disparities; and greater flexibility than in the past in how this is delivered. The new regional policy was outlined by the Treasury in 2004:

> to be successful government intervention has to complement and promote structural development and change. Programmes to build regional economic capacity and human and social capital need to be complemented by policies to build a network of firms capable of sustaining high levels of growth, without persistent government finance. (Treasury 2004: 113)

Much of the policy was concerned with changing economic cultures, creating a new entrepreneurial mood as well as providing infrastructure rather than simply channelling money into poorer regions.

The Mayor of London and London Assembly

After the demise of the Greater London Council (GLC), it was frequently pointed out that London was the only major capital in the world which did not have its own multi-purpose city-wide elected authority. In its place, London was governed by Government Ministers, its 32 boroughs and a number of joint authorities for specific functions creating a 'highly fragmented' structure which left 'powers drifting to Whiethall' (Pimlott and Rao 2002: 45). Labour favoured re-establishing a democratically elected London authority but over time it moved away from recreating something similar to the GLC and towards a less bureaucratic structure (Ibid.: 55–56). The idea of a directly elected mayor was supported by a range of political positions. Peter Walker, former Conservative Minister, had advocated directly elected mayors in the 1960s and Michael Heseltine argued for them in 1990 after Prime Minister John Major gave him responsibility for the Department of the Environment. However, Major rejected the idea and it was left to Tony Blair and New Labour to make the case for directly elected mayors: Blair was attracted to the idea of US-style elected mayors who would use their personal electoral mandate to provide leadership and coherence in local government, though Frank Dobson, Labour's Environment and London spokesman after 1994, opposed the idea, preferring an indirectly elected mayor. The idea of elected mayors was not restricted to London: under the Local Government Act, 2000 the option became available to local authorities in England and Wales. Twelve English authorities opted, after referendums, to have directly elected mayors, though most authorities refused to take advantage of the opportunity to introduce this innovation despite strong support for it from the Prime Minister and Government.

In 1996, Labour published *A Voice for London*, a consultation document, which proposed a Greater London Authority with a wide range of responsibilities and gave lukewarm support to the possibility of a directly elected mayor. Blair, however, had been converted and firmed up the proposal and by January 1997 was giving it strong backing. Labour's 1997 manifesto stated:

> London is the only Western capital without an elected city government. Following a referendum to confirm popular demand, there will be a new deal for London, with a strategic authority and a mayor, each directly elected. Both will speak up for the needs of the city and plan its future. They will not duplicate the work of the boroughs, but take responsibility for London-wide issues – economic regeneration, planning, policing, transport and environmental protection. London-wide responsibility for its own government is urgently required. We will make it happen. (Labour Party 1997)

Dobson became Health Secretary and responsibility for London was given to Nick Raynsford. Ken Livingstone, the GLC's Labour leader at the time of its demise, used his election as an MP as a platform to make the case for the return of a London authority: he disagreed with the policy of a directly elected mayor though strongly favoured a London-wide elected authority.

A referendum was held in May 1998 at the same time as elections to the London boroughs. Londoners supported the proposals for a directly elected mayor and London Assembly: on a turnout of only 34 per cent, 72 per cent voted in favour of the Government's proposals with the highest support recorded in working-class areas, though clear majorities were recorded in all London boroughs. The new structure of London government involved both an elected mayor and an assembly with 25 members, together constituting the Greater London Authority (GLA). The GLA was given executive powers over four main bodies: Transport for London; London Development Agency; Metropolitan Police Authority; and London Fire and Emergency Planning Authority. The scope for pursuing priorities radically at odds with central government was severely circumscribed as revenue-raising powers were limited and there was no scope for transferring money set by the Government between these bodies.

The first elections were held in May 2000 and both the Labour and Conservative Parties experienced problems in selecting candidates. Lord Archer was initially selected as the Tory candidate but had to resign following his arrest for perjury. Ken Livingstone sought the Labour nomination but was strongly opposed by Tony Blair and Gordon Brown who backed Frank Dobson as Labour's candidate, provoking William Hague, Tory leader, to suggest to Blair in late 1999, 'Why not split the job in two, with Frank Dobson as your day mayor and Ken Livingstone as your nightmare?' (D'Arcy and MacLean 2000). Dobson was chosen by Labour despite majority support amongst ordinary members because the system gave Labour MPs and MEPs greater weight. Livingstone stood as an Independent and won the election comfortably under the Supplementary Vote system whereby voters express their first and second preferences and, if no candidate has more than half the ballots cast with first preferences, all but the top two candidates are elimated with eliminated candidates' second preferences distributed between the two remaining candidates. Dobson won under 13 per cent of the vote leaving Livingstone, with 38 per cent of first preferences, facing Steven Norris of the Tories, with 26 per cent. In the second round, Livingstone won 58 per cent of the vote. In the second mayoral elections, Labour decided to readmit Livingstone to the party and to have him stand as its candidate and he once more topped the poll.

Despite his limited formal powers, Livingstone had the advantage of being mayor of the capital city where the media was concentrated and could command considerable attention. The main area of controversy was transport. Livingstone challenged in the courts the Government's proposals for Private-Public Partnerships (PPPs) to fund the London underground. The Government won the court case. However, a report by the Commons' Public Accounts Committee in March 2005 suggested that PPPs should have been restricted to upgrading work and that publc sector bonds ought to be considered in future (House of Commons 2005). Livingstone managed to secure additional funding from the Government as part of a deal which involved dropping possible legal action (Sandford 2004: 159). Another more successful policy venture was Livingstone's plan to introduce congestion charging to reduce traffic congestion in central London. Motorists entering central London were charged a fee per day. While other cities have been reluctant to follow London's lead, the policy has generally been deemed a success.

New Labour and the English Question

Different views had been expressed by Labour's leaders on the English Question. In his book written in the aftermath of the 1979 Scottish devolution referendum with Henry Drucker, Gordon Brown criticised the first devolution legislation on the grounds that it had evaded the West Lothian Question:

> Most of all, a revised Scotland Act could embody some form of the 'in-and-out' principle. Under such a principle the remaining Scottish MPs at

Westminster would not be allowed to take part in the proceedings of the House when it was debating English or Welsh domestic matters. The 'in-and-out' principle ought to be attractive to Conservatives since it would ensure them a semi-permanent majority on most social issues at Westminster – no small prize. Labour remains formally committed to devolution and may be expected to consider a plan along these lines in the future. (Drucker and Brown 1980: 127)

The idea was later abandoned by Brown. In January 1995, Brown argued that a Scottish Parliament and Welsh Assembly 'go hand in hand with the offer of greater regional democracy throughout Britain' and thus the West Lothian Question should not be a barrier to change (*Scotsman*, 13 January 1995). Two months later, Tony Blair said that he did not see Scottish devolution 'in any way, shape or form dependent upon what happens in the English regions' (*Scotsman*, 8 March 1995). Blair disagreed with Brown on the relationship between devolution and English regional government: 'That is not really a basis for legislating for the English regions. You are not going to answer one question by going for another. The answer to the West Lothian question is what is happening in Northern Ireland ... the Government will not reduce the number of MPs there. Scots MPs will still be coming to Westminster to decide the main parts of economics, foreign affairs and defence policy and all the rest of it' (Ibid.). The reduction in numbers of Scottish MPs at Westminster after devolution became the 'solution' to the West Lothian Question and appeared to have been successful in the early years. However, this appearance may simply have been a function of Labour's strength in England at the time.

A view has been developing since devolution amongst English Conservative politicians, supporters and others which is similar to that found in Wales and Scotland in the 1980s. The feeling that Scottish and Welsh MPs are able to impose policies against the wishes of majority opinion in England may not have become politically significant in the early years of devolution because there have been few parliamentary votes on matters affecting England which were won only because of the support of Scottish MPs (Russell and Lodge 2006). Under different circumstances however, the temptation to play the 'English card' may prove attractive even if the official Conservative position is less shrill than some Conservatives would prefer.

In February 2006, Lord (Kenneth) Baker introduced his Parliament (Participation of Members of the House of Commons) Bill in the House of Lords which sought to prevent Scottish and Welsh MPs voting on matters affecting England that had been devolved to Scotland and Wales. The debate in the Lords heard many criticisms of the Bill, not least its practicability. The official Tory position was ambivalent, supporting the principle of English votes for English laws but unclear on whether the official policy would be similar in detail to Baker's Bill (See Lord Strathclyde,

Hansard, Lords, 10 February 2006, cols 943–946). There have been a number of critiques of the Conservatives' position (Hazell 2006: 224–226) and some evidence that, while there may be strong support inside the party for the principle of English votes for English laws, there is some unease too. When Shadow Trade Secretary Alan Duncan suggested that it was 'almost impossible' to have a Scottish Prime Minister, it was stressed that he was not speaking for his party (*Daily Mail*, 4 July 2006). Sir Malcolm Rifkind, former Scottish Secretary who followed a long line of defeated Scottish Tories to seek a safe seat in England, voiced his concerns (*Evening Standard*, 5 July 2006) though later fell into line with the official party position when he developed proposals for an English Grand Committee, an elaborate version of English votes for English laws (*Sunday Express*, 30 September 2007; *The Herald*, 3 October 2007). Liam Fox, another Scot representing an English constituency, criticised Alan Duncan, warning that the 'Conservative Party needs to remember that it is a Unionist party ... If it becomes used for short term political knockabout it could have consequences for the cohesion of the UK' (Ibid.). The journalist Peter Oborne, writing before Gordon Brown became Prime Minister, summed up the mood of the Conservative Party: 'Some genuinely think it is unfair that Scottish MPs can vote on English health and education, while England MPs have no say in Scotland. Others will be pleased that Cameron is embarrassing Gordon Brown, probably the next leader of the Labour Party and a very obvious Scot. But I don't like it at all. The fact that Brown is Scottish is no barrier to becoming Prime Minister. He is every bit as patriotic as any Englishman. The Conservative Party believes, above all else, in the union and Cameron – with a name like his, he should know better – is playing with fire' (*Evening Standard*, 3 July 2006). The possibility of the West Lothian Question becoming salient has encouraged some Labour politicians to re-open the issue. Michael Wills, Labour MP and 'confidante of the Chancellor' (*Scotsman*, 21 June 2006) called for an answer to the West Lothian Question. Wills referred to devolution as containing 'unfinished business' (Wills 2006: 22).

The difficulty of finding a solution has left the issue unresolved with considerable potential to undermine the legitimacy of a Westminster Government relying on Scottish and Welsh MPs. While it is widely accepted that there is little prospect of solving the West Lothian Question short of fundamental constitutional change, any response short of this is likely only to succeed if agreement can be found amongst the political elites at Westminster.

Conclusion

England remains one and indivisible though London, as ever, remains a place apart. There have been two quite distinct sets of English Questions.

The first concerns the familiar problems associated with governing a large territory with a large, diverse population in an advanced liberal democratic state. Central government cannot operate without some regional tier of government but the tier which is appropriate for one service may be inappropriate for another, creating multiple networks of territorial government and administration. Rationalising these networks has been a perennial objective of successive governments but this has been set against recognition that this might diminish efficacy in the provision of some services. Underlying these matters has been that of the legitimacy of regional structures of government and whether these require elected democratic institutions. This could only work in the event of rationalising the system under single boundaries. Further complicating matters has been the role of elected local government in a system of elected regional government.

A second and quite different set of issues has arisen since devolution was granted to Scotland, Wales and Northern Ireland. This is often summed up in the West Lothian Question but goes much deeper. Devolved government has territorialised UK politics, made England more apparent as a polity and created anomalies. In essence, devolution may have resolved matters of legitimacy elsewhere in the UK but this has occurred only by shifting the problem elsewhere. This has been insignificant during the early years of devolution when the governing party has commanded a majority in England, at least in terms of seats, but might raise issues of fairness and legitimacy in a different context.

It was argued in the introduction that England had been the prototypical unitary state and that this legacy continued to inform understandings of territorial politics in England. The state of unions which created the United Kingdom involved very different conceptions of union which operated harmoniously pre-devolution but may prove to create problems in the future.

10

Ever looser union

As a theoretical proposition the United Kingdom would probably win few converts because it seems such a fragile concoction. Imagine the reaction to a political scientist who proposed to create a country from the following design: three and a half nations, multiple religions, a number of languages, two separate legal systems and the whole thing ruled by a highly centralised government in the city in the south of the largest nation. (Morgan and Mungham 2000: 21)

Devolution does not cede ultimate sovereignty. The decisions Parliament takes have consequences for all the people of our nation. The great strength of our constitution is its effectiveness. It can accommodate difference and rough edges in support of wider goals of national unity, affiliation to the institutions of the state and the service of those institutions to the public. (Governance of Britain White Paper, 2007: 43)

Introduction

The central argument of this book is that devolved government was the culmination of processes that had evolved over many decades but devolution was never inevitable. There was no single 'track' which the United Kingdom started down. England has been the archetypal unitary polity. It would be an exaggeration to describe it as uniform but it has been a highly centralised polity in which the myth of parliamentary sovereignty easily gained adherents. By the beginning of the twentieth century, the empirical evidence of England as a unitary polity had taken on a normative quality and England could hardly be perceived as anything other than a unitary polity. The Anglo-Welsh union was assimilationist, though less so than the many unions which had created England. The Welsh language, religion and other distinguishing features ensured that despite political assimilation, Wales retained sufficient distinctiveness at key choice points to ensure that a base of Welsh distinctiveness was preserved. The unions of Scotland and Ireland were far from assimilationist ensuring that pre-union rights and institutions were preserved and served as important references when choices were made as to the nature of these unions. Choices were constantly being made, whether these were concerned consciously with the nature of the unions or whether they concerned other matters but had consequences for the unions.

The original different unions have been important in the development of the UK's territorial politics but so too have been other forces. As has been shown throughout this book, social and economic pressures gave rise to different conceptions of what the state at the centre should do, how much it should intervene in society and the economy, and this had consequences for its territorial constitution and issues of territorial management. At times these pressures have undermined these constituent unions, while at other times have served to strengthen the unions. Faith in centralised demand management had very different consequences for the territorial constitution than belief in a free market.

Thinking constitutionally

David Edwards has suggested that we have become 'constitutionally illiterate' in the United Kingdom (Edwards 2005: 9). Despite this, the UK embarked on a significant programme of constitutional reform after 1997, with devolution at its heart. The most striking consequence of constitutional change without constitutional thinking has been the *ad hoc* nature of changes brought about and its consequent incoherence. A valid response is that this is the British way, captured in Nevil Johnson's notion of a customary constitution. The UK's component nations have developed incrementally and separately. Leaving 'principles inexplicit, relying instead on what people feel from past experience, to be appropriate in the circumstances' (Johnson 2004: 19) was the hallmark of the UK constitution.

The thinking that led to devolution was political, rather than constitutional, in the sense that it was informed by political pressures rather than any coherent system-wide constitutional thinking. It built on the customary constitution rather than replaced it. Just as the customary constitution had developed with inexplicit principles, so too did devolution. Each devolution statute, leaving aside other aspects of constitutional reform, was a response to pressures within each component of the UK with little consideration for its implications for the UK as a whole. It is in this very basic sense that devolution was enacted with little constitutional thought and within the traditions of the 'political constitution' (Griffith 1979). Prior to devolution, it was possible for diverse autarchic institutions to operate under a centralised system of government. The central core provided constraints and limited significant centrifugal tendencies though the existence of autarchic institutions, to use the term as introduced by Mackenzie and Chapman (1951: 186), created institutions around which grievances developed. Autarchic institutions in Scotland had the effect of encouraging the development of what James Kellas called a 'Scottish polit-ical system' (Kellas 1973). Whether it was, indeed, a system is doubtful but these autarchic institutions, at the heart of Kellas's political system, created expectations, especially when the govering party at Westminster had relatively little support in Scotland, which could not be realised within the context of autarchic bodies.

There has been some codification of past practice as a consequence of devolution. It is hardly surprising that Whitehall accommodated devolu-tion easily during the early years, not only because considerable additional sums of public money were available and Labour was in power in London, Cardiff and Edinburgh but crucially because it had experience of working with autarchic institutions in Northern Ireland, Wales and Scot-land. The key difference was that the devolved bodies had their own legitimacy but still operated under the shadow of parliamentary sover-eignty. Devolution involved the creation of autarchic institutions in the sense that they are creatures of Westminster statute rather than bodies entrenched by fixed principles but, as Bogdanor noted, devolution should be viewed 'through political rather than constitutional spectacles' and 'power retained at Westminster might be very difficult to exercise' (Bogdanor 1979: 217). He predicted that had the Scottish Assembly legis-lated for in the 1970s come into being then 'power will be transferred, and it cannot, except under pathological circumstances, be recovered' (Ibid.: 217). That applies at least as much with devolved government established after 1997.

The late night amendments to the Scotland Act, 1998 introducing Joint Ministerial Committees (JMCs) and after-thoughts such as the concordats can be seen as making explicit long-standing arrangements. Ministers serving the territorial departments had always had an input into policy-making at the centre; the JMCs ensured that this practice might continue. They have no legal standing but made long-standing practice more explicit. This represents a small, tentative step towards making the 'implicit principles' explicit but the customary constitution remins the bedrock on which devolution has been built. What has been most notable is the extent to which these new institutions have not been used. The pref-erence for 'inexplicit principles' of the customary constitution appears to have won out over a more codified constitution in the early years of devo-lution.

One change that has come about has been in the understanding of the con-stitution. There is now greater appreciation that the UK consists of a num-ber of unions each with its diverse institutions. While the myth of the UK as a unitary state still persists, especially the myth that it was a unitary state be-fore devolution, there is far greater awareness in England of the diversity of the state. The strength of the myth of the pre-devolution unitary state has meant that devolution has been perceived as far more radical than it actually has been.

Year Zero assumptions have contributed to misunderstandings. The UK has not changed from being a unitary state to a devolved state but from a state with autarchic institutions to one in which these institutions created by the state take on the properties of autonomous institutions. However, the change in mythology has been greater than institutional change. This may prove an important dynamic.

What kind of constitution does the UK have post-devolution?

The establishment of devolved government constitutes a critical juncture in UK constitutional history. The nature of the significant change with distinct legacies can be explained by focusing on a number of key questions. In his polemic against devolution, Dicey asked three questions about Gladstone's 1886 Home Rule Bill:

i.   is sovereignty of Parliament preserved?
ii.   does the home rule constitution secure justice?
iii. does it hold out fair hopes of finality? (Dicey 1886: 238–273)

His first question can be reinterpreted and widened to focus on the nature of the constitution. The argument presented here is that the UK today is more emphatically a state of unions than ever before. The diverse nature of the unions is not only more evident but this has become much more politically salient than ever before. Old notions of the customary constitution, discussed in the introduction, have given way to troublesome and unresolved questions concerning the ability of the state to cope with different conceptions of sovereignty post-devolution. These different conceptions existed before devolution but had little political impact. It matters less whether sovereignty is viewed as an unhelpful concept, as has been argued elsewhere (Laski 1948: 44; Crick 1968: 70, 81; Nettl 1968: 560; Mitchell 1992), than that conceptions of sovereignty continue to inform understandings of the UK. In essence, Dicey's concern that Parliamentary sovereignty should be preserved and his insistence that this is of vital importance might actually serve to undermine the very state he strenuously defended. Given the prospect of a clash of sovereignties, or interpretation of sovereignties, as a result of the increased salience of territorial political conflict, the question may be whether some conception of sovereignty is more important than the UK itself.

Assertions of parliamentary sovereignty in the context of devolution are symptoms of the resilience of ideas associated with the unitary state. They speak of a failure to come to terms with the new institutions of devolution, not to mention Europe. Continuities have tended to be played down in the early discussion of the new arrangements while newness has been exaggerated. This partly reflects the obvious nature of the new formal institutions – new sets of politicians operating in new buildings. But it hides continuities from the old system of territorial government in the UK. The early years of devolution have made it difficult to judge whether a new culture of devolution has developed because of the absence of much overt conflict between London and the devolved polities. New formal institutions need not involve the creation of new politics.

Justice and legitimacy

Dicey's second question should also be expanded. Justice and legitimacy are closely related and what may prove important is whether the new constitutional arrangements are not only deemed just but legitimate. The justification for the diverse nature of devolution and its asymmetries is that they are deemed legitimate. But legitimacy has a number of meanings. David Beetham distinguished between 'legal validity', 'moral justifiability' and 'legitimation' (Beetham 1991: 4–5). 'Power can be said to be legitimate to the extent that: i) it conforms to established rules ii) the rules can be justified by reference to beliefs shared by both dominant and subordinate, and iii) there is evidence of consent by the subordinate to the particular power relation ... The three levels are not alternatives, since all contribute to legitimacy; all provide the subordinate with moral grounds for compliance or cooperation with the powerful' (Ibid.: 15–16). It is worth recalling that the pre-devolutionary constitutional order was legally valid but whether it was morally justifiable was questioned by supporters of devolution: the strength of feeling and nature of the challenge to its justification differed in the components of the UK.

This is worth recalling when considering issues of justice and legitimacy post-devolution. It is difficult for those who questioned the justice and legitimacy of pre-devolution constitutional arrangements to deny the injustice of existing arrangements for England, the largest component of the state. The argument that the UK contains anomalies is a statement of fact rather than a justification. The territorial dimension of UK politics has become more important and may lead to an expectation that much that exists is unfair and might easily become politically salient and require attention.

Hopes of finality

Dicey's third question might be easily dismissed with reference to the difficulties, indeed, dangers of insisting on expecting finality. Constitutions will evolve even if they remain rooted in arrangements determined at some critical juncture. But Dicey's question is relevant when understood as concerning stability. Has the post-devolved UK become more or less stable? The answer to this lies in the answer to the second of his questions. The early years of devolution have been remarkably stable but, as Michael

Forsyth, the last Conservative Scottish Secretary before devolution, used to argue, devolution is not just for Christmas and its real test lies in whether it provides long-term stability. Two conclusions can be drawn. First, while devolution has gone a considerable way to repair damage done to the legitimacy of the UK constitution in those parts of the UK with devolved government today, this may have been done at the expense of creating new problems of legitimacy elsewhere. In other words, devolution may have simply shifted the problem of legitimacy rather than resolved it. Secondly, territorial politics has created new expectations that cannot hope to be fulfilled which in time may create new pressures. However, what appears to have become more entrenched has been the sense that the different components of the UK should be treated as distinct polities. This might prove the key legitimising idea behind the new constitutional arrangements. Instead of creating pressure for equality of rights, devolved government may create pressure for or at least an acceptance of more diversity. In essence, the stability of the new devolved polity may depend on the extent to which the idea of a state of unions takes root.

Dicey was well aware of inconsistencies and anomalies in the constitution:

> The constitution, it may be retorted, is full of anomalies. So be it. The idea that one unreasonable arrangement is justified by pointing to the existence of a hundred other equally unreasonable arrangements is characteristic of certain modes of thought. It is a notion which has found favour in turn with the opponents of every reform, but which has always lost its force from the moment that men became earnestly bent on the removal of some glaring abuse. Grant, however, to the apologist for things as they stand that an anomaly, though requiring defence, need not of necessity be an abuse. (Dicey 1901: 360)

This Diceyan response is used by opponents of institutional responses to the 'English Question' today. Anomalies may be acceptable but only so long as the central tenets of the constitution are not undermined and these anomalies may be embraced as key features of the constitution. However, it will be difficult to do this so long as the myth of parliamentary sovereignty retains its hold.

The consequences of devolution will only begin to become clear after a period of experience. The first eight years were unusual in that Labour was in power in London as well as in power or sharing power in Cardiff and Edinburgh. Additionally, and more significantly, these were eight years when public spending across the UK, including the budgets of the devolved administrations, grew considerably. These conditions had consequences for the nature of devolution. The strains of territorial politics were largely hidden in a system that appeared more unified and settled than would have been the case in different curcumstances. Nonetheless, evidence emerged that there remained much unfinished business. The consequences of devolution for the UK as a whole and for England in particular have not been fully worked out and have the potential to create instability. Supporters of devolution would have to acknowledge the injustice of policy made for England on matters devolved to Scotland and Wales on the strength of Scottish and Welsh MPs' votes. It does not follow that there will be an English backlash. There would be nothing illegal or unconstitutional in a situation in which Scottish and Welsh votes determined the outcome of English domestic affairs. But, as discussed above, the legitimacy of the current arrangements will be tested in less favourable times than the early years of devolution. A key choice in politics is between anticipating and reacting to events. Waiting to see how and whether a backlash occurs means that any response will have to be made in a context less propitious to achieving agreement.

Ever looser union

The greatest problem with the idea of the UK as a union state is that it focuses exclusively on only some or even one of the unions which created the state. If the unitary state understanding of the UK was inadequate because it only described the English polity, the union state understanding is inadequate because it ignores England and Wales. The absence of either an English Parliament separate from Westminster or absence of directly elected English regional government is poorly accounted for in the notion of a union state. The description of the UK post-devolution as a union state has come to resemble past complacent descriptions of the UK as a unitary state.

The UK's devolved polity has inherited pre-devolution features and might appear to be little more than the continuity of old institutions with a new democratic veneer. This may, indeed, have been the intention of at least some of its founders. Former Prime Minister Tony Blair was no enthusiast for devolution and insisted that parliamentary sovereignty remained. This also appears to be evident in the mindset of those who have yet to come to terms with the probable, if not inevitable, consequences of deepening divergence in public policy. Creating new devolved institutions is not the same as creating a new devolved political culture. Much commentary on the radical nature of devolution focuses on the obvious changes in the formal institutions of devolution while failing to take account of continuities in the informal institutions.

However, the establishment of devolved government has significant implications. The probability of greater policy divergence, institutional diversity and differences in the party systems across the UK all suggest that over the long term diversity within this state of unions will become more pronounced, more entrenched. This is not the same as suggesting that the UK will break up. Indeed, it suggests that even if some part of the

UK was to secede, relations between the seceding part and the rest of the state would remain close and that such a new dispensation would be marked by continuities.

The most likely scenario is perhaps best understood by analogy. The UK's constitution may come to resemble that of the European Union's in one respect at least. 'Ever closer union' is the objective set out in the Treaty of Rome, the founding treaty of the modern EU. The meaning of this objective has been contested but its practice has not meant and will probably never mean the creation of some centralised unitary polity much feared by its opponents nor some federal body envisaged by its most ardent supporters, but something much less precise, an elusive and never to be achieved end point but a direction. Ever looser union, as imprecise as ever closer union, might not be the aim of devolution but may prove to be its consequence.

Bibliography and sources

Files in the following archives were consulted:
Public Record Office of Northern Ireland (PRONI) Papers
The National Archives (TNA) Papers
National Archives of Scotland (NAS) Papers
Dicey Papers, Glasgow University Library

In addition, various newspapers, publications of political parties, pressure groups and official papers were consulted.

Adkins, Sir W. Ryland (1920), 'Home Rule for England', *The Contemporary Review*, March, pp. 326–331.

Alexander, Alan (1982), *Local Government in Britain since Reorganisation*, London, George Allen & Unwin.

Alford, Robert (1963), *Party and Society: The Anglo-American Democracies*, Chicago, Rand McNally & Company.

Allison, Graham (1971), *Essence of Decision: Explaining the Cuban Missile Crisis*, Boston, MA, Little, Brown and Company.

Ambrosini, Gaspare (1946), *Autonomia Regionale e Federalismo*, Rome, Tip. Dell'Universita.

Anderson, C., A. Blais, T. Donovan and L. Listhaug (2005), *Losers' Consent: Elections and Democratic Legitimacy*, Oxford, Oxford University Press.

Anderson, Perry (1994), 'The Invention of the Region, 1945–90', *EUI Working Papers European Forum*, EUF no. 94/2, Florence, European University Institute.

Andrews, Leighton (1999), *Wales Says Yes: The Inside Story of the Yes for Wales Referendum Campaign*, Bridgend, Seren.

Anthony, Gordon and John Morison (2005), 'Here, There, and (Maybe) Here Again: The Story of Law Making for Post-1998 Northern Ireland', in Robert Hazell and Richard Rawlings (eds), *Devolution, Law Making and the Constitution*, Exeter, Imprint Academic.

Arbuthnott Commission (2006), *Putting Citizens First: Boundaries, Voting and representation in Scotland*, Commission on Boundary

Differences and Voting Systems, Edinburgh, the Stationery Office.

Arthur, W. Brian (2000), *Increasing Returns and Path Dependence in the Economy*, Ann Arbor, University of Michigan Press.

Ashby, Edgar (1929), 'Regional Government: or The Next Step In Public Administration', *Public Administration*, vol. 7, pp. 365–375.

Bagehot, Walter (1981 [1867]), *The English Constitution*, London, Fontana.

Baldwin, Stanley (1926), *On England*, London, Philip Allan & Co. Ltd.

Balfour (1954), *Report of the Royal Commission on Scottish Affairs* London, HMSO, Cmnd. 9212.

Balls, Ed (2000), 'Britain's New Regional Policy', in E. Balls and J. Healet (eds), *Towards a New Regional Policy: Delivering Growth and Full Employment*, London, Smith Institute.

Balsom, Denis (1985), 'The Three-Wales model', in John Osmond (ed.), *The National Question Again*, Llandysul, Gomer.

Barnett, Joel (1982), *Inside the Treasury*, London, André Deutsch.

Barnett, Lord (1985), Letter to the author, 8 February 1985.

Barnett, Lord (1997), 'Evidence to Treasury Select Committee', in *Treasury Committee, The Barnett Formula*, Second Report of Session 1997–98, HC 341 of Session 1997–98, London, Stationery Office, pp. 1–7.

Barton, Brian (1996), 'The Impact of World War II on Northern Ireland and Belfast–London Relations', in Peter Catterall and Sean McDougall (eds), *The Northern Ireland Question in British Politics*, Basingstoke, Macmillan.

Beetham, David (1991), *The Legitimation of Power*, Basingstoke, Palgrave Macmillan.

Berriedale Keith, Arthur (1940), *The Constitution of England from Queen Victoria to George VI*, London, Macmillan.

Bew, Paul, Peter Gibbon and Henry Patterson (1995), *Northern Ireland, 1921–1994: Political Forces and Social Classes*, London, Serif.

Billig, Michael (1995), *Banal Nationalism*, London, Sage.

Birrell, Derek and Murie, Alan (1980), *Policy and Government in Northern Ireland: Lessons of Devolution*, Dublin, Gill and Macmillan.

Black, Edwin and Alan Cairns (1966), 'A Different Perspective on Canadian Federalism', *Canadian Public Administration*, vol. 9, pp. 27–44.

Bloomfield, Kenneth (1994), *Stormont in Crisis: A Memoir*, Belfast, Blackstaff Press.

Bloomfield, Kenneth (2007), *A Tragedy of Errors: The Government and Misgovernment of Northern Ireland*, Liverpool, Liverpool University Press.

Bogaards, Matthhijs (2000), 'The Uneasy Relationship between Empirical and Normative Types of Consociational Theory', *Journal of Theoretical Politics*, vol. 12, pp. 395–423.

Bogdanor, Vernon (1979), *Devolution*, Oxford, Oxford University Press.

Bogdanor, Vernon (2004), 'Our New Constitution', *Law Quarterly Review*, vol. 120, pp. 242–262.

Borthwick, R.L. (1978), 'When The Short Cut May Be A Blind Alley: The Standing Committee on Regional Affairs', *Parliamentary Affairs*, vol. 31, pp. 201–209.

Bowman, John (1989), *De Valera and the Ulster Question, 1917–1973*, Oxford, Oxford University Press.

Bradbury, Jonathan (1997), 'Conservative Governments, Scotland and Wales: A Perspective on Territorial Management', in J. Bradbury and J. Mawson (eds), *British Regionalism and Devolution*, London, Jessica Kingsley Publishers.

Bradbury, Jonathan and James Mitchell (2007), 'The Constituency Work of Members of the Scottish Parliament and Assembly for Wales', *Regional and Federal Studies*, vol. 17, pp. 117–145.

Bradley, A.W. and D.J. Christie (1979), *The Scotland Act, 1978*, Edinburgh, W. Green and Son/Sweet and Maxwell.

Bradley, John (1996), *An Island Economy: Exploring Long-term Economic and Social Consequences of Peace and Reconciliation Consultancy Studies No. 4*, Dublin, Dublin Castle.

Brivati, Brian (1997), *Hugh Gaitskell*, London, Richard Cohen Books.

Brown, Gordon (2001), 'Enterprise and the regions', speech to UMIST, 29 January. www.hm-treasury.gov.uk/Newsroom_and_Speeches/Press/2001/press_02_01.cfm (accessed 2 February 2001).

Brown, Gordon (2004), 'Foreword' to Treasury, *Microeconomic Reform in Britain: Delivering Opportunities for All*, Houndmills, Palgrave.

Brown, Gordon and Henry Drucker (1980), *The Politics of Nationalism and Devolution*, London, Longman.

Buckland, Patrick (1979), *The Factory of Grievances: Devolved Government in Northern Ireland, 1921–39*, Dublin, Gill and Macmillan.

Bulpitt, Jim (1983), *Territory and Power in the United Kingdom*, Manchester, Manchester University Press.

Bunbury, Sir Henry (1957), *Lloyd George's Ambulance Wagon: Being the Memoirs of William J. Braithwaite, 1911–12*, London, Methuen and Co.

Burk, Kathleen (ed.) (1982), *War and the State: The Transformation of British Government, 1914–1919*, London, Routledge.

Butler, David and Dennis Kavanagh (1975), *The British General Election of October 1974*, London, Macmillan.

Butt Philip, Alan (1975), *The Welsh Question: Nationalism in Welsh Politics, 1945–1970*, Cardiff, University of Wales Press.

Cabinet Office (1999), *Modernising Government*, London, HMSO.

Callaghan, James (1973), *A House Divided: The Dilemma of Northern Ireland*, London, Collins.

Callaghan, James (1987), *Time and Chance*, London, Collins.

Calvert, Harry (1968), *Constitutional Law in Northern Ireland: A Study in Regional Government*, London and Belfast, Stevens & Sons Ltd and Northern Ireland Legal Quarterly Inc.

Cameron, Ewen (1996), 'The Scottish Highlands: From Congested District to Objective One', in T.M. Devine and R.J. Finlay (eds), *Scotland in the 20th Century*, Edinburgh, Edinburgh University Press.

Cameron, Lord (Chairman) (1969), *Disturbances in Northern Ireland: Report Commissioned by the Governor of Northern Ireland*, Belfast, HMSO, Cmd. 532.

Campaign for a Scottish Assembly (1988), *A Claim of Right for Scotland*, Edinburgh, CSA.

Campbell, James (1995), 'The United Kingdom of England: The Anglo-Saxon Achievement', in Alexander Grant and Keith J. Stringer (eds), *Uniting the Kingdom? The Making of British History*, London, Routledge.

Carmichael, Paul (2002), 'The Northern Ireland Civil Service: Characteristics and Trends Since 1970', *Public Administration*, vol. 80, pp. 23–49.

Castle, Barbara (1980), *The Castle Diaries, 1974–1976*, London, Weidenfeld and Nicolson.

Catterall, Peter (2003), *The MacMillan Diaries: The Cabinet Years, 1950–1957*, Basingstoke, Macmillan.

Cawson, A. (1992), 'Interests, Groups and Public Policy-Making: The Case of the European Consumer Electronics Industry', in J. Greenwood, J.R. Grote, and K. Ronit (eds) *Organized Interests and the European Community*, London, Sage.

Chappell, Edgar L. (1943), *The Government of Wales*, London, Foyle's Welsh Co., Ltd.

Chester, Sir Norman (1968), *The Organisation of Central Government, 1914–64*, London, Allen & Unwin.

Chester, Sir Norman (1975), *The Nationalization of British Industry, 1954–51*, London, HMSO.

Clarke, John (1948), *The Local Government of the United Kingdom*, fourteenth edition, London, Sir Isaac Pitman & Sons, Ltd.

Cochrane, Feargal (1997), *Unionist Politics and the Politics of Unionism Since the Anglo-Irish Agreement*, Cork, Cork University Press.

Collier, Ruth Berins and David Collier (2002), *Shaping the Political Arena: Critical Junctures, the Labour Movement, and Regime Dynamics in Latin America*, Princeton, NJ, Princeton University Press.

Constitution Unit (1996), *An Assembly for Wales*, London, The Constitution Unit.

Constitutional Convention (1989), *Towards a Scottish Parliament*, Edinburgh, COSLA.

Consultative Steering Group (1998), *Shaping Scotland's Parliament*, Edinburgh, Scottish Office.

Cornford, James (1996), 'Constitutional Reform in the UK', in Stephen Tindale (ed.), *The State and the Nations*, London, IPPR.

Cosgrove, Richard (1980), *The Rule of Law: Albert Venn Dicey, Victorian Jurist*, London, Macmillan.

Council of Wales and Monmouthshire (1957), *Third Memorandum on its activities*, London, HMSO, Cmnd. 53.

Council of Wales and Monmouthshire (1959), *Fourth Memorandum Government Administration in Wales*, London, HMSO, Cmnd. 631.

Coupland, Sir Reginald (1954), *Welsh and Scottish Nationalism: A Study*, London, Collins.

Crick, Bernard (1968), 'Sovereignty', in *International Encyclopedia of Social Sciences*, vol. 15.

Crossman Richard (1975), *The Diaries of a Cabinet Minister: vol. I Minister of Housing, 1964–66*, London, Hamish Hamilton and Jonathan Cape.

Crossman, Richard (1976), *The Diaries of a Cabinet Minister: vol. II, Lord President of the Council and Leader of the House of Commons, 1966–68*, London, Hamish Hamilton and Jonathan Cape.

Crowther-Hunt, Lord and A.T. Peacock (1973), *Royal Commission on the Constitution, vol. II: Memorandum of Dissent*, London, HMSO, Cmnd. 5460–I.

Culls, R. and P. Dodd (eds) (1986), *Englishness: Politics and Culture, 1880–1920*, Beckenham, Croom Helm.

Cunningham, George (1989), 'Burns Night massacre', *The Spectator*, 18 January.

Curtice, John (2006), 'What the People Say – If Anything', in Robert Hazell (ed.), *The English Question*, Manchester, Manchester University Press.

D'Arcy, M. and R. MacLean (2000), *Nightmare: The Race to Become London's Mayor*, London, Pimlico.

Davies, John (2007), *A History of Wales*, London, Penguin.

Davies, Norman (1996), *Europe: A History*, Oxford, Oxford University Press.

Davies, Ron (1999), *Devolution – A Process not an Event*, Cardiff, Institute of Welsh Affairs.

Davis, J.H. (1988), *Reforming London: The London Government Problem, 1855–1900*, Oxford, Clarendon Press.

Day, John Percival (1918), *Public Administration in the Highlands and Islands of Scotland*, London, University of London Press.

Deacon, Russell (2002), *The Governance of Wales: The Welsh Office and the Policy Process, 1964–99*, Cardiff, Welsh Academic Press.

Denver, D., J. Mitchell, C. Pattie and H. Bochel (2000), *Scotland Decides: The Devolution Issue and the 1997 Referendum*, London, Frank Cass.

DETR (1997), *Building Partnerships for Prosperity*, London, HMSO, CM. 3814.

Devolution Brief (2005), *Why the North East said 'No': the 2004 referendum on an Elected Regional Assembly*, no. 19, February.

Dicey, A.V. (1881), 'Two Acts of Union: A Contrast', *Fortnightly Review*, vol. 36, pp. 168–178.

Dicey, A.V. (1886), *England's Case Against Home Rule*, London, John Murray.

Dicey, A.V. (1887), *Letters on Unionist Delusions*, London, Macmillan.

Dicey, A.V. (1901), 'The Due Representation of England', *National Review*, vol. 38, November, pp. 359–382.

Dicey, A.V. (1923), *Introduction to the Study of the Law of the Constitution*, eighth edition, London, Macmillan and Co.

Dicey, A.V. (1973 [1886]), *England's Case Against Home Rule*, Richmond, Richmond Publishing Company edition.

Dicey, A.V. and R.S. Rait, (1920), *Thoughts on the Union Between England and Scotland*, London, Macmillan and Co.

Dixon, Paul (2001), 'British Policy towards Northern Ireland 1969–2000: Continuity, Tactical Adjustment and Consistent "Inconsistencies"', *British Journal of Politics and International Relations*, vol. 3, pp. 340–368.

Dixon, Paul (2005), 'Why the Good Friday Agreement in Northern Ireland is not Consociational', *Political Quarterly*, vol. 76, pp. 357–367.

Donoughue, Bernard (2005), *Downing Street Diary: With Harold Wilson in No. 10*, London, Jonathan Cape.

Donoughue, Bernard and George Jones (2001), *Herbert Morrison: Portrait of a Politician*, London, Weidenfeld and Nicolson.

Drower, G.M.F. (1984), *Neil Kinnock: The Path to Leadership*, London, Weidenfeld and Nicolson.

Drucker, Henry (n.d.), *Breakaway: the Scottish Labour Party*, Edinburgh, EUSPB.

Drucker, Henry and Gordon Brown (1980), *The Politics of Nationalism and Devolution*, London, Longman.

Duchacek, Ivo D. (1986), *The Territorial Dimension of Politics: Within, Among, and Across Nations*, Boulder, CO, Westview Press.

Edwards, Andrew and Duncan Tanner (2006), 'Defining or Dividing the Nation? Opinion Polls, Welsh Identity and Devolution, 1966–1979', *Contemporary Wales*, vol. 18, pp. 54–71.

Edwards, David (2005), 'Thinking about Constitutions', European Essay no. 34, London, The Federal Trust.

Elliot, Sydney and W.D. Flackes (1999), *Northern Ireland: A Political Directory 1968–1999*, fifth edition, Belfast, The Blackstaff Press.

English, Richard (2003), *Armed Struggle: A History of the IRA*, London, Pan Macmillan.

Evans, Geoffrey and Dafydd Trystan (1999), 'Why was 1997 Different? A Comparative Analysis of Voting behaviour in the 1979 and 1997 Welsh Referendums', in Bridget Taylor and Katarina Thomson (eds), *Scotland and Wales: Nations Again?*, Cardiff, University of Wales Press.

Evans, Gwynfor (1996), *For The Sake of Wales: The Memoirs of Gwynfor Evans*, Cardiff, Welsh Academic Press.

Evans, John Gilbert (2006), *Devolution in Wales: Claims and Responses, 1937–1979*, Cardiff, University of Wales Press.

Falconer, Lord (2006), Speech to Final Conference of the ESRC Devolution and Constitutional Change Programme, Queen Elizabeth II Conference Centre, London, 10 March: www.dca.gov.uk/speeches /2006/sp060310.htm (accessed 10 March 2006).

Farrell, Michael (1976), *Northern Ireland: The Orange State*, London, Pluto Press.

Faulkner, Brian (1974), *Memoirs of a Statesman*, London, Weidenfeld and Nicolson.

Ferguson, William (1990), *Scotland: 1689 to the Present*, Edinburgh: Mercat Press.

Fielding, Steve (2000), 'A New Politics?', in P. Dunleavy, A. Gamble, I. Holliday and G. Peele, *Developments in British Politics 6*, Basingstoke, Palgrave.

Flynn, Norman, Steve Leach and Carol Vielba (1985), *Abolition or Reform?: The GLC and the Metropolitan County Councils*, London, George Allen & Unwin.

Follis, Bryan A. (1995), *A State Under Siege: The Establishment of Northern Ireland, 1920–1925*, Oxford, Clarendon Press.

Foulkes, David (1983), 'An Analysis of the Wales Act 1978', in D. Foulkes, J. Barry Jones and R.A. Wilford (eds), *The Welsh Veto: The Wales Act 1978 & The Referendum*, Cardiff, University of Wales Press.

Garnett, Mark and Ian Aitken (2003), *Splendid! Splendid!: The Authorized Biography of Willie Whitelaw*, London, Pimlico.

Gay, Oonagh and James Mitchell (2007), 'Stormont, Westminster and Whitehall', in P. Carmichael, C. Knox and R. Osborne (eds), *Devolution and Constitutional Change in Northern Ireland*, Manchester, Manchester University Press.

Gibbon, Gwilym (1938), 'Regional Government', *Public Administration*, vol. 16, pp. 415–419.

Gibson, Edward Leon (1968), *A Study of the Council for Wales and Monmouthshire, 1948–1966*, Unpublished LLB thesis, University College of Wales, Aberystwyth.

Godson, Dean (2004), *Himself Alone: David Trimble and the Ordeal of Unionism*, London, HaperCollins.

Gowan, Ivor (1965), *Government in Wales*, Inaugural Lecture as Professor of Political Science, University College, Wales, December.

Greer, Scott (2003), 'Policy Divergence: Will It Change Something in Greenock?', in Robert Hazell (ed.), *The State and the Nations: The Third Year of Devolution in the United Kingdom*, Exeter, Imprint Academic.

Griffith, J.A.G. (1979), 'The Political Constitution', *Modern Law Review*, vol. 42, pp. 1–21.

Griffiths, Dylan (1996), *Thatcherism and Territorial Politics: A Welsh Case Study*, Aldershot, Avebury.

Griffiths, James (1969), *Pages From Memory*, London, J.M. Dent & Sons Ltd.

Grodzins, Morton (1966), *The American System: A New View of Government in the United States*, Chicago, Rand McNally.

Guthrie, R. and I. MacLean (1978), 'Another part of the periphery: reactions to devolution in an English Development Area', *Parliamentary Affairs*, vol. 31, pp. 190–200.

Hacker, Jacob (1998), 'The Historical Logic of National Health Insurance: Structure and Sequence in the Development of British, Canadian, and US Medical Policy', *Studies in American Political Development*, vol. 12, pp. 57–130.

Hadfield, Brigid (1989), *The Constitution of Northern Ireland*, Belfast, SLS.

Hadfield, Brigid (ed.) (1992), *Northern Ireland: Politics and the Constitution*, Buckingham, Open University.

Hailsham, Lord (1990), *A Sparrow's Flight: Memoirs*, London, Collins.

Halkier, Henrik (2006), *Institutions, Discourse and Regional Development: The Scottish Development Agency and the Politics of Regional Policy*, Brussels, Peter Lang.

Hall, Peter (1986), *Governing the Economy: The Politics of State Intervention in Britain and France*, Oxford, Oxford University Press.

Hall, Peter (1989), *The Power of Economic Ideas*, Princeton, Princeton University Press.

Hall, Peter (1992), 'The Movement from Keynesianism to Monetraism: an Institutional Analysis and British Economic Policy in the 1970s', in S. Steinmo, K. Thelen and F. Longstreth (eds), *Structuring Politics: Historical Institutionalism in Comparative Politics*, Cambridge, Cambridge University Press.

Hall, Sir Robert (chairman) (1962), *Report of the Joint Working Party on the Economy of Northern Ireland*, Belfast, HMSO, Cmnd. 446.

Hammond, J.L. (1938), *Gladstone and the Irish Nation*, London, Longmans, Green and Co.

Hanham, H.J. (1965), 'The Creation of the Scottish Office, 1881–87', *Juridical Review*, 1965, pp. 205–244.

Hansard (1991), *The Report of the Hansard Commission on Election Campaigns*, London, Hansard Society.

Harrison, H. (1939), *Ulster and the British Empire*, London, Robert Hale.

Harvie, Christopher (1994), *Scotland and Nationalism*, London, Routledge.

Hayes, Maurice (1995), *Minority Verdict: Experiences of a Catholic Public Servant*, Belfast, The Blackstaff Press.

Hazell, Robert (2006), 'Introduction: What is the English Question?', in Robert Hazell (ed.), *The English Question*, Manchester, Manchester University Press.

Hazell, Robert (2006), 'What Are The Answers To The English Question?', in Robert Hazell (ed.), *The English Question*, Manchester, Manchester University Press.

Heald, David (1980), *Territorial Equity and Public Finances: Concepts and Confusion*, Studies in Public Policy no. 75, Glasgow, University of Strathclyde.

Heasman, D.J. (1962), 'The Ministerial Hierarchy', *Parliamentary Affairs*, vol. 15, pp. 307–330.

Heath, Edward (1998), *The Course of My Life*, London, Hodder and Stoughton.

Heclo, Hugh and Aaron Wildavsky (1981), *The Private Government of Public Money*, Basingstoke, Macmillan.

Heffer, Simon (1999), *Nor Shall My Sword*, London, Weidenfeld and Nicolson.

Hennessy, Peter (1996), *The Hidden Wiring: Unearthing the British Constitution*, London, Indigo.

Hennessy, Thomas (1997), *A History of Northern Ireland*, 1920–1996, Basingstoke, Macmillan.

Herbert, Sir Edwin (1960), *Report of the Royal Commission on Local Government in Greater London, 1957–1960*, London, HMSO, Cmnd. 1164.

Heuston, R.F.V. (1964), *Essays in Constitutional Law*, second edition, London, Stevens & Sons.

Hirschman, Albert (1970), *Exit, Voice, and Loyalty: Responses to Decline in Firms, Organizations, and States*, Cambridge, MA: Harvard University Press.

HMSO (1937a), Report of the Royal Commission to Investigate the Conditions of Local Government on Tyneside, *Local Government in the Tyneside Area*, Cmd. 5402.

HMSO (1937b), Report of the Committee on Scottish Administration (Gilmour), Cmd. 5563.

HMSO (1948), White Paper on Scottish Affairs.

HMSO (1969), Northern Ireland: Text of a Communiqué and Declaration issued after a meeting held at 10 Downing Street on 19 August 1969, Cmnd. 4154.

HMSO (1975), *Our Changing Democracy*.

HMSO (1976), *Devolution: The English Dimension (A Consultative Document).*

HMSO (1985), Agreement Between the Government of the United Kingdom of Great Britain and Northern Ireland and the Government of the Republic of Ireland, Cmnd. 9690.

Hogg, Quintin (1978), *The Dilemma of Democracy: Diagnosis and Prescription*, London, Collins.

Hogwood, Brian (1994), 'Whatever Happened to Regional Government?: Developments in Regional Administration in Britain since 1979', *Strathclyde Papers on Government and Politics*, Glasgow, Dept. of Government, University of Strathclyde, no. 97.

Hogwood, Brian (1995), 'Regional Administration in Britain since 1979: Trends and Explanations', *Regional and Federal Studies*, vol. 5, pp. 267–91.

Hogwood, Brian and Peter Lindley (1980), 'Which English Regions? An Analysis of Regional Boundaries used by Government', *Studies in Public Policy* no. 50, Glasgow, Strathclyde University.

Home, Sir Alec Douglas (1976), *The Way the Wind Blows*, London, Collins.

Hood, Christopher (1991), 'Concepts of Control over Public Bureaucracies: "Control" and "Interpolable Balance"', in Franz-Xaver Kauffmann (ed.), *The Public Sector*, New York, Walter de Gruyter.

House of Commons (2005), *London Underground Public Private Partnerships, 17th Report of Public Accounts Committee 2004–05*, HC 446, 9 March.

House of Lords (2001), *Reviewing the Constitution: Terms of Reference and Methods of Working*, First Report of the Select Committee on the Constitution, HL Paper 11, Session 2001–02.

Hughes-Parry, Sir David (Chairman) (1965), *Report of the Committee on the Legal Status of the Welsh Language*, London, HMSO, Cmnd. 2785.

Hume, Ian (1981), 'The Welsh Experience', in John Bochel, David Denver and Allan Macartney (eds), *The Referendum Experience, Scotland 1979*, Aberdeen, Aberdeen University Press.

Hutchison, I.G.C. (2001), *Scottish Politics in the Twentieth Century*, Basingstoke, Palgrave.

Irvine of Lairg, Lord (1998), *Government's Programme of Constitutional Reform*, London, Constitution Unit.

Jackson, Alvin (1999), *Ireland, 1798–1998*, Oxford, Blackwell.

Jalland, Patricia (1979), 'United Kingdom Devolution 1910–14: Political Panacea or Tactical Diversion?', *English Historical Review*, no. 73, pp. 757–785.

James, Mari and Peter Lindley (1983), 'The Parliamentary Passage of the Wales Act 1978', in D. Foulkes, J. Barry Jones and R.A. Wilford (eds), *The Welsh Veto: The Wales Act 1978 & The Referendum*, Cardiff,

University of Wales Press.

Jenkins, Brian (2001), 'The Chief Secretary', in D. George Boyce and Alan O'Day (eds), *Defenders of the Union: A survey of British and Irish unionism since 1801*, London, Routledge.

Johnson, Nevil (2000), 'Then and Now: the British Constitution', *Political Studies*, vol. 48, pp. 118–131.

Johnson, Nevil (2004), *Reshaping the British Constitution*, Basingstoke, Palgrave Macmillan.

Jones, Edwin (1998), *The English Nation*, Stroud, Sutton Publishing.

Jones, G.H., B.C. Smith and H.V. Wiseman (1967), 'Regionalism and Parliament', *Political Studies*, vol. 38, pp. 403–410.

Jones, J. Barry and Michael Keating (1979), 'The British Labour Party as a Centralising Force', *Studies in Public Policy*, no. 32, Glasgow, University of Strathclyde.

Jones, J. Barry and R.A. Wilford (1983), 'The Referendum Campaign: 8 February – 1 March 1979', in D. Foulkes, J. Barry Jones and R.A. Wilford (eds), *The Welsh Veto: The Wales Act 1978 & The Referendum*, Cardiff, University of Wales Press.

Jones, Peter (1994), 'Smith pledge over Scottish Parliament', *Scotsman*, 12 March.

Jones, R. Merfyn and Ioan Rhys Jones (2000), 'Labour and the Nation', in D. Tanner, C. Williams and D. Hopkin (eds), *The Labour Party in Wales, 1900–2000*, Cardiff, University of Wales Press.

Jones, Richard Wyn and Dafydd Trystan (1999), 'The 1997 Welsh Referendum Vote', in Bridget Taylor and Katarina Thomson (eds), *Scotland and Wales: Nations Again?*, Cardiff, University of Wales Press.

Jones, Timothy and Jane Williams (2005), 'The Legislative Future of Wales', *The Modern Law Review*, vol. 68, pp. 624–653.

Jordan, Grant (1979), 'The Committee Stage of the Scotland and Wales Bill (1976–77), *Waverley Papers*, Edinburgh, Edinburgh University.

Judge, David (2005), *Political Institutions in the United Kingdom*, Oxford, Oxford University Press.

Keating, Michael (1988), *State and Regional Nationalism*, Hemel Hempstead, Wheatsheaf.

Keating, Michael (2005), *The Government of Scotland: Public Policy Making After Devolution*, Edinburgh, Edinburgh University Press.

Keating, Michael and David Bleiman (1979), *Labour and Scottish Nationalism*, London, Macmillan.

Kellas, James (1973), *The Scottish Political System*, Cambridge, Cambridge University Press.

Kendle, John (1975), *The Round Table Movement and Imperial Union*, Toronto, University of Toronto Press.

Kendle, John (1989), *Ireland and the Federal Solution: The Debate Over the United Kingdom Constitution, 1870–1921*, Kingston and

Montreal, McGill-Queen's University Press.

Kenny, Anthony (1986), *The Road to Hillsborough: The Shaping of the Anglo-Irish Agreement*, Oxford, Pergamon.

Kiernan, Victor (1993), 'The British Isles: Celt and Saxon', in Mikuláš Teich and Roy Porter (eds), *The National Question in Europe in Historical Context*, Cambridge, Cambridge University Press.

Kilbrandon, Lord (1973), *Report of the Royal Commission on the Constitution*, London, HMSO, Cmnd. 5460.

King, Anthony (2001), *Does the United Kingdom Still Have a Constitution?*, London, Sweet & Maxwell.

Labour Party (1962), *Signposts to the New Wales*, London, Labour Party.

Labour Party (1974), *Britain Will Win With Labour*, London, Labour Party.

Labour Party (1992), *It's Time to Get Britain Working Again*, London, Labour Party.

Labour Party (1995), *A Parliament for Scotland: Labour's Plan*, Glasgow, Labour Party.

Labour Party (1996), *A New Voice for England*, London, Labour Party.

Labour Party (1997), *Britain Will Be Better With New Labour*, London, Labour Party.

Labour Party in Wales (1970), *Memorandum Submitted by the Labour Party in Wales to the Kilbrandon Commission*, Minutes of Evidence V, 26–27 June, London, HMSO.

Lang, Ian (2002), *Blue Remembered Years*, London, Politicos.

Laski, Harold (1948), *The Grammar of Politics*, fifth edition, London, Allen & Unwin.

Lawrence, R.J. (1965), *The Government of Northern Ireland: Public Finance and Public Services, 1921–1964*, Oxford, Clarendon Press.

Lee, J.J. (1990), *Ireland: 1912–1985*, Cambridge, Cambridge University Press.

Lessing, Doris (1994), *Prisons we Choose to Live Inside*, London, Flamingo.

Levi, Margaret (1997), 'A Model, a Method, and a Map: Rational Choice in Comparative and Historical Analysis', in Mark I. Lichbach and Alan S. Zuckerman (eds), *Comparative Politics: Rationality, Culture and Structure*, Cambridge, Cambridge University Press.

Lijphart, Arend (1977), *Democracy in Plural Societies*, New Haven, CT, Yale University Press.

Lijphart, Arend (1996), 'The Framework Documents on Northern Ireland and the Theory of Power Sharing', *Government and Opposition*, vol. 31, pp. 267–275.

Lipset, S.M. and S. Rokkan (1967), 'Cleavage Structures, Party Systems, and Voter Alignments: An Introduction' in S.M. Lipset and S. Rokkan (eds), *Party Systems and Voter Alignments: Cross-National Perspec-*

tives, New York, Free Press.

Lipsky, Martin (1980), *Street-Level Bureaucrats*, New York, Russell Sage.

Lodge, Guy and James Mitchell (2006), 'Whitehall and the Government of England', in Robert Hazell (ed.), *The English Question*, Manchester, Manchester University Press.

Low, Sidney (1904), *The Governance of England*, London, T. Fisher Unwin.

Lowther, Speaker T.W. (1920), *Conference on Devolution: Letter from Mr Speaker to the Prime Minister*, London, HMSO, Cmd. 692.

MacCormick, James and Wendy Alexander (1996), 'Firm Foundations – Securing the Scottish Parliament', in Stephen Tindale (ed.), *The State and the Nations: The Politics of* devolution, London, IPPR.

MacCormick, Neil (1978), 'Does the United Kingdom have a Constitution? Reflections on MacCormick v. Lord Advocate', *Northern Ireland Legal Quarterly*, vol. 29, pp. 1–20.

MacCormick, Neil (1999), *Questioning Sovereignty*, Oxford, Oxford University Press.

MacDonald, Henry (2000), *Trimble*, London, Bloomsbury.

MacDonald, Mary and Adam Redpath (1979), 'The Scottish Office, 1954–79', in *Scottish Government Yearbook, 1979*, Edinburgh, Paul Harris.

Mackenzie, W.J.M. and B. Chapman (1951), 'Federalism and Regionalism: A Note on the Italian Constitution of 1948', *The Modern Law Review*, vol. 14, pp. 182–194.

Mackenzie, W.J.M. and J.W. Grove (1957), *Central Administration in Britain*, London, Longmans.

Mackintosh, J.P. (1968), *The Devolution of Power: Local Democracy, Regionalism and Nationalism*, Harmondsworth, Penguin.

Mackintosh, John (1975), 'Obstacle to an Effective Assembly', *Scotsman*, 8 December.

Mackintosh, John (1976), 'The Power of the Secretary of State', *New Edinburgh Review*, no. 31, pp. 9–16.

MacPherson, Andrew and Charles Raab (1988), *Governing Education: A Sociology of Policy since 1945*, Edinburgh, Edinburgh University Press.

Mahoney, James (2000), 'Path dependence in historical sociology', *Theory and Society*, vol. 29, pp. 507–548.

Mahoney, James (2001), *The Legacies of Liberalism: Path Dependence and Political Regimes in Central America*, London, Johns Hopkins Press.

Mahoney, James and Dietrich Rueschemeyer (2003), 'Comparative Historical Analysis', in J. Mahoney and D. Rueschemeyer (eds), *Comparative Historical Analysis in the Social Sciences*, Cambridge, Cambridge University Press.

Maitland, F.W. (1900), 'Introduction', in Otto Friedrich von Gierke, *Polit-*

ical Thought of the Middle Ages, Cambridge, Cambridge University Press.

Major, John (1996), *Speech to Conservative Party Conference*, October.

Mansergh, Nicholas (1936), *The Government of Northern Ireland*, London, George Allen & Unwin.

Mansergh, Nicholas (1991), *The Unresolved Question: the Anglo-Irish Settlement and its Undoing, 1912–72*, London, Yale University Press.

March, James G. and Johan P. Olsen (1989), *Rediscovering Institutions: The Organisational Basis of Politics*, New York, Free Press.

Marshall, Geoffrey (1984), *Constitutional Conventions*, Oxford, Clarendon Press.

Marshall, Geoffrey (2002), 'The Constitution: Its Theory and Interpretation', in Vernon Bogdanor (ed.), *The British Constitution in the Twentieth Century*, Oxford, Oxford University Press/The British Academy.

Marshall, T.H. (1992), *Citizenship and Social Class*, London, Pluto Press.

Martin, R. and Tyler, P. (1991), 'The Regional Legacy of the Thatcher Years', *Land Economy Discussion Paper 36*, Cambridge, Department of Land Economy, University of Cambridge.

Mason, Roy (1999), *Paying the Price*, London, Robert Hale.

Mawson, John and Ken Spencer (1997), 'The Origins and Operation of the Government Offices for the Regions', in J. Bradbury and J. Mawson (eds), *British Regionalism and Devolution*, London, Jessica Kingsley Publishers.

May, John (1973), 'Opinion Structure of Political Parties: The Special Law of Curvilinear Disparity', *Political Studies*, vol. 21, pp. 135–151.

McAllister, Laura (1998), 'The Perils of Community as a Construct for the Political Ideology of Welsh Nationalism', *Government and Opposition*, vol. 33, pp. 497–517.

McAllister, Laura (2005), 'Proving the Potential of Independent Commissions: A Critical Review of the Richard Commission on the Powers and Electoral Arrangements of the National Assembly for Wales', *Pubic Management*, vol. 83, pp. 493–512.

McCrone, Gavin (1976), *Regional Policy in Britain*, fifth impression, London, George Allen & Unwin.

McCrone, Gavin (1985), 'The Role of Government', in Richard Saville (ed.), *The Economic Development of Modern Scotland, 1950–1980*, Edinburgh, Edinburgh University Press.

McDonald, J.F. (1979), 'The Lack of Political Identity in English Regions: Evidence from MPs', *Studies in Public Policy*, no. 33, Glasgow, Strathclyde University.

McGarry, John and Brendan O'Leary (1995), *Explaining Northern Ireland*, Oxford, Blackwell.

McGarry, John and Brendan, O'Leary (2006a), 'Consociational Theory,

Northern Ireland's Conflict, and its Agreement. Part 1. What Consociationalists can learn from Northern Ireland', *Government and Opposition*, vol. 41, pp. 43–63.

McGarry, John and Brendan O'Leary (2006b), 'Consociational Theory, Northern Ireland's Conflict, and its Agreement. Part 2. What Critics of Consociation can Learn from Northern Ireland', *Government and Opposition*, vol. 41, pp. 249–277.

McGilvray, James (1975), 'Sowing the seeds of conflict', *Scotsman*, 10 December.

McIvor, Basil (1998), *Hope Deferred: Experiences of an Irish Unionist*, Belfast, The Blackstaff Press.

McLean, Bob (1991), *Labour and Scottish Home Rule*, Part 2, Broxburn, Scottish Labour Action.

McLean, Bob (2005), *Getting It Together*, Edinburgh, Luath Press Limited.

McLean, Iain (1995), 'Are Scotland and Wales Over-represented in the House of Commons?', *Political Quarterly*, vol. 66, pp. 250–268.

McLean, Iain and Alistair McMillan (2005), *State of the Union*, Oxford, Oxford University Press.

McLeish, Henry (2004), *Scotland First: Truth and Consequences*, Edinburgh, Mainstream.

Mény, Yves and Vincent Wright (1985), 'General Introduction', in Y. Mény and V. Wright (eds), *Centre-Periphery Relations In Western Europe*, London, George Allen & Unwin.

Midwinter, A., M. Keating and J. Mitchell (1991), *Politics and Public Policy in Scotland*, Basingstoke, Macmillan.

Millan, Bruce (Chair) (1996), *Renewing the Regions: Report of the Regional Policy Commission*, Sheffield, Sheffield Hallam University.

Miller, Bill, Jack Brand and Maggie Jordan (1981), 'Government Without a Mandate: its Causes and Consequences for the Conservative Party in Scotland', *Political Quarterly*, vol. 52, pp. 203–213.

Milne, Sir David (1957), *The Scottish Office And Other Scottish Government Departments*, London, George Allen & Unwin.

Milosz, Ceslaw (1980), *Nobel Lecture*, New York, Farrar Straus Giroux.

Mitchell, James (1990), *Conservatives and the Union*, Edinburgh, Edinburgh University Press.

Mitchell, James (1992), 'Shibboleths and Slogans: Sovereignty, Subsidiarity and Constitutional Debate', in *Scottish Government Yearbook 1992*, Edinburgh, Unit for the Study of Government in Scotland.

Mitchell, James (1996), *Strategies for Self-Government*, Edinburgh, Polygon.

Mitchell, James (1997), 'Conceptual Lenses and Territorial Government in Britain' in Ulrike Jordan and Wolfram Kaiser (eds), *Political Reform in Britain, 1886–1996: Themes, Ideas, Policies*, Bochum, Universitätsverlag Dr. Brochmeyer.

Mitchell, James (1998), 'The Evolution of Devolution: Labour's Home Rule Strategy in Opposition', *Government and Opposition*, vol. 33, pp. 479–496.

Mitchell, James (2003), *Governing Scotland: the Invention of Administrative Devolution*, Basingstoke, Palgrave Macmillan.

Mitchell, James (2006), 'Undignified and Inefficient: Financial Relations Between London and Stormont', *Contemporary British History*, vol. 20, no. 1, pp. 57–73

Mitchell, James and Lynn Bennie (1996), 'Thatcherism and the Scottish Question', in *British Elections and Parties Yearbook, 1995*, Ilford, Essex, Frank Cass.

Molyneaux MP, James (1983), *Unionist Party Conference Speech by the Leader of the Party*, 19 November. Copy sent to the author by James Molyneaux.

Moore, Chris and Simon Booth (1989), *Managing Competition: Meso-Corporatism, Pluralism, and the Negotiated Order in Scotland*, Oxford, Clarendon Press.

Morgan, Kenneth (1982), *Rebirth of a Nation: Wales 1880–1980*, Oxford, Oxford University Press and University of Wales Press.

Morgan, Kenneth (1989), *The Red Dragon and the Red Flag: The Cases of James Griffiths and Aneurin Bevan*, Aberystwyth, National Library of Wales, The Welsh Political Archive Lecture 1988.

Morgan, Kenneth (1997), *Callaghan*, Oxford, Oxford University Press.

Morgan, Kevin and Geoff Mungham (2000), *Redesigning Democracy: The Welsh Labour Party and Devolution*, Bridgend, Seren Books.

Morgan, Kevin and Ellis Roberts (1993), *The Democratic Deficit: a Guide to Quangoland*, Cardiff, Cardiff School of City and Regional Planning, no. 144.

Mulholland, Marc (2000), *Northern Ireland at the Crossroads: Ulster Unionism in the O'Neill Years, 1960–9*, Basingstoke, Macmillan.

Munro, Robert (1930), *Looking Back: Fugitive Writings and Sayings*, London, Oceana Publications.

Murray, Gerard (1998), *John Hume and the SDLP: Impact and Survival in Northern Ireland*, Dublin, Irish Academic Press.

Needham, Richard (1998), *Battling for Peace*, Belfast, The Blackstaff Press.

Nettl, J.P. (1968), 'The State as a Conceptual Variable', *World Politics*, vol. 20, pp. 559–592.

Newark, F.H. (1955), 'The Law and the Constitution', in Thomas Wilson (ed.), *Ulster Under Home Rule: a Study of the Political and Economic Problems of Northern Ireland*, Oxford, Oxford University Press.

New Ireland Forum (1984), *Report of the New Ireland Forum*, Dublin, Stationery Office.

Newsam, Sir Frank (1954), *The Home Office*, London, George Allen & Unwin Ltd.

North, Douglass (2002), *Institutions, Institutional Change and Economic Performance*, Cambridge, Cambridge University Press.

Northern Ireland Office (1972), *The Future of Northern Ireland: A Paper for Discussion*, London, NIO.

O'Day, Alan and John Stevenson (1992), *Irish Historical Documents Since 1800*, Dublin, Gill and Macmillan.

O'Kane, Eamonn (2004), 'Anglo-Irish Relations and the Northern Ireland Peace Process: From Exclusion to Inclusion', *Contemporary British History*, vol. 18, pp. 78–99.

O'Leary, Brendan (1997), 'The Conservative Stewardship of Northern Ireland, 1979–1997: Sound-bottomed Contradictions or Slow Learning?', *Political Studies*, vol. 45, pp. 663–676.

O'Leary, Brendan (1999), 'The Nature of the British Irish Agreement', *New Left Review*, vol. I/233, pp. 66–96.

O'Leary, Cornelius, Sydney Elliott and R.A. Wilford (1988), *The Northern Ireland Assembly, 1982–1986: A Constitutional Experiment*, London and Belfast, C. Hurst & Company and Queen's University Bookshop.

Oliver, Dawn (2003), 'The Project: Modernizing the UK Constitution', in Dawn Oliver (ed.), *Constitutional Reform in the United Kingdom*, Oxford, Oxford University Press.

Oliver, John (1978), *Working at Stormont, Memoirs*, Dublin, Institute of Public Administration.

O'Neill, Terence (1969), *Ulster at the Crossroads*, London, Faber and Faber.

O'Neill, Terence (1972), *The Autobiography of Terence O'Neill: Prime Minister of Northern Ireland, 1963–1969*, London, Rupert Hart-Davis.

Orwell, George (1941), *The Lion and the Unicorn: Socialism and the English Genius*, London, Secker & Warburg.

Osmond, John (2005), 'Provenance and Promise', in John Osmond (ed.), *Welsh Politics Come of Age*, Cardiff, Institute of Welsh Politics.

Palley, Claire (1972), 'The Evolution, Disintegration and Possible Reconstruction of the Northern Ireland Constitution', *Anglo-American Law Review*, vol. 1, pp. 368–476.

Parsons, Wayne (1988), *The Political Economy of British Regional Policy*, London, Routledge.

Patterson, Henry (2006), *Ireland Since 1939*, London, Penguin.

Pattie, Charles and James Mitchell (2006), 'Electoral Reform Reformed? The Arbuthnott Commission and Scottish Parliamentary Elections', *Representation*, vol. 42, pp. 195–208.

Peters, B. Guy (1999), *Institutional Theory in Political Science: The 'New*

Institutionalism', London, Pinter.

Pierson, Paul (2000), 'Increasing Returns, Path Dependence, and the Study of Politics', *American Political Science Review*, vol. 94, pp. 251–267.

Pimlott, Ben (1986), *Hugh Dalton*, London, Jonathan Cape Ltd.

Pimlott, Ben (1992), *Harold Wilson*, London, HarperCollins.

Pimlott, Ben and Nirmala Rao (2002), *Governing London*, Oxford, Oxford University Press.

Poirier, Johanne (2001), 'The Functions of Intergovernmental Agreements: Post-Devolution Concordats in a Comparative Perspective', *Public Law*, pp. 134–157.

Pollak, Andy (ed.) (1993), *A Citizens' Inquiry: The Opsahl Report on Northern Ireland*, Dublin, The Lilliput Press.

Powell, Enoch (1996), 'Britain and Europe', in M. Holmes (ed.), *The Eurosceptical Reader*, Houndmills, Macmillan.

Powell, Enoch (1998), 'The Spell of England', speech given on 22 April, 1961 to dinner of the Royal Society of St George in London, reproduced in the *Daily Telegraph*, 9 February.

Prescott, John and Tom Pendry (1982), *Alternative Regional Strategy*, London, Labour Party.

Prestwich, Roger and Peter Taylor (1990), *Introduction to Regional and Urban Policy in the United Kingdom*, Harlow, Longman.

Pryde, George S. (1960), *Central and Local Government in Scotland Since 1707*, London, Cox & Wyman Ltd.

Purdie, Bob (1986), 'The Irish Anti-partition League, South Armagh and Abstentionism', *Irish Political Studies*, vol. 1, pp. 67–77.

Purdie, Bob (1990), *Politics in the Streets*, Belfast, Blackstaff Press.

Quekett, Sir Arthur (1928), *The Constitution of Northern Ireland*, Belfast, HM Stationery Office.

Quigley (1976), *Economic and Industrial Strategy for Northern Ireland: Report of a Review Team*, Belfast, HMSO.

Rait, Robert (ed.) (1925), *Memorials of Albert Venn Dicey: Being Chiefly Letters and Diaries*, London, Macmillan and Co. Ltd.

Rallings, Colin and Michael Thrasher (2000), *British Electoral Facts*, Aldershot, Ashgate.

Randall, P.J. (1969), *The Development of Administrative Decentralisation in Wales from the Establishment of the Welsh Department of Education in 1907 to the Creation of the Post of Secretary of State for Wales in October 1964*, Unpublished M.Sc. thesis, University of Wales.

Randall, P.J. (1972), 'Wales in the Structure of Central Government', *Public Administration*, vol. 50, pp. 353–372.

Rawlings, Rick (2003), *Delineating Wales: Constitutional, Legal and Administrative Aspects of National Devolution*, Cardiff, University of Wales Press.

Rawlings, Rick (2005), 'Hastening Slowly: The Next Phase of Welsh

Devolution', *Public Law*, pp. 824–852.

Redcliffe-Maud, Lord (Chairman) (1969), *Report of the Royal Commission on Local Government in England*, London, HMSO, Cmnd. 4040.

Redwood, John (1999), *The Death of Britain?*, Basingstoke, Macmillan Press.

Reich, Robert (1998), *Locked Inside the Cabinet*, New York, Vintage Books.

Renan, E. (1939), 'What is a Nation?', in Zimmern, Alfred (ed.), *Modern Political Doctrines*, Oxford, Oxford University Press.

Richard, Lord Ivor (Chair) (2004), *Commission on the Powers and Electoral Arrangements of the National Assembly for Wales*, Report of the Richard Commission, Cardiff, National Assembly for Wales.

Robbins, Keith (1988), *Nineteenth-Century Britain: Integration and Diversity*, Oxford, Clarendon Press.

Roberts, Andrew (2000), *Salisbury: Victorian Titan*, London, Orion Books.

Roberts of Conwy, Lord (2006), *Right From the Start: The Memoirs of Sir Wyn Roberts*, Cardiff, University of Wales Press.

Rokkan, Stein (1970), *Citizens, Elections, and Parties*, New York, David Mackay.

Rokkan, Stein (1999), *State Formation, Nation-Building, and Mass Politics in Europe: The Theory of Stein Rokkan*, based on his collected works and edited by Peter Flora with Stein Kuhnle and Derek Urwin, Oxford, Oxford University Press.

Rokkan, Stein and Derek Urwin (1982), "Introduction: Centres and Peripheries in Western Europe', in Stein Rokkan and Derek Urwin (eds), *The Politics of Territorial Identity: Studies in European Regionalism*, London, Sage.

Rose, Peter (1996), 'Labour, Northern Ireland and the Decision to Send in the Troops', in Peter Catterall and Sean McDougall (eds), *The Northern Ireland Question in British Politics*, Basingstoke, Macmillan.

Rose, Richard (1971), *Governing Without Consensus: An Irish Perspective*, Boston, Beacon Press.

Rose, Richard (1975), *Northern Ireland: A Time of Choice*, Basingstoke, Macmillan.

Rose, Richard (1982), *Understanding the United Kingdom*, London, Longman.

Ross, Jim M. (1985), Letter to the author, 11 January.

Ross, William (1978), 'Approaching to Arch-angelic?', in *Scottish Government Yearbook 1978*, Edinburgh, Paul Harris Publishing.

Rowlands, E. (1972), 'The Politics of Regional Administration: The Establishment of the Welsh Office', *Public Administration*, vol. 50, pp. 333–351.

Rowlands, Ted (2004), 'Whitehall's Last Stand: The Establishment of the

Welsh Office, 1964', *Contemporary Wales*, vol. 16, pp. 39–52.

Rowthorn, Bob (1981), 'Northern Ireland: an Economy in Crisis', *Cambridge Journal of Economics*, vol. 5, pp. 1–31.

Russell, Meg (2005), 'A Constitution by any other name …', *Political Quarterly*, vol. 76, p. 457.

Russell, Meg and Guy Lodge (2006), 'The government of England by Westminster', in Robert Hazell (ed.), *The English Question*, Manchester, Manchester University Press.

Sahlins, Peter (1989), *Boundaries: The Making of France and Spain in the Pyrenees*, Berkeley and Los Angeles, University of California Press.

Sandford, Mark (2004), 'The Governance of London', in Alan Trench (ed.), *Has Devolution Made a Difference?*, Exeter, Imprint Academic.

Sandford, Mark (2005), *The New Governance of the English Regions*, Basingstoke, Palgrave Macmillan.

Sandford, Mark (2006), 'Facts on the Ground: the Growth of Institutional Answers to the English Question in the Regions', in Robert Hazell (ed.), *The English Question*, Manchester, Manchester University Press.

Scottish Constitutional Convention (1989), *Towards a Scottish Parliament*, Edinburgh, Convention of Scottish Local Authorities.

Scottish Office (1997), *Scotland's Parliament*, Edinburgh, HMSO, Cm. 3658.

Scottish Unionist Party (1949), *Scottish Control of Scottish Affairs*, Edinburgh, Scottish Unionist Party.

Seawright, David (1999), *An Important Matter of Principle: The Decline of the Scottish Conservative and Unionist Party*, Aldershot, Ashgate.

Shea, Patrick (1981), *Voices and the Sound of Drums*, Belfast, Blackstaff.

Sillars, Jim (1986), *The Case for Optimism*, Edinburgh, Polygon.

Smith, B.C. (1964), *Regionalism in England: Regional Institutions: A Guide*, London, Acton Society Trust.

Smith, Fintan (2005), *The North East Referendum: Initiation and Control*, dissertation submitted for award of M.Phil., Strathclyde University.

Smith, Llew (1995), *The Welsh Assembly: Why It Has No Place in Wales*, London, Llew Smith.

Smith, Sheriff Guthrie (1885), 'Scotland and the National Government', *Journal of Jurisprudence*, vol. 29, pp. 225–241.

Steel, David (2001), 'A Dozen Differences of Devolution', 4 June: www.scottish.parliament.uk/nmCentre/news/news-01/pa01–031.htm (accessed 5 July 2005).

Stewart, A.T.Q. (1981), *Edward Carson*, Belfast, Blackstaff.

Stewart, A.T.Q. (1989), *The Narrow Ground: The Roots of Conflict in Ulster*, London, Faber and Faber.

Stinchcombe, Arthur L. (1968), *Constructing Social Theories*, New York, Harcourt, Brace and World.

Supreme Court (1990), *McGimpsey v. Ireland, IESC 3*, 1 March: www.bailii.org/ie/cases/IESC/1990/3.html (accessed 6 January 2005).

Swank, Duane (2002), *Global Capital, Political Institutions, and Policy Change in Developed Welfare States*, Cambridge, Cambridge University Press.

Symmons, Clive (1992), 'International Treaty Obligations and the Irish Constitution: the McGimpsey Case', *International and Comparative Law Quarterly*, vol. 41, pp. 311–342.

Tanner, Duncan (2006a), 'How Devolution Died: the British Labour Party's Constitutional Agenda, 1900–45', in D. Tanner, C. Williams, W.P. Griffith and A. Edwards (eds), *Debating Nationhood and Governance in Britain, 1885–1939*, Manchester, Manchester University Press.

Tanner, Duncan (2006b), 'Richard Crossman, Harold Wilson and Devolution, 1966–70: The Making of Government Policy', *Twentieth Century British History*, vol. 17, pp. 545–578.

Taylor, Charles (1993), *Reconciling the Solitudes: Essays on Canadian Federalism and Nationalism*, London, McGill-Queen's University Press.

Taylor, Rupert (2001), 'Consociation or Social Transformation?', in John McGarry (ed.), *Northern Ireland and the Divided World: Post-Agreement Northern Ireland in Comparative Perspective*, Oxford, Oxford University Press.

Taylor, Rupert (2006), 'The Belfast Agreement and the Politics of Consociationalism: A Critique', *Political Quarterly*, vol. 77 pp. 217–226.

Thatcher, Margaret (1993), *The Downing Street Years*, London, Harper-Collins.

Thelen, Kathleen (2003), 'How Institutions Evolve' in James Mahoney and Dietrich Rueschemeyer (eds), *Comparative Historical Analysis in the Social Sciences*, Cambridge, Cambridge University Press.

Thomas, George (1985), *Mr Speaker: The Memoirs of Lord Tonypandy*, London, Harmondsworth.

Thomas, Ian C. (1981), 'The Creation of the Welsh Office: Conflicting Prposes in Institutional Change', Studies in Public Policy, no. 91, Glasgow, Centre for the Study of Public Policy, University of Strathclyde.

Tilly, Charles (1975), 'Reflections on the History of European State Making', in Charles Tilly (ed.) , *The Formation of National States in Europe*, Princeton, Princeton University Press.

Tilly, Charles (1992), *Coercion, Capital, and European States, AD 990–1992*, Oxford, Blackwell.

Tindale, Stephen (ed.), *The State and the Nations*, London, IPPR.

Todd, Jennifer (1987), 'Two Traditions in Unionist Political Culture', *Irish Political Studies*, vol. 2, pp. 1–26.

Tomaney, John (2006), 'The Idea of English Regionalism', in Robert Hazell (ed.), *The English Question*, Manchester, Manchester University Press.

Tomaney, John and Hetherington, Peter (2004), 'English Regions: The Quiet Revolution?' in Alan Trench (ed.), *Has Devolution Made A Difference?*, Exeter, Imprint Academic.

Tomkins, Adam (2005), *Our Republican Constitution*, Oxford, Hart Publishing.

Toothill, J.N. (1961), *Inquiry into the Scottish Economy*, Edinburgh, Scottish Council (Development and Industry).

Treasury (2004), *Microeconomic Reform in Britain: Delivering Opportunities for All*, Houndmills, Palgrave.

Trench, Alan (2005), 'Whitehall and the Process of Legislation after Devolution', in Robert Hazell and Richard Rawlings (eds), *Devolution, Law Making and the Constitution*, Exeter, Imprint Academic.

Trench, Alan (2007a), 'Old Wine in New Bottles? Wales–Whitehall Relations After the Government of Wales Act, 2006', *Contemporary Wales*, vol. 20, pp. 31–51.

Trench, Alan (2007b), 'Washing Dirty Linen in Private: The Processes of Intergovernmental Relations and the Resolution of Disputes' in Alan Trench (ed.), *Devolution and Power*, Manchester, Manchester University Press.

Trimble, David (2001), *To Raise up a New Northern Ireland*, Belfast, Blackstaff Press.

Trystan, Dafydd, Richard Wyn Jones and Roger Scully (2003), 'Explaining the Quiet Earthquake: Voting Behaviour in the First Election to the National Assembly for Wales', *Electoral Studies*, vol. 22, pp. 635–650.

Wales Office (2005), *Better Governance for Wales*, Cardiff, HMSO, Cm. 6582.

Walker, Graham (2004), *A History of the Ulster Unionist Party: Protest, Pragmatism and Pessimism*, Manchester, Manchester University Press.

Wallace, Martin (1967), 'Home Rule in Northern Ireland – Anomalies of Devolution', *Northern Ireland Legal Quarterly*, vol. 18, pp. 159–176.

Watkins, Sir Percy E. (1944), *A Welshman Remembers*, Cardiff, W. Lewis Ltd.

Weight, Richard (2002), *Patriots: National Identity in Britain, 1940–2000*, London, Macmillan.

Wheare, Sir Kenneth (1963), *Federalism*, fourth edition, Oxford, Oxford University Press.

Whyte, John (1991), *Interpreting Northern Ireland*, Oxford, Clarendon Press.

Wichert, Sabine (1991), *Northern Ireland Since 1945*, London, Longman.

Wilford, Rick and Robin Wilson (2000), 'A "Bare Knuckle Ride": Northern Ireland', in Robert Hazell (ed.), *The State and the Nations: The*

First Year of Devolution in the United Kingdom, Exeter, Imprint Academic.

Wilford, Rick and Robin Wilson (2003), 'Northern Ireland: Valedictory?', in Robert Hazell (ed.), *The State and the Nations: The Third Year of Devolution in the United Kingdom*, Exeter, Imprint Academic.

Wilford, Rick and Robin Wilson (2005), 'Northern Ireland: While You Take The High Road . . .', in Alan Trench (ed.), *The Dynamics of Devolution: The State of the Nations 2005*, Exeter, Imprint Academic.

Williams, D. (1950), *Modern Wales*, London, John Murray.

Williams, Gwyn (1991), *When Was Wales?*, London, Penguin.

Williams, Hywel (1998), *The Guilty Men*, London, Arium Press.

Wills, Michael (2006), *A New Agenda: Labour and Democracy*, London, IPPR.

Willson, F.M.G. (1955), 'Ministries and Boards: Some Aspects of Administrative Development Since 1832', *Pubic Administration*, vol. 33, pp. 43–58.

Wilson, Andrew (1995), *Irish America and the Ulster Conflict, 1968–1995*, Belfast, the Blackstaff Press.

Wilson, Robin and Rick Wilford (2001), 'Northern Ireland: Endgame', in Alan Trench (ed.), *The State of the Nations 2001: The Second Year of Devolution in the United Kingdom*, Exeter, Imprint Academic.

Wilson, Robin and Rick Wilford (2004), 'Northern Ireland: Renascent?', in Alan Trench (ed.), *Has Devolution Made a Difference? The State of the Nations 2004*, Exeter, Imprint Academic.

Index